DATA PROCESSING BUDGETS: HOW TO DEVELOP AND USE BUDGETS EFFECTIVELY

(A Management Perspective)

William E. Perry

Prentice-Hall, Inc., Englewood Cliffs, N.J. 07632

Library of Congress Cataloging in Publication Data

PERRY, WILLIAM E.
Data processing budgets.

Includes index.
1. Electronic data processing departments—Finance.
2. Budget in business. I. Title.
HF5548.2.P47282 1985 658′.054 84-22276
ISBN 0-13-196874-2

Editorial/production supervision and
interior design: Dee A. Josephson
Cover design: Wanda Lubelska Design
Manufacturing buyer: Gordon Osbourne

Printed in the United States of America

10 9 8 7 6 5 4 3 2 1

ISBN 0-13-196874-2 01

Prentice-Hall International, Inc., *London*
Prentice-Hall of Australia Pty. Limited, *Sydney*
Editora Prentice-Hall do Brasil, Ltda., *Rio de Janeiro*
Prentice-Hall Canada Inc., *Toronto*
Prentice-Hall Hispanoamericana, S.A., *Mexico*
Prentice-Hall of India Private Limited, *New Delhi*
Prentice-Hall of Japan, Inc., *Tokyo*
Prentice-Hall of Southeast Asia Pte. Ltd., *Singapore*
Whitehall Books Limited, *Wellington, New Zealand*

This book is dedicated to my daughter, Debra, who taught me the relationship between the importance of the budget and the economic plushness of the organization. Budgets grow more important in poor economic times and less important in good economic times. Nice going, Debra!

Contents

Preface ***ix***

Part 1 Budgeting for the DP Function ***1***

1 Budgeting—An Essential DP Ingredient ***1***

The Underlying Cause of DP Budgetary Difficulties 2
Impediments to Successful Budgeting 3
Budgeting Is the Principal Tool of Management 6
The Golden Rules of Budgeting 6
Budgets versus Financial Statements 8
Road Map through the Book 10
DP Department Budgetary Process Self-Assessment 12
DP Management Budget Actions 17
On to the Wonderful World of Budgeting 20

2 Budgeting and Planning Strategies ***21***

What's Different about DP Budgeting? 21
Budgetary Problems Associated with the DP Budgeting Challenge 25
Budgeting Strategies to Address Unique Problems in DP Budgeting 27
DP Budgeting Strategies 31
Implementing the Budgeting Strategies 34
The Value of Budgeting 35

Part 2 The Budget as a Management Tool 36

3 The Dimensions and Components of DP Budgeting 36

Budgeting the DP Department versus Budgeting DP Expenditures 36
Allocation of DP Funds 37
Controllable DP Components 39
The Three Dimensions of Budgeting 49
The Risk Dimensions of the Controllable Budget Components 52
Preparing for the Budget Process 56
Relating Budgeting to the DP Mission 57

4 Budgeting as a Management Tool 58

Budgeting Information Systems versus Budgeting the DP Function 58
Methods for Using the Budget as a Managerial Tool 60
Managerial Procedures Used to Accomplish Managerial Objectives 64
Uses and Abuses of Budgeting 69
Budgeting as a Management Tool to Achieve Quality 70
SDLC Budgetary Control Case Study 73
The Responsibility for Using Budgetary Principles 76
Good Budgeting Does Not Just Happen 76

5 Managing the Budget Process 77

Defining Management's Budgetary Responsibilities 77
The Eight Keys to Successful Management of the Budgetary Process 79
The Budgetary Cycle 81
Quality Factors That Need to Be Managed 82
Managing the Budgetary Requirements Phase 84
Managing the Budgetary Preparation Process 89
Managing the Budgetary Approval Process 91
Managing the Use of the Budget 93
What Is the Process That Should Be Managed? 96

Part 3 The DP Budget Process 98

6 Building a Budget 98

The Budgetary Process versus the Budget Product 98
Why Budgetary Processes Fail 99
Integrating DP Budgets into Corporate Budgets 100
Interrelationship between Budgeting and Planning 104
Special Budgetary Considerations 106
The Steps in Building a Budget 109
Aren't Accountants Supposed to Build the Budgetary Process? 112

7 Step 1: Budget Planning 114

Budget Planning—The Most Important Step 114
The Budget Planning Step 116
Budgetable Components Planning Considerations 117
Planning the Quality of the Budget Process 122
Task 1: Assign Budget Responsibilities 123
Task 2: Train Budget Participants 125
Task 3: Determine Reliability/Validity of Budget 126
Task 4: Schedule and Staff the Budgetary Process 127
Task 5: Customize the Budget Process 128
Ensuring the Quality of the Budget Planning Step 129
Budget Planning Impediments and Counterstrategies 129
The Results of Planning 131

8 Step 2: Data Gathering 132

You Cannot Control What You Cannot Measure 132
Identifying Controllable Budget Line Items 133
Data Collection Considerations 134
Conducting the Data-Gathering Step 139
Task 1: Identify Budget Participants 140
Task 2: Distribute Budget Requirements to Participants 142
Task 3: Collect Budget Data 142
Task 4: Evaluate the Quality of the Collected Data 146
Ensuring the Quality of the Budget Process 146
Data-Gathering Impediments and Counterstrategies 146
How Do I Know that the Data Gathered Are Correct? 149

9 Step 3: Estimating Costs and Benefits 150

Estimating—An Art or a Science? 150
Budgets—Should They Include Benefits? 151
Methods to Estimate Costs and Benefits 152
Selecting an Estimating Method 157
The Estimating Tasks 158
Ensuring the Quality of the Estimating Step 174
Estimating Impediments and Counterstrategies 174
The Value of a Good Estimate 176

10 Step 4: Classification, Consolidation, and Presentation of a Budget 177

Adding the Finishing Touches to the Budget 177
Preparing a Winning Budget 178
Another Important Element of Success—Prioritization 180
Performing the Classification, Consolidation, and Preparation Step 182
Task 1: Analyze and Approve Budget Items 183

Task 2: Classify Budget Items 183
Task 3: Consolidate Budget Items 184
Task 4: Organize Budget Items 185
Task 5: Ensure the Quality of the Final Budget Document 186
Ensuring the Quality of the Classification, Consolidation, and Budget Preparation Process 187
Impediments and Counterstrategies to Classifying, Consolidating, and Preparing a Budget 187

11 Step 5: Marketing the Budget 189

The Key to Selling the Budget 189
Anticipating Management's Budget Challenge 191
Conducting the Marketing-the-Budget Step 194
Task 1: Package the Budget 194
Task 2: Present the Budget 196
Task 3: Negotiate the Budget 198
Marketing Impediments and Counterstrategies 199

Part 4 Using and Evaluating the Budget 201

12 Living with Your Budget 201

So Now Your Budget Is Approved! 201
Task 1: Allocating Budgetary Funds 202
Task 2: Managing the DP Department with a Budget 205
Task 3: Managing the Changing Workload 210
Task 4: Surviving Managerial Budget Edicts 211

13 Assessing the Effectiveness of the Budgetary Process 213

Evaluate the Process, Not the Participants 213
Methods for Evaluating the Budgetary Process 214
Method 1: Judgment 215
Method 2: Participant Survey 215
Method 3: Attributes 217
Method 4: Budgetary Metrics 218
Use of the Evaluation 219

Preface

The average worker believes that senior management spends their time devising impediments for their subordinates to fight through in order to accomplish their stated mission. Of all the impediments, budgets normally rank number one. This reaction is associated with the fact that most subordinates do not understand budgeting, and most managers abuse it.

When senior managers are asked how they control the subordinates, the answer is almost always, "Through budgets." Of all the managerial tools, it is the strongest and the most versatile. Executives come from widely differing backgrounds, but once promoted to the executive suite they quickly become budgeting experts—or fail as executives.

Successful managers understand budgeting, unsuccessful managers never master the skill. This book explains the budgeting process and shows how to use that process effectively within the data processing function. The process is so important to the function's success that the subject should be mandatory in a computer science curriculum, but is not. Properly used, all parties to the budget can win.

The lessons presented in this book are drawn from a wide range of corporations and governmental units. The principles should be practiced every day of the year, because budgeting is an everyday part of managing. It is my hope that these principles applied to the data processing profession will result in the revitalization and integration of data processing within organizations.

William E. Perry

Part 1 Budgeting for the DP Function

1

Budgeting—An Essential DP Ingredient

Budgets are the battleground on which the war for organizational resources is fought. The winners walk away with a large piece of the pie, while the losers must scratch for the funds needed to accomplish their mission. Budgeting, while frequently viewed as a necessary evil, is a game whose winner will probably move up the organizational ladder.

Budgeting is a managerial tool. It is used by managers to fulfill their planning, directing, and controlling responsibilities. A budget shows how an approved plan will be accomplished. It directs performance by allocating resources, and it controls organizations by limiting costs and measuring benefits.

Accounting is the common language spoken by senior management. It is a language that crosses all disciplines, including data processing (DP). Budgeting is a subfunction within the accounting function, but much more. Budgeting is closely related to planning, as it relates funding to plans, and is used by management to direct and control their organization.

Budgeting, unlike many of the other accounting functions, does not reside solely in the domain of accountants. Almost all managers are involved in the budgetary process. In data processing, this includes project leaders, operations supervisors, and many of the technical support managers, such as the data base administrator.

You cannot win at budgeting if you do not know the rules of the game. The objective of this book is to help the data processing professional stand nose to nose with senior management and the accountants throughout the budgetary process. To a senior manager and an accountant, a budget tells a story. This book will help data processing construct and present the proper budgetary story.

Budgeting should be viewed as a data processing project. As such, the requirements must be defined, the specifications determined, and a budgetary process designed, implemented, tested, and operated. Budgeting, like any other project, must be maintained throughout the life of the project. When viewed as a project, it can be properly managed to ensure that data processing personnel will be allocated sufficient resources to accomplish their mission properly.

THE UNDERLYING CAUSE OF DP BUDGETARY DIFFICULTIES

During the early 1960s, the U.S. Internal Revenue Service wanted to capitalize data processing project costs. The argument of the IRS was that funds were being expended to build a system that had a useful life of more than one year. U.S. corporations countered with the argument that although the system lasted more than a year, it had no value. It was argued that a data processing system development project was like any other use of administrative resources, and as such should be expensed. The U.S. corporations won, but both the IRS and the data processing profession lost.

In many corporations, the data processing systems are one of the most valuable assets of the corporation. Yet, unfortunately, programs and data do not show up on the financial records of the organization, and thus are not managed as a capitalized financial asset would be managed.

Let's look at an example of the value of the systems asset in a typical corporation. Let us assume that there are approximately twenty-five systems analysts and programmers who over a twenty-year period have built up an inventory of 500,000 source statements. Note that in larger organizations single systems may contain this number of source statements. The replacement cost of a source statement varies. Estimates to replace a source statement range from $20 to $70, so that $20 is a conservative estimate of the value of a source code statement. Simple arithmetic shows us the replacement cost of the applications inventory for our company:

500,000 source statements
× $20 replacement cost per source statement

$10 million application system replacement cost

What this says is that our hypothetical corporation has a $10 million asset not recorded on the books of the corporation. In most organizations, it would be difficult to find a record of the applications that comprise that unrecorded $10 million asset.

Now let's compare the treatment of this $10 million data processing asset with that of a $10 million factory. The maintenance of the factory equipment is well understood as being essential to preserve the asset; the equipment is safeguarded to protect the asset from destruction and loss. In addition, the capital budget provides funds to upgrade continually to improve the efficiency and performance of the equipment. The responsibility for the equipment is usually under the direction of a single person who is responsible for managing that resource. In most instances, this will be a vice president or general manager.

The $10 million data processing asset is not considered an asset, but an expense. As such, senior management has failed to recognize the need to preserve and upgrade the performance of that asset. The responsibility for it is frequently delegated to groups of users who also do not consider it an asset, and in fact many of them do not consider it "their" system. In contrast to the general manager of the factory, the application system is managed by a systems analyst or project leader who may be relatively far down the corporate chain of command. Although no one would consider letting the factory deteriorate, that same concern has not been directed at data processing applications. In many instances, the applications have significantly deteriorated, only to be saved from extinction by the huge increases in hardware performance.

The bottom line of expensing data processing system development costs is that the program and data assets developed by the DP function are undermanaged, frequently underbudgeted, and undercontrolled. This is a correctable situation that is addressed extensively in this book. The management of the data processing assets must be budgeted and controlled in the same manner as any other asset of equal significance in the organization.

The key points presented in this book are illustrated as budgetary principles. These principles capture and present good budgetary principles in an easy-to-find and read format. The learning and use of these budgetary principles will significantly enhance the use of budgeting to accomplish the data processing mission. The first budgetary principle follows.

> **Budgetary Principle**
>
> What is not measured is not controlled. Measuring the replacement cost of application systems establishes the need to manage and control those systems as a capital asset of the organization.

IMPEDIMENTS TO SUCCESSFUL BUDGETING

Many managers are unhappy with the budgetary process. It is frequently viewed as a restriction placed on them by senior management, as opposed to a tool to help each manager do his or her job better. The problem for many of these managers is that they are not prepared academically or psychologically to use the budget properly.

Effective use of the budgetary process by a manager involves:

1. *Budget strategy:* the planning and forethought that a manager puts into preparing for the budgetary process. The strategy includes the approaches that a manager will use in developing a budget, together with how that budget will be used in operating the manager's function, and how that manager will use the budgetary process as a communication vehicle between himself or herself and senior management.
2. *Budget process:* the process of gathering, organizing, preparing, presenting, maintaining, and using the budget in the day-to-day operation of the manager's

area of responsibility. The operation part of the budgetary process involves the mechanics of gathering and using the budgetary numbers.

When the budgetary process is unsatisfactory, it can usually be traced to either of two budgetary impediments. The first impediment is poor budgetary strategy and the second is the misuse of the budgetary process.

The impediments to successful budgeting associated with a poor budgetary strategy include:

1. *Lack of accounting skills:* Budgeting requires a basic understanding of the accounting process. It is an internal estimate of the income and expense of organizational activities. Without an understanding of how those numbers relate to the financial statements of the organization, it may be difficult to put budgets into the proper managerial perspective.
2. *Inability to reflect the true needs of DP:* A budget is a means of expressing plans in financial terms. The justification of the budget involves the justification of the data processing plan. Thus budgetary failures are normally planning failures for the data processing function.
3. *Failure to recognize the importance of budgeting to senior management:* As people move into senior management, their concerns shift toward financial matters. The budgetary process is one means used by management to ensure the profitability of the organization and to help determine how profitable the organization will become. When lower-level managers fail to recognize this importance, they may find themselves out of step with senior management's desires.
4. *Failure to fit the data processing budget into the needs of the organization:* Data processing serves most of the areas within an organization. Its budget has an impact on the success of other areas in the organization. Failure to recognize those needs and include them in the data processing budget can affect the credibility of the data processing function.

The impediments associated with the poor operation of the budgetary process include:

1. *Complex budgetary process:* Each function, including data processing, must implement management's budgetary requirements in their area. Because data processing contains a lot of systems people, they may make the budgetary process too complex. This adds an extra workload burden to the staff, which in turn may result in inadequate preparation and input to the budgetary process.
2. *Failure to integrate budgeting into work procedures:* Budgeting is a day-to-day function of an organization. It should be an integral part of all processes, not an after-the-fact or as-time-is-available process. Separating budgeting from the daily work functions of the data processing staff reduces the effectiveness of the budgetary process.

3. *Failure to use the budget as a data processing management tool:* Many data processing managers view the budget as a tool of senior management, as opposed to a data processing management tool. When viewed as a constraint rather than a managerial tool, it becomes more of a device to circumvent than a tool to help manage.

The result of these impediments can be illustrated as shown in Figure 1.1. This figure indicates what is necessary to build a successful budgetary program, or why it may not work. The budgetary process is comprised of both strategy and operation. Either can be effective or ineffective.

The matrix shows the results of having an effective or ineffective budgetary strategy and operation. The results of the four combinations are shown within the matrix. If both the budgetary strategy and operation are ineffective, the budgetary process will be a failure. If one of the two variables is effective and the other ineffective, the result will be budgetary problems. When both the strategy and operation are effective, the budgetary process will be successful. It is that success formula that is described in this book.

The matrix in Figure 1.1 is also a predictor of success and failure for the data processing manager. Managers who use budgeting effectively to implement an effective budget strategy tend to create an environment in which their subordinates can be successful. Budgeting failures normally lead to morale problems and system failures. Not doing budgeting right normally means that the data processing manager is more

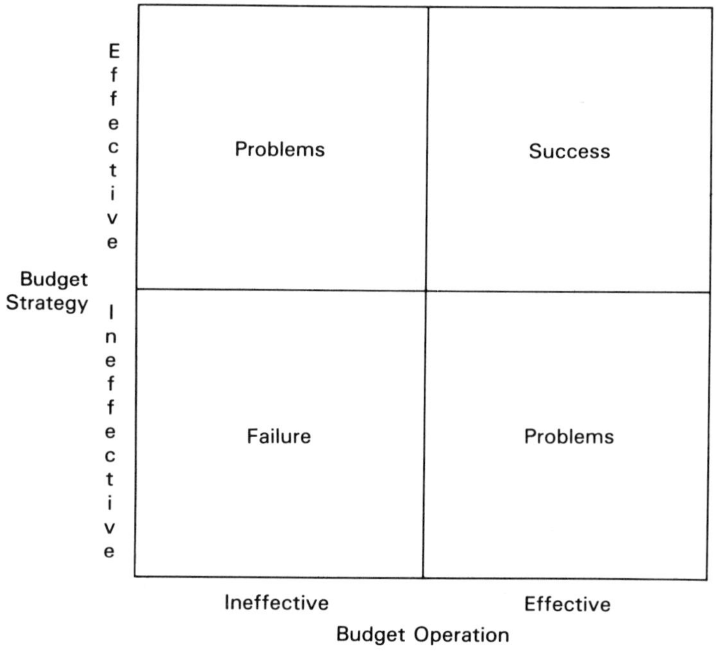

Figure 1.1 Building a successful budgetary process.

of a technician than a manager and does budgeting only because it is necessary. This lack of managerial skill is usually directly translatable into mediocrity within the data processing function.

BUDGETING IS THE PRINCIPAL TOOL OF MANAGEMENT

The majority of managers state that the tool they rely on the most to control their organization is the budget. The budget is not just an accounting process for justifying and regulating funding. It is the vehicle for controlling organizations. It is used to estimate revenue, plan expansions, change directions during the year, reprioritize tasks, and evaluate performance. There is no other tool in the organization nearly as versatile as the budget for controlling how organizations function.

The power of the budget can best be summarized in the following budgetary principle.

Budgetary Principle

He or she who owns the gold rules!

Senior managers rule by owning the gold. The budget is the process by which they measure the expected income, and control the outflow. It is a language in which production can be related to the medical department, personnel department, and the office manager.

Budgeting involves every aspect of managing the data processing function. The problems associated with poor budgeting are usually attributable to the fact that the manager involved does not understand budgeting. This book provides the solution to that dilemma. Although it is presumptuous to state that "everything you need to know about budgeting" is included within the covers of this book, there is probably not much else that one needs to know to be successful at budgeting. Winning at any function is a combination of acquiring a skill and using that skill. This book teaches the skills of budgeting and then provides the practical advice needed to overcome the impediments and problems described earlier in this chapter.

THE GOLDEN RULES OF BUDGETING

In many professions, knowledge is passed from the senior people to the junior people only after the latter have served an apprenticeship. In many professions, such as that of magician, how to perform the various activities may not even be written down, but passed along by word of mouth.

Figure 1.2 lists the ten golden rules of effective budgeting, which are explained briefly below.

1. Budgets should be believable.
2. Budgets should be based on accounting principles.
3. Budgets should be reproducible.
4. Budgets should provide for contingencies.
5. Budgets should be used.
6. Budgets should be anticipated by management.
7. Budgets should be consistent with plans.
8. Budgets should encourage efficiency and economy.
9. Budgets should be easy to prepare, monitor, and maintain.
10. Budgets should be understandable.

Figure 1.2 Golden rules of budgeting.

1. *Golden rule:* Budgets should be believable.
   Explanation: The person approving the budget should be led to the conclusion that the figures on the budget are correct, thus believable.
2. *Golden rule:* Budgets should be based on accounting principles.
   Explanation: Budgeting is a subset of accounting, so that budgeting should be based on good accounting principles.
3. *Golden rule:* Budgets should be reproducible.
   Explanation: The justification and buildup for each budgetary item should be easy to obtain. In other words, anyone who followed the same process would arrive at the same budgetary amounts.
4. *Golden rule:* Budgets should provide for contingencies.
   Explanation: Budgets should not assume that everything will work perfectly, because it won't. The budget should include funds for contingencies.
5. *Golden rule:* Budgets should be used.
   Explanation: The budgeting process should go on every day of the year, and use of the budget as a management tool should be utilized each workday of the year.
6. *Golden rule:* Budgets should be anticipated by management.
   Explanation: The amounts in the budget should not surprise anyone. Managers approving the budget should be apprised of what is coming long before they see the budget for approval.
7. *Golden rule:* Budgets should be consistent with plans.
   Explanation: The budget and the plans should be consistent. For each item in the plan there should be something in the budget, and vice versa.
8. *Golden rule:* Budgets should encourage efficiency and economy.
   Explanation: The budgetary process should have as an objective to help improve the economy, effectiveness, and efficiency of the data processing organization.
9. *Golden rule:* Budgets should be easy to prepare, monitor, and maintain.
   Explanation: The process for preparing and using a budget should not be cumbersome and time consuming. The easier the budget is to prepare, the more likely it is that it will be used.

10. *Golden rule:* Budgets should be understandable.
    Explanation: The budget should be comprehensible by anyone with a basic knowledge of accounting in the area being budgeted. If people do not understand what the budget is attempting to say, it is not a good budget.

These golden rules work. However, they are not meant to be used separately. It is the total effect of all ten golden rules of budgeting that make the concept work. They are not presented as a shopping basket of good principles in which management selects some and rejects others but, rather, as a package for which the use of all the golden rules is essential in ensuring the effective use of budgeting.

Budgetary Principle

No budget should be presented to management before the proper time. In other words, DP managers will regret the day they submitted an ill-prepared budget to senior management.

BUDGETS VERSUS FINANCIAL STATEMENTS

Three major financial documents are used in organizations:

- Balance sheet
- Statement of income and expenses
- Annual budget

Two of these three financial statements represent the external performance of the business. These are the balance sheet and statement of income and expense. The balance sheet is a list of the assets, liabilities, and stockholders' interest in the business at the end of the accounting period, which for many corporations is December 31. The statement of income and expense shows the results of business operations for the period reported, usually a year. The statement of income and expense shows revenue from all sources, and all the expenses involved in generating that revenue. The difference between revenue and expenses is the profit or loss generated by business operations.

The budget is a measure of the internal performance of the business. This shows how the organization did in regard to its business plan. The budget is a projection or estimate of what the revenue and expenses will be for the accounting period. The statement of income and expense represents the actual revenue and expenses for the same period.

The differences between the budgetary information and the financial amounts included on the statement of income and expense is commonly referred to as *budget overage* or *underage.* It is a variance from actual expenses. Therefore, we can state that a budget is an estimate of what will happen, and the statement of income and expense is what actually happened.

Figure 1.3 shows an illustrative DP budget in a profit and loss statement for the company.

DP BUDGET FOR THE YEAR 19XX

Item	Budget	Actual	Variance
Personnel	$ 500,000	$ 503,000	$ 3,000
Hardware	200,000	187,000	(13,000)
Software	200,000	206,000	6,000
Supplies	50,000	54,000	4,000
Facilities	150,000	160,000	10,000
	$1,100,000	$1,110,000	$ 10,000

XYZ COMPANY

STATEMENT OF INCOME AND EXPENSE YEAR ENDED 12/31/XX

Revenue:		$12,000,000
Less cost of sales		8,000,000
Gross Profit:		$ 4,000,000
Less administrative costs		
Accounting	$ 200,000	
Management	500,000	
DP	1,110,000	
Other	890,000	
		$ 2,700,000
Net Profit		$ 1,300,000

Figure 1.3 Budget versus statement of income and expense.

The DP budget is for the year 19XX. It shows five items, the budgeted amount for those items, the actual amount expended during the year, and the variance. For example, the DP department budgeted $500,000 for personnel but actually spent $503,000, resulting in a variance of $3,000 over budget. The result for the year was an overrun of $10,000 on a budget of $1,100,000, resulting in an actual expenditure in the DP department of $1,110,000.

The statement of income and expense for the XYZ Company, of which the DP department is a part, shows a revenue of $12 million, cost of sales of $8 million, and administrative expenses of $2,700,000, resulting in a net profit of $1,300,000. Note that this statement of income and expense is designed to illustrate the data processing input to that statement, not to be representative of the cost categories included on most income and expense statements.

The statement of income and expense shows that DP is an administrative cost of the business, as opposed to the cost of sales. *Cost of sales* represents the cost to develop and sell the company's products. *Administrative costs* are frequently referred to as *overhead,* or management-type expenses. We see that the actual expenditures as shown in the DP department budget is the same amount as that included on the statement of income and expense. The budget items and the variance do not show on the statement of income and expense or on the balance sheet. These include only the actual expenses. The two repeat a previous statement; the statement of income and expense shows the results of external operations, and the budget shows the results of internal operation. The external operation in the business generated a net profit of $1,300,000. The internal operation of the DP department resulted in a budget variance of $10,000. For a budget of this size, a variance of $10,000 would normally be considered reasonable. It would be indicative of a well-managed department, assuming that the department accomplished its mission with the $1,110,000 of resources expended by the department.

ROAD MAP THROUGH THE BOOK

This book on DP budgeting is designed for the following four audiences:

1. *Senior management:* The book is designed to explain the unique considerations in DP budgeting and why it may be more difficult than budgeting other activities in the organization. The book provides guidance to senior management on working with data processing management to establish an effective budgetary process. The book is also designed to help senior managers assess the effectiveness of the DP budgetary process.
2. *User management:* Many users pay for data processing services. What they pay will be partially dependent on the mechanics of budgeting and cost allocation. The book will explain to users the difficulty in developing a good DP budget and how they can help provide the input needed to prepare more realistic budgets. The book also explains to users the processes involved in estimating projects when new technology is involved.
3. *DP management:* The primary audience for this book is DP management. It is designed to be a primer on why to budget, how to budget, and how to budget effectively. It is designed to help data processing managers develop good budgeting strategies and to offer methods to implement those strategies.
4. *DP staff:* The detailed work in preparing a budget will be borne by the DP staff. This book outlines in step-by-step format the mechanics of preparing the budget and then developing the arguments needed to convince senior management of the need to adopt the budget.

The book is divided into four parts, comprising thirteen chapters. A brief explanation of these four parts follows.

Part 1: Budgeting for the DP Function

This part of the book explains why budgeting is important to the DP function, what is different about budgeting, and how to develop an effective budgeting strategy in DP. Part 1 is comprised of the following two chapters:

Chapter 1 Budgeting—An Essential DP Ingredient
Chapter 2 Budgeting and Planning Strategies

Part 2: The Budget as a Management Tool

This part of the book is directed at data processing management. The three budgeting dimensions of resource, time frame, and risk are described. Management is provided with a solution when addressing each of these dimensions. In addition, Part 2 explains how data processing managers can use the budget as an audit tool. Guidance is provided in how to organize and manage the development and use of the budget. This part comprises the following three chapters:

Chapter 3	The Dimensions and Components of DP Budgeting
Chapter 4	Budgeting as a Management Tool
Chapter 5	Managing the Budget Process

Part 3: The DP Budget Process

This part of the book is devoted to an explanation of how to prepare a budget. A five-step process is provided, together with the forms and methods needed to build an effective DP budget. This part contains six chapters explaining the proposed five-step budgetary process:

Chapter 6	Building a Budget
Chapter 7	Step 1: Budget Planning
Chapter 8	Step 2: Data Gathering
Chapter 9	Step 3: Estimating Costs and Benefits
Chapter 10	Step 4: Classification, Consolidation, and Presentation of a Budget
Chapter 11	Step 5: Marketing the Budget

Part 4: Using and Evaluating the Budget

This part of the book is designed to help managers use the budget in day-to-day management of the data processing function. The chapter also explains how data processing management can evaluate the effectiveness of the budgetary process. Some measurements are recommended that will provide a mathematical assessment of the effectiveness of the budget. This part contains the following two chapters:

Chapter 12	Living with Your Budget
Chapter 13	Assessing the Effectiveness of the Budgetary Process

The parts of the book that will be of most interest to various audiences are indicated in Figure 1.4. This matrix provides chapter-by-chapter guidelines for those readers for whom the book is designed. The audiences indicated by a P are primary

		Audience[a]			
Chapter	Title	Senior management	User management	DP management	DP staff
1	Budgeting—An Essential DP Ingredient	S	S	P	S
2	Budgeting and Planning Strategies	S	S	P	S
3	The Dimensions and Components of DP Budgeting	S	S	P	S
4	Budgeting as a Management Tool			P	S
5	Managing the Budget Process			P	S
6	Building a Budget			S	P
7	Step 1: Budget Planning			S	P
8	Step 2: Data Gathering			S	P
9	Step 3: Estimating Costs and Benefits		S	S	P
10	Step 4: Classification, Consolidation, and Presentation of a Budget			S	P
11	Step 5: Marketing the Budget			S	P
12	Living with Your Budget		S	P	S
13	Assessing the Effectiveness of the Budgetary Process	S		P	S

[a]P, primary audience; S, secondary audience.

Figure 1.4 Chapter-by-chapter guidelines for readers.

audiences for a given chapter; those indicated by an S are secondary audiences but should benefit from reading the chapter.

> **Budgetary Principle**
>
> The data processing manager who can speak of the DP budget from an authoritative perspective will be listened to. When a knowledgeable person speaks, people listen.

DP DEPARTMENT BUDGETARY PROCESS SELF-ASSESSMENT

The importance of the DP budget is frequently overlooked by data processing managers. They view it as one of many tools used by management to control the direction of an activity. What they fail to understand is that it is a fundamental control, perhaps the single most important control, used by management to accomplish the objectives of an organization.

The power and prestige of an activity can often be measured by the success of its budgetary process. The favored functions rarely have monetary problems, whereas those activities that have fallen out of favor often operate with bare-bone budgets. Although it is overly simplistic to state that the budgetary process is the primary ingredient, it is realistic to state that the judicious use of budgeting is a principal factor in the success of many business activities.

Managers need to step back and evaluate the success of their budgetary process. This self-assessment should be part factual and part judgmental. Following are the questions that need to be asked in this self-assessment.

1. *Question:* Are actual expenditures within plus or minus 5 percent of budget estimates?
   Consideration: The estimates made in a budget should be realistic. A 5 percent tolerance is a reasonable tolerance.
2. *Question:* Are project managers held accountable for operating within the budget?
   Consideration: Data processing managers should measure the performance of their subordinates on meeting their budgetary objectives. Both the total budget and the individual line item should be considered.
3. *Question:* Are budgetary results used to identify inefficiencies in the DP function?
   Consideration: If budgetary estimates vary significantly from actual costs, the reasons should be investigated. Deficiencies uncovered in this investigation should be improved to help both the budgetary process and the procedures being conducted.
4. *Question:* Must every budget item be justified each year?
   Consideration: Zero-based budgeting is a good practice if the budget is to be used as a managerial tool.
5. *Question:* Is one member of the DP department responsible for the quality of the budgetary process?
   Consideration: Until one person is held accountable for the budget, it will be a committee effort for which no one is responsible, and frequently about which no one cares.
6. *Question:* Is the DP budget based on the short- and long-range plans of the data processing department?
   Consideration: Budgeting is a financial implementation of a plan. The plans and the budget should be developed together and should reflect the same objectives.
7. *Question:* Are both the short- and long-range plans of the organization given to the DP department so that the DP budget is consistent with the business plans of the organization?
   Consideration: Data processing is an integral part of an organization. Information is needed for the organization to accomplish its mission. Therefore, the DP plans and budget should be a subset of the entire organization's plans and budget. The organization's plans and budget should be considered in developing the DP budget.
8. *Question:* Are the data needed for budgeting collected throughout the year through the DP internal information systems?
   Consideration: Budget information should be a by-product of the information

system and collected throughout the year. The collection procedure should not be a crash project done a few days or weeks prior to the submission date for the budget.

9. *Question:* Has the budgetary process been formalized and documented?
   Consideration: It is as important to tell people how to perform the budget process as it is to tell them how to design systems or write programs.
10. *Question:* Do DP personnel attend formal training classes in how to prepare and use budgets?
    Consideration: Data processing personnel should be trained in how to prepare and use budgets.
11. *Question:* If budgets are reduced, are DP plans changed at the same time?
    Consideration: To reduce budgets and not adjust plans accordingly makes a mockery of the budget process.
12. *Question:* Are budget reductions done item by item rather than as across-the-board reductions?
    Consideration: As a budget goes through the analysis process, reductions are normally required. These should not be across-the-board reductions, such as "reduce all budget items by 10 percent," but, rather, all items should be examined individually and the least important items cut.
13. *Question:* If DP plans are changed, is the budget changed at the same time?
    Consideration: Whenever plans are changed, budgets should be changed accordingly to provide the needed resources.
14. *Question:* Is DP management satisfied with the budgetary process?
    Consideration: The budgetary process should produce those budgets that provide the information needed for the manager to manage the department. It should be a fair process producing realistic results.
15. *Question:* Are DP staff members satisfied with the budgetary process?
    Consideration: If the staff members are dissatisfied with the process and procedures they must go through to develop budgets, they may not devote the needed resources or attention to the development of a good budget.
16. *Question:* Do you believe that the budgetary process is fair?
    Consideration: The budgetary process should provide reasonable resources to accomplish the plans and objectives of the activities being budgeted. If it is not fair, the budget and budgetary process will lack credibility in the eyes of the users.
17. *Question:* Are you successful in getting management to approve your budget?
    Consideration: The budgetary process should be such that the ensuing budget is realistic, in accordance with the organization's plans and budgetary guidelines, and presents proposals that management is prepared to receive. If the department managers are not successful in getting what they want, they have probably not put enough effort into the budgetary process.
18. *Question:* Do you have the relevant information readily available to support your budget requests?

ITEM	RESPONSE			
	YES	NO	N/A[a]	COMMENTS
1. Are actual expenditures within plus or minus 5 percent of budget estimates?				
2. Are project managers held accountable for operating within the budget?				
3. Are budgetary results used to identify inefficiencies in the DP function?				
4. Must every budget item be justified each year?				
5. Is one member of the DP department responsible for the quality of the budgetary process?				
6. Is the DP budget based on the short- and long-range plans of the data processing department?				
7. Are the short- and long-range plans of the organization given to the DP department so that the DP budget is consistent with the business plans of the organization?				
8. Are the data needed for budgeting collected throughout the year through the DP internal information systems?				
9. Has the budgetary process been formalized and documented?				
10. Do DP personnel attend formal training classes in how to prepare and use budgets?				
11. If budgets are reduced, are DP plans changed at the same time?				
12. Are budget reductions done item by item rather than across the board?				
13. If DP plans are changed, is the budget changed at the same time?				
14. Is DP management satisfied with the budgetary process?				
15. Are DP staff members satisfied with the budgetary process?				
16. Do you believe that the budgeting process is fair?				
17. Are you successful in getting management to approve your budget?				
18. Do you have the information readily available to support your budget requests?				
19. Is meeting the real operating goals of the data processing function more important than meeting the budget?				

[a]N/A, not applicable.

Figure 1.5 Self-assessment of the DP budgetary process.

Consideration: The budgetary process should produce adequate support for each line item in the budget. That information should be available before the budget is submitted to senior management for approval.

19. *Key question:* Is meeting the real operating goals of the data processing function more important than meeting the budget?
    Consideration: Data processing is charged both with meeting its operating goals and meeting them within budgetary constraints. Just as it would be foolish not to meet an operating goal because it would require exceeding the budget, it is foolish to meet goals if it is not cost-effective to do so. The intent of this question is to ensure that meeting operating goals is put into the proper perspective in the budgeting process.

A self-assessment checklist that includes the foregoing questions is provided as Figure 1.5. (See page 15.) This checklist should be completed by the data processing manager or another manager in the data processing department who has overall responsibility for planning and budgeting. The objective of the self-assessment is to provide an initial look at the budgetary process to determine whether any significant enhancements or changes appear to be needed.

Before reading further, the self-assessment checklist should be completed. If the items in the checklist are representative of the practices, attitudes, or results of the budgetary process, the item should receive a "yes" response. If the item is not representative of the data processing department, a "no" response should be given. If the item is not applicable to the organization the N/A column should be checked, meaning not applicable. Where appropriate, and for the respondent's later reference, a comments column is provided to explain the response. Complete the self-assessment checklist now.

Evaluating the Results of the Self-Assessment

The self-assessment checklist is designed so that "yes" responses are representative of good budgetary practices, and "no" responses are indicative of potential budgetary vulnerabilities. The respondent should total the number of "no" responses checked on Figure 1.5 and then consult the following table for an interpretation of those responses.

Number of "no" responses	Interpretation of self-assessment results
0–3	Your organization appears to have a well-established budgetary process, which is properly implemented in the data processing function. There may be some fine tuning to do, but in general you are doing the right things. This book should reinforce that opinion and provide you with some suggestions on how to increase the efficiency of the budgetary process.
4–6	You have some potential weaknesses in your budgetary process. Although it would appear to be basically sound, you probably experience some minor grumbling and dissatisfaction during the preparation of the budget or

Number of "no" responses	Interpretation of self-assessment results
	when your staff is evaluated on adherence to the budgetary figures. Some restructuring of your budgetary process and methods seems indicated, which this book can provide.
7–9	You are probably experiencing some significant dissatisfaction with the budgetary process. It may be viewed as a senior management tool, not as a tool of the data processing department. You should consider some serious restructuring of your budgeting strategy and budgetary methods. Put particular emphasis on Chapters 6 through 12 as a basis for redesigning the process used by your department to develop and use the DP budget.
10–13	You have some very serious flaws in your budgetary process. There is probably major dissatisfaction with the whole process, and a lack of interest on the part of your subordinates in developing and using budgets. The budgets are probably being developed because they are required, not for use as a management tool. Your organization would probably be better off to scrap its current strategy and methods and restructure them in line with those suggested by this book (note that they must also be consistent with your organization's budgetary concepts).
14–19	You do not have a budgetary process. If you collect numbers at all, it is because someone is making you do it. Seriously consider the strategy concepts discussed in Chapters 2 through 5 to rethink the whole budgetary process.

DP MANAGEMENT BUDGET ACTIONS

The process of preparing a budget is basically the same in all organizations, even though the methods vary significantly. The forms to be completed and the methods used to record that information are customized by most organizations. In the later chapters of the book, a proposed method for preparing budgets will be presented.

What is common in the budgetary process are the actions taken by management in preparing a data processing budget. The actions are described briefly below and explained in more detail together with a proposed methodology in Chapters 6 through 12. As we discuss the six budgetary actions, an example of budgeting for programmer supplies will be discussed.

Action 1: Identification of Budget Items

The budgetary process begins with a mission and plan for the budgetary period. The items involved in accomplishing that mission must then be identified. Note that in most data processing departments budgeting involves primarily the cost of operating the function, but in other parts of an organization the budgetary process also estimates income.

The planning process should have identified the categories of costs. In the data processing function, those would include people, machine time, supplies, service contracts, software purchase and/or rental, space, administrative facilities, employee benefits, and other costs associated with performing the data processing function. Unfortunately, many key items are not identified and thus are lumped into larger budget categories and lost. For example, the cost of testing applications is usually not identified, thus not budgeted, and thus becomes hard to control.

Normally, budgets are assembled from the bottom up. The individual work projects are identified, and the cost items associated with that product are then determined. Note that some items are departmental, whereas others are oriented by specific projects.

Let us assume that we were budgeting for a developmental project. In this action we would identify all the cost items associated with that project. Let us assume that one of the items of cost for developing the project is programmer supplies, such as templates, coding pads, and so on.

Action 2: Classification of Costs

Each of the costs must be classified into a budgetary account. The accounts used will be those specified by the organization's accounting department. However, at lower levels of budgetary development, these items can be customized for the department. This is important because as a managerial tool the classification of costs is a basic aspect of controlling costs. We will see in a later section of this chapter that incorrect classification can lead to the inability of management to control some data processing variables.

In our example of programmer supplies, we would probably classify those costs as data processing technical supplies. This would differentiate it from administrative supplies such as pencils, paper, and paper clips. The person responsible for preparing the budget should have a *chart of accounts* to be used in classifying budget costs. A chart of accounts is a list of the categories for which costs will be collected.

Action 3: Recording Costs

The recording of budgetary information is a mechanical function. Normally, forms are provided for the people preparing the budget, and the cost items, which were identified and classified earlier, are now recorded on those forms. At this point in the budgetary process, the data are collected at the lowest controllable activity in the department. In our example, the project leader would be asked to estimate the amount of funds that would be required for programmer supplies for that project. These would be recorded on a project budget form and classified as programmer supplies.

Most data processing costs are expensed. As mentioned previously, the failure to show the capital value of data processing assets has led to neglect of many important assets.

Senior management of a corporation reads only two documents: the statement of income and expense and the balance sheet. The fact that data and programs are not included on those documents means that senior management is not reading about them. Although those capital costs cannot appear directly on the balance sheet, they can appear as a recorded asset on budgetary reports.

Action 4: Consolidation of Budgetary Costs

The estimated budgetary amounts for each project must be consolidated into a departmental budget. In many organizations, this step is performed on a computer. It is a mechanical process of accumulating all the individual items for use in preparing a consolidated data processing department budget.

At this point in our example, the programmer supplies for our project would be combined with all other budgetary requests for programmer supplies. The result would be a total dollar amount that the department now estimates would be spent for programmer supplies during the forthcoming budgetary period. In the consolidated budget, we could not identify the supplies for an individual project. That identification would require budgetary breakdowns. In these budgetary breakdowns that should be used as a managerial tool.

Action 5: Analysis and Modification

The consolidated budget shows the resources necessary to accomplish the departmental mission for the budgetary period based on the departmental staff members' best estimate. At this point, the people involved have spoken, stating what they perceive to be their resource requirements. Management must now analyze that for reasonableness and for acceptability by senior management.

The types of constraints that management must consider during this analysis and modification process include:

1. *Reasonableness of costs among the various estimates:* For example, if two similar projects have widely varying budget estimates, management should investigate the cause.
2. *Organization's budgetary constraints:* For example, the requirement that this year's budget cannot exceed last year's budget may not be ignored.
3. *Desirability of attempting to accomplish all the items included in the budget:* Organizations can grow only in a controlled manner at a certain pace. If the budget estimates appear to be causing too rapid growth, the organizational managerial structure may not be able to handle the acquisition and integration of the additional resources into the department.
4. *Reasonableness of estimates:* Management must be sure that the estimates are neither padded nor overly optimistic. Major variances in actual cost from budget estimates affect the credibility of the department.

In our example, the data processing managers would examine the total request for programmer technical supplies. One of the things they would do is compare this year's budget in that category versus last year's budget. This analysis would take into account any growth or reduction in department staff or workload. If that amount appeared to be out of line, management might request additional study or justification for that budgetary line item. This means that each project leader who submitted budget requests in that category would be asked to reconsider the importance of expenditures. The types of requests management may make include:

- A stated across-the-board cut. This is a no-option alternative presented by management.
- Asking project leaders to reconsider the importance of an expenditure.
- Asking project leaders to justify the expenditure in more detail.

Action 6: Acceptance and Presentation of Budget

The last action in the budgetary process by the department is acceptance by DP management. Once the managers have agreed that the budget is reasonable, it is prepared in finalized format and forwarded to senior management for approval.

This is not the end of the budgetary process, merely the end of the preparation of the budget within the department. The same type of analysis that data processing management went through in approving the budget, senior management must now perform. This may require several iterations before a final budget is passed. Even then, there may be modifications made throughout the year, depending on the revenue generated by the organization.

ON TO THE WONDERFUL WORLD OF BUDGETING

Many data processing technicians and managers see budgeting as a necessary evil in fulfilling their mission. Many never even dreamed that budgeting would become such an important part of determining their personal performance. However, these attitudes are normal in the maturing of a manager. The remainder of the book is the yellow brick road leading to successful budgeting. Follow the path and watch the budgetary impediments drop by the wayside as you master the intricacies of *using* budgeting rather than *being used by* the budget.

2
Budgeting and Planning Strategies

Budgeting is normally a standardized process. The person responsible for budgeting in the organization is the comptroller. This person prepares the procedures, the forms, and the schedules, and then instructs the managers of the activities within the organization on how and when to prepare budgetary information. The comptroller distributes the forms and instructions at the appropriate time and is actively involved in the consolidation and senior management reviews of the activity budgets.

The process sounds cut and dried. It would appear that if the managers of the various activities complete the forms by following the instructions, they would have fulfilled their budgetary responsibilities. However, DP is different from many other activities and those differences must be addressed in the budgetary process. If they are going to be addressed, it will be the data processing manager who must address them.

In this chapter what is different about budgeting for DP is explained and then strategies on how to deal with those differences are provided. The budgetary differences lead to some specific budgeting problems. If these problems are not addressed, it can and does affect the credibility of the data processing department. How to turn these budgeting adversities into budgeting advantages is explained.

WHAT'S DIFFERENT ABOUT DP BUDGETING?

The early differences in DP budgeting dealt with the rapid growth of data processing and the mystique of the process being budgeted. These problems still occur in the newer data processing functions, but have been dealt with and solved in the more mature functions. Unfortunately, that learning experience may have cost the jobs of one or more data processing managers.

The rapid growth of data processing posed not only budgetary problems but also planning and management problems. The organizational structure, plans, and budgets that work well for a staff of twenty-five crumbled when the staff grew to one hundred. One of the painful lessons of DP maturity was the need for constant reorganization, replanning, and rebudgeting as departments grow in size. In addition, it was learned that departments could not assimilate to rapid growth. It was far better to have a controlled growth than a rapid buildup of staff.

The growth of DP posed other budgeting challenges to senior management. When data processing started, it was an insignificant portion of the total organization budget. However, as senior management began to plot the projected growth of data processing, it became apparent that data processing was growing too rapidly. One company projected that at the current rate of growth, the data processing budget would exceed the organization's revenue in twelve years. The way senior management handles these types of problems is to put a cap on the budget rather than dealing with the true problem.

Data processing, to many, was a black art. The computer was referred to as a black box. Those who controlled the black box were the high priests and priestesses of the data processing profession (note that many senior managers called them prima donnas). The complexity this added was that senior managers did not understand where the funds went—but they did know that a lot of funds went into data processing. Again, the solution was to cap the budget rather than address the true budgetary problems of data processing. The true differences between budgeting the DP department and budgeting most other activities within an organization are discussed next.

Projects Are Expensed

Data processing personnel have, do, and will continue to expend large amounts of money to develop application system projects. Although the actual dollars vary significantly from organization to organization, it is generally a significant amount in relation to the organization in which the project is developed. The question that needs to be asked is: Why are these large costly projects expensed rather than capitalized?

In the early 1960s, the U. S. Internal Revenue Service attempted to rule that data processing projects should be capitalized. A group of major corporations banded together to fight this ruling. Their argument was that computer projects were no different from any other administrative project that is expensed. The corporations argued further that these systems had no resale value and thus should not be capitalized. The major corporations won.

The result of this landmark decision was that computer systems are not capitalized. Since they are not capitalized, they are not recorded on the books as an asset. Because they are not recorded on the books as an asset, they are not subject to the same managerial control as are other assets of similar value.

The bottom line of this problem is that because the asset is not capitalized, management cannot equate the need to maintain that asset in the same context in which assets of comparable value require maintenance. The problem is further complicated by the fact that software systems do not wear out in the same manner as do buildings, furniture, and equipment. Obsolescence occurs in a different way, but what management must recognize is that if the system asset is properly maintained, it has an almost infinite life.

Multidepartment Projects

Single data processing projects interrelate with multiple departments. This frequently means that no one is in charge of a complete project. Figure 2.1 illustrates a primary responsibility dilemma for computer projects. The figure shows that most organizational structures are hierarchical in nature. On the other hand, computer systems flow horizontally through the organizational structure. Figure 2.1 shows one large integrated system encompassing four different organizational units. Let us assume that a problem in system A affects the comptroller's division, department H. If department H and department A cannot resolve their difference with the data processing department, the only person who can is the president of the corporation. Since the president does not want to be a data processing project leader, it may become necessary to establish alternative organizational structures to solve such problems.

Many organizations form planning committees or task forces to address this

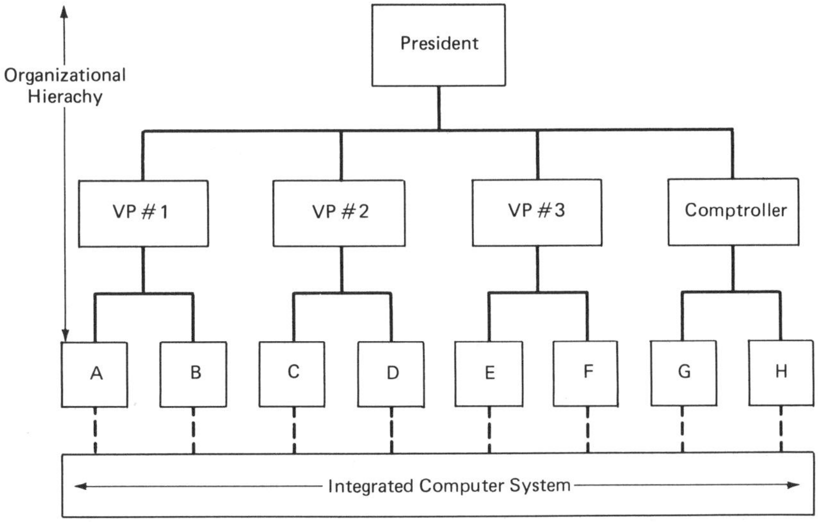

Figure 2.1 Primary responsibility dilemma.

issue. IBM has a recommendation called Business Systems Planning (BSP). In Figure 2.1, the three vice presidents and the comptroller would sit on the Business Systems Planning Committee to establish priority, direction, and resolve differences. If there is such a committee, it can also address budgetary problems; if not, the data processing department has a new budgetary challenge.

Clouding this issue is the fact that many data processing functions are generic in nature, affecting the entire organization. For example, data base administration, the information center concept for user-developed systems, and certain common systems such as those that maintain customer lists are developed for the use of the entire organization. In other words, costs directly associated with data processing are for the sole benefit of helping other parts of the organization fulfill their mission. This complicates justification and explanation of those budgetary items.

Uniqueness of Products

Data processing organizations build one-of-a-kind systems. It matters little whether they are purchased and then customized for the organization, or whether they are built in-house. Each system is unique, having unique operating characteristics, problems, and challenges.

There are few routine, repetitive operations in a data processing department. The motto of many data processing departments is that the only thing that is constant is change. This makes it difficult for data processing personnel to estimate and budget resources effectively, because each set of circumstances is unique.

In the past, many project leaders have attempted to compensate for these job shop variables by skipping some of the project development steps. This is the same process as that used by contractors when they use inferior materials or increase the distance between joists in order to cut costs. However, with the new emphasis on quality in data processing, it is becoming more difficult to shortcut the process. This, in turn, may make it more difficult to meet budgetary estimates.

Changing Technology

The rate of change of computer technology over the last thirty years has been phenomenal. Speeds and capabilities exist today which were not even dreamed of twenty-five years ago. The projection for the future is even a greater rate of change.

One of the most significant changes in data processing that will occur in the 1980s is voice recognition by machines. People will be able to communicate directly to computers by voice and receive responses back by voice. This will further accelerate the use of computers by non-DP professionals.

Managing and budgeting for this change poses continuous challenges for DP management. In some organizations, users already control over 50 percent of the data processing resources. The type of support and costs associated with this rapidly changing technology is hard to estimate.

BUDGETARY PROBLEMS ASSOCIATED WITH THE DP BUDGETING CHALLENGE

The four major differences between budgeting in a DP department versus budgeting in a non-DP department cause data processing management budgeting problems. These problems are rarely recognized in organizations' budgetary procedures. If the data processing managers fail to recognize and address these problems, they are probably having difficulties in preparing, justifying, and using DP budgets properly. The four differences mentioned in the preceding section lead to the corresponding four specific problems.

Managing an Unrecorded Asset

Maintenance of existing computer applications consumes the majority of data processing people resources. In some organizations up to 80 percent of the data processing staff is dedicated to maintenance. Note that this percentage can be changed significantly by redefining the word "maintenance." As used in this context it means managing operational systems. It includes all the activities required to keep operational systems technically current and current to meet changing business requirements. There is truly little new development going on in many data processing departments.

The application system asset that is being maintained is an unrecorded, undefined asset. If one were maintaining a piece of equipment in a factory, one would know the original cost of the equipment, the expected life of the equipment, and the replacement cost of the system. Maintenance of that equipment could be justified on increasing the uptime of the equipment and extending the life of the equipment. If the replacement cost of a machine were $200,000, and the life of that machine could be extended from five years to ten years, the savings could easily be calculated. Maintenance would not be difficult to justify.

In a computer system, the original cost of the system may be known, the replacement cost is rarely known, and the life of the system is unknown. The major factor that is known is the cost of maintenance, and it appears high.

The damaging effect of this unrecorded asset is that data processing has given the rights of maintenance to the user. Even most of the maintenance needed to keep applications technologically current has been given to the user. If the user does not desire to spend money to increase the architecture of the application system, it probably will not be done. The net result is that data processing management is left to manage a continually deteriorating asset.

Budgetary Principle

The cost of fixing a continually deteriorating application system architecture increases significantly the longer the system is allowed to remain in operation without upgrading it technologically. Data processing managers should not let their application portfolio deteriorate.

Managing Diverse Functions

The data processing department is not a single entity but, rather, a conglomerate of many different activities. It has been described by many as a "business within a business." A later section of this chapter will describe that business as being comprised of thirteen subfunctions, each of which must be managed and budgeted differently.

The data processing department staff members probably interact with every other department of the organization. They are involved in providing data processing services for all those organizations. In some businesses, the data processing function charges for its services; in others it absorbs all the costs. Regardless of the method of reallocating costs to users, those costs are dependent on the needs and requirements of most other departments within the organization. In many instances, the same system has multiple users.

Estimating Unique Project Requests

Many comptrollers joke that data processing estimates are good. The problem, they say, is with estimating the factor used to multiply the estimates to get the true cost. Data processing has been notorious for developing poor estimates.

This problem has two basic causes. First, there may be little precedence on which to base an estimate. For example, the system being built today will use tomorrow's technology, for which there is no experience on which to base the estimate. For example, if you were asked to estimate what it would cost to get 15 percent of the market share for a specific new product, but were not told what the new product was, your estimate could only be a guess. Second, most data processing professionals have never been trained in estimating and budgeting. They are not accountants, do not understand accounting, and suffer significantly from a lack of accounting knowledge. On the other hand, when their estimates are wrong they are chided for not understanding accounting principles.

Managing Unknown Risk

Risk is the probability that a loss might occur. For example, acts of nature, such as flooding, are risks that must be dealt with in data processing. Although risks are ever present, their probability of occurrence may not be known. When risks turn into losses it can have a disastrous effect on budgeting.

Let's look at the security risk and how it can affect application development and budgets. The probability that a system may be destroyed, defrauded, or compromised is an ever-present risk. The specifications for an application may address the need for security. The data processing project leader estimates the costs based on the current security level. However, newspaper articles about "hackers" breaking into computer systems increase management's awareness of the security risk. The need for security increases significantly, requiring the project to expend much more money, resulting in overruns of budgets. In another instance, a piece of purchased software fails to function according to specifications, requiring the data processing department to expend large amounts of money to make the appropriate changes, again overrunning the budget.

Senior management expects data processing management to anticipate these risks. When they are not anticipated, and more funds are requested, data processing management is frequently viewed as inept rather than viewed as doing the best job possible given the uncertainties of new technology.

BUDGETING STRATEGIES TO ADDRESS UNIQUE PROBLEMS IN DP BUDGETING

Budgeting is too important to DP management to let the corporate comptroller decide the strategy. Data processing managers should develop their own budgetary policies and strategies to deal with the unique problems within the data processing function. The difficulty in many data processing departments has been the failure to recognize and address the budgeting problems unique to the data processing function.

Budgeting policies and strategies exist in all data processing departments. Most of them are informal and probably could not be stated by either the management or staff of the function. In many instances, the strategies may vary from project to project and from manager to manager. This unstructured environment is subject to the same chaos as that which occurred when each data processing project leader was allowed to develop systems in any way that he or she wished.

We will look at budgeting strategies from three perspectives. The first will be the games people play in budgeting. In this area we will look at both the games used by preparers of budgets, and the games played by management as they review and react to budgets. Second, we will introduce the concept of fit, so data processing managers can help ensure that their budget fits into the overall organizational plan and budget. Third, we will discuss some specific strategies that should be considered in addressing the previously identified problems unique to DP budgeting.

Budgeting Games People Play

Budgeting is sometimes viewed as a cat-and-mouse game. The preparer of the budget is the mouse trying to get away with some things without being caught by the cat. Many budgeteers are very successful at this game; others end up by being eaten by the management cat.

Let's first look at some of the games played by the people preparing budgets, which include the following theories:

- *Double-cut theory:* With this theory the person preparing the budget asks for twice as much as he or she wants so that management can cut the budget in half and the requester will still receive the desired amount of money. For example, if the DP manager wants to send one person to a specific conference, the manager requests budget funds for two. Management then cuts it back to one—thus performing the managerial function of cutting the budget—and the DP manager gets what he or she wants.

- *Rathole theory:* The rathole theory states that you ignore all past costs. In other words, past costs are considered as having gone down the rathole. For example, if a project that was supposed to return $100,000 of benefits had $100,000 expended on it last year, that $100,000 can be considered to have been thrown down the rathole. This year, you budget $50,000 to complete the project, and show a $100,000 return on that $50,000 investment.
- *Creeping commitment theory:* The creeping commitment theory states that you never tell senior management all that you are intending to do. For example, if the data processing manager wants to convert to a data base environment, the current budget might request only sufficient funds to buy a data base management system. Next year the budget can call for hiring a data base administrator and one or two staff members. The following year the computer is upgraded, storage added, and applications are started to be converted. Within a five-year period, several million dollars may be expended, without ever having a plan.
- *Trial-balloon theory:* With this theory a trial balloon—a new concept or idea—is inserted into the budget. For example, funds may be included to study the acquisition of voice-recognition equipment. If the trial balloon is not shut down in the budgetary process, DP management can undertake an extensive effort and push forward rapidly in this new area.
- *Gimme theory:* The "gimme" is an intentional ploy inserted into the budget that is designed to catch management's attention. It is usually something unwanted by the person requesting the budget. The objective is to let management find something quickly and reject it, with the hope that the rest of the budget will go through unscathed.

Budgetary Principle

If people play games to achieve their budgetary objectives, it is usually because the budgeting process is not well planned and managed.

Managers are not fools. They recognize the budgetary games of subordinates and develop counterstrategies to address those games. Some of management's budgetary games include:

- *Across-the-board-cut theory:* In many cases, management does not understand the implications or detail behind the budgetary figures and justification. All management may know is that most activities ask for more money than they require. Rather than attacking the budget piecemeal, management just requires an across-the-board cut of 10 percent, for example. This avoids making a decision and at the same time pressures activities to reduce their budget.

- *Pioneer/pathfinder theory:* In the early days of the old west, the pioneers went where the whites had never been before. Unfortunately, many were killed by the Indians. Some time later, the pathfinder, following in the steps of the pioneer, would locate new areas and live to tell about it. Thus the pathfinder became the hero while the pioneer was forgotten. In many organizations, management shoots the first person to come up with a new scheme or idea. However, that plants the seed so that when the pathfinder comes along some time later, he or she gets credit for having a wonderful idea. A variation of this theory is for management to shoot the pioneer and then appoint the pathfinder to work on a project.
- *Counterattack theory:* In an effort to shoot down budgetary requests, management attacks the data presented in the budget. The statistical validity of the information is challenged, and if it cannot be supported quickly and undeniably, management eliminates the proposal from the budget.
- *Turn-the-tide theory:* Frequently, budgetary requests are not to the liking of managers. However, they are reluctant to dictate change, and therefore ask for more data, investigations, and so on, in order to attempt to change the requester's request or to get more factual information that can be used to convince the requester of the merits of a management-preferred alternative. Under this theory, management uses a variety of ploys to turn the requester's opinion in the direction desired by management.
- *New-ballgame theory:* If managers are unable to get what they want from the original budgetary process, they can always change the ground rules. For example, they might decide after the initial budgets have been prepared that the budget should not exceed last year's budget, sending the requesters back to the drawing board to meet the new rules.

People are people, and the games will continue to be played. Even in the fairest and best of systems, someone will try to beat the rules. On the other hand, most of the games are played because the budgetary system does not take into account the special needs and requirements of the areas doing the budgeting. It is toward this goal that data processing managers can make a significant contribution. What they must do is fit the data processing needs into the needs of the organization.

Concept of Budget Fit

The concept of fit means that the data processing budget fits into its organization's budget. This preassumes that the data processing short- and long-range plans fit into its organization's short- and long-range plans. If management perceives the lack of fit, the credibility of the data processing function is affected.

Loss of credibility occurs when the data processing management team is not considered part of the organization's management team. Senior management may view data processing as a technical function that supports the organization, not as an integral part of the organization. It is this attitude of senior management that has resulted in the elevation of very few data processing managers into senior management.

The lack of fit occurs when:

- The data processing short- and long-range plans are technical plans, not business plans.
- The data processing budget is service oriented, not benefit oriented.
- The data processing budget is prepared without consultation with the other operating activities served by the data processing department.

The concept of fit in the budgetary process is illustrated in Figure 2.2. This figure shows the budget and the four components of fit, which are:

1. *Planning:* The budget must be representative of both the data processing and business plan. The budgetary items should be traceable directly to both data processing and business planning activities.
2. *Performance measurement:* The budget must be presented in a format that is conducive to measuring the performance of the data processing function. If the budget is expressed in such terms, the performance can be determined only by whether or not the budgetary amounts have been achieved. The budget lacks credibility as a good managerial tool.
3. *Usability:* The budget must be usable to all parties involved in the budget. It should be a tool that can be used by the requester, data processing manage-

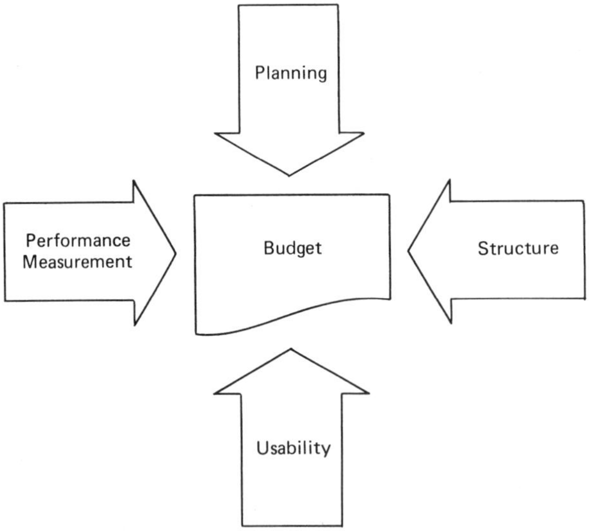

Figure 2.2 Concept of fit.

ment, and senior management to assist them in the performance of their mission and/or job responsibilities.

4. *Structure:* The budget must be prepared in the structure specified by the organization. Even though the data processing function has some differences and unique problems in the budgeting process, the end product must conform to the organization's budgeting structure. However, within that structure, the uniqueness of data processing must be addressed.

DP BUDGETING STRATEGIES

Strategies are the approaches and direction that data processing management will utilize in budget preparation and usage. These strategies should be defined and the procedures established to implement those strategies. Without strong direction from data processing management, the budget may fail to address adequately the department's mission.

There are three general strategies and four specific strategies that need to be addressed by data processing management. The general strategies are those that apply to any activity within the organization. The specific strategies are those unique to data processing and address the four budgetary problems described previously.

General Budgeting Strategies

The general budget strategies describe the philosophy that data processing management wants followed in budget preparation. These general strategies should be confidential and discussed only with those subordinates responsible for budget preparation. To disclose these general strategies would be like showing the other players in a card game your hand and then betting against them.

The general budgetary strategies that need to be determined within data processing include the following.

Tight versus ample budgets. This strategy relates to how data processing managers want to manage their staff. Some managers believe that people work best when they are under pressure. In a budgetary context, this means that the project personnel will have slightly less than is really needed to do the job. One philosophy says that this tends to make people work harder. The other strategy is to provide people with ample resources or in some cases extra resources to handle expected contingencies. In preparing the budgets, managers must decide whether their strategy is to request projects to budget at the minimal level possible to do the project, or whether they want their project personnel to provide ample funds to ensure that the project can be adequately developed. Experience has shown that the difference between a minimal budget and a high-quality budget estimate is normally 10 percent or less.

Short-term versus long-term budgeting strategies. Budgets tend to be planned on an annual basis. On the other hand, data processing projects frequently extend more than a year. Governmental agencies are particularly troubled by this dilemma because although they budget and get their money on an annual basis, many of the programs are ongoing. When the funding is uncertain from year to year, it is difficult to do adequate planning for project development. If managerial strategy is multiyear planning, the project personnel need not be concerned about annualizing what they need. This becomes a subset of the budgetary process, but the plans and budgeting from a staff perspective are a multiyear process. The alternative strategy is to think of planning in twelve-month increments, which although effective in many areas, may not be effective in the data processing area.

DP-directed versus user-directed budgeting. Data processing management must decide who will take control over the data processing budget. If the strategy is for users to make decisions on the use of data processing resources, the users will provide the primary budgetary input. Although data processing managers may actually calculate the cost, the requirements come directly from the users. The other alternative strategy is for data processing managers to assume control of their function. When this is done, information processing is viewed from an organizational perspective, and the budget becomes a subset of the organization's budget with data processing determining what must be done to provide the information processing needs as specified in the organizational plan and budget.

Specific Budgeting Strategies

In an earlier discussion, we stated that the problems associated with budgeting for data processing were: managing an unrecorded asset, coordinating diverse functions, estimating the use of new technology, and managing some new risks. Each of these problems must be addressed with a specific budgeting strategy. Following are recommended strategies for dealing with these four unique budgetary problems.

Strategy for budgeting for unrecorded assets. The application system requirements from a business perspective are a user responsibility. In other words, the payroll department has responsibility for specifying, prioritizing, and requesting changes and enhancements to the payroll system. On the other hand, one of the maintenance requirements is maintaining the technological currentness of the application system. This is not a responsibility of the user area but, rather, a responsibility of the data processing department.

The need for product features should be separate from the need to maintain that product technically. For example, if the organization acquired a limousine for the president, the president would be responsible for the features included, such as an automobile telephone. On the other hand, the president would rarely have responsibility for maintaining the engine and transmission. In data processing, the user has no responsibility for hardware selection and operation. It is reasonable to deduce from these analogies that the user, due to the lack of technical knowledge, should not have responsibility for the technological currentness of application systems.

A recommended budgetary strategy is for users to budget for the changes and enhancements to business features, and for the data processing department to budget for technologically upgrading application software. This does not mean that the user does not pay the entire cost. What it is suggesting is that strategically it is better for the user to specify business concerns, and for data processing to specify and budget for technological considerations.

Strategies for coordinating diverse functions. The data processing department is comprised of many different processing components. These components are involved in servicing most areas within the organization. For some systems, many of the activities within the organization are involved. The net result is that the interaction of activities becomes a budgeting nightmare. For example, many users may interface with the data base administration activity, yet that activity is not under the direct control of a single user. Therefore, a problem exists as to how to collect and allocate charges for those activities among multiple users.

The recommended strategy for dealing with this problem is to put each functional activity on a pay-as-you-go basis. This means that the activity must be able to recoup its cost if it is going to continue to exist. This is a simple budgetary procedure of cost allocation among multiple users. It uses cost accounting concepts to allocate costs based on services rendered.

This concept requires data processing to view itself as a profit center rather than as a cost center. This is more of a mental orientation than a revised accounting approach. As a cost center, data processing is responsible for expending monies of the organization in order to provide information processing services. In a profit center services that are not cost-effective will be satisfied through other means. Thus the profit center concept means that if data processing cannot be competitive with similar organizations, it will go out of business.

When data processing views itself as a profit center, it reallocates all its expenditures back to those areas using the services. This concept is frequently referred to as charging for data processing services, or *charge-out*. In this context, data processing operates as a business within a business.

Strategies for estimating costs involving new technology. Estimating data processing costs for the use of new technology has been a risky business. Experience has shown that many data processing professionals are ill equipped to develop good estimates when new technology is involved. On the other hand, management needs realistic estimates in order to make logical business decisions.

The challenge facing data processing professionals is that if they make an estimate for which they do not have a good basis, and that estimate proves to be wrong, theirs and the data processing department's credibility has been lessened. A strategy is needed for budgeting to increase the probability of these estimates involving the use of new technology. Since technology is accelerating rapidly, this will be a continuing challenge for data processing.

The recommended budget strategy is to use risk as a budgeting criterion. If all projects are estimated using the same yardstick, and then adjusted by the degree of risk, the probability of making a realistic estimate will be increased. For example, if a project using known technology could be installed for $50,000, that estimate could be adjusted by a risk factor if the risk of the new technology could be equated to the risk of the known technology. For example, if the new technology has twice the risk of the current technology, a risk factor of 2 might be used. If we multiplied the $50,000 estimate by 2, we would produce a $100,000 estimate to do that project using new technology.

Strategies relating to the budgeting for new technology. New technology will always pose a high risk for the data processing function. Organizations must learn how to deal with this risk in the budgetary process. An unfortunate fact of budgeting is that many managers are conditioned to believe that the budget is a high-precision tool. This may not be a realistic approach when dealing in unknown areas.

A suggested strategy for addressing unknown technology is to qualify the budget precision. Some parts of the data processing budget can be estimated to very high precision, such as hardware costs. It may even be possible to develop an entire data processing budget for which the overall precision is very high. On the other hand, the precision of the individual line items may be very low. A strategy that qualifies precision by line items may be very positive strategy for data processing. This will avoid leading management to perceive that the budget estimates are finite, when in fact they may not have a reliability greater than plus or minus 50 percent.

Adopting the appropriate budgetary strategies is an essential part of effective budgeting for data processing. Data processing management must determine the type of image they desire to express in their budgetary process. It is recommended that these strategies recognize the uniqueness of data processing, and utilize those differences as budgetary strengths, as opposed to ignoring them with the resulting potential loss of DP management credibility.

IMPLEMENTING THE BUDGETING STRATEGIES

Strategies are broad, general guidelines provided by management to provide direction in the performance of budgeting. These strategies must be interpreted and applied to everyday budgetary problems. The implementation of strategies involves the reconciliation of budgetary line items with data processing responsibilities.

Budgetary line items address components such as salaries, hardware costs, communication costs, software costs, and so on. Data processing functions deal with maintaining a payroll system, developing an automatic inventory replenishment system, overseeing the organization's personal computer program, and so on.

Budgeting is easy at the line-item level, for example, salaries. Unfortunately, this does not help manage the data processing department, nor does it address some of its unique problems. For example, salaries may be easy to determine, but the cost of implementing voice-recognition technology can be very difficult. However, management wants to monitor the voice-recognition program, but can do little to manage salaries other than at the total dollar level.

The strategies should be implemented for each data processing function, not at the traditional organizational budgetary line-item level. This requires that each function (e.g., payroll system) be broken up into its component parts. If budgeting is performed at the component level, it can then be combined and presented in any format desirable by the organization's comptroller. However, if the functional aspect of budgeting is lost, it loses value as a managerial tool, and does not become the means of communicating data processing problems, needs, and benefits to senior management.

Budgetary Principle

The budget should be prepared first, to meet the needs of data processing management, and second, restructured and presented in the structure decreed by the organization's comptroller. It is the former that becomes a DP management tool, and the latter that meets the needs of the organization's budgetary procedures.

THE VALUE OF BUDGETING

The resources expended to perform any process should add value to the products produced by that function. If the value of any job cannot be demonstrated, it is difficult to justify performing that job. Budgeting is no exception to this business principle.

The "value added" to budgeting increases as the budget is used to manage the data processing function. When the comptroller makes all the budgeting rules, the comptroller owns the budget. No product will become valuable until the user of that product accepts ownership of the product. In other words, if data processing managers are going to use the budget, they must feel that the budget is theirs—in other words, they own it.

Ownership of the budget comes from customizing the organizational budgetary process to meet specific data processing needs. This customization process should add value to the department from the effort expended on budgeting. The remaining chapters in the book provide the steps to be used in implementing the strategies described in this chapter.

Budgetary Principle

People utilize products they own more effectively than they utilize products they do not own. Budgetary ownership comes from customizing the organization's budgetary process for the unique needs of the data processing function.

Part 2 The Budget as a Management Tool

3 The Dimensions and Components of DP Budgeting

Budgeting is a tool for use by managers in controlling their activities. This presumes that the activities or components of their business can be adequately defined. For the purpose of budgeting in a DP department, we will define these budgeted activities as controllable components. A controllable component is defined as an activity, area, or segment within the data processing department that can be identified and controlled as an entity.

Budgeting for these controllable components of the DP department must take into account the three dimensions of budgeting. Many managers view budget as a single-dimensional activity—a single activity and a single amount of money for that activity. However, this concept does not take into account some of the uniqueness of data processing. The data processing budget is three-dimensional, including the resources, the time frame, and the risk associated with each controllable component.

In this chapter the sixteen components of data processing that are controllable and budgetable, and the three dimensions of budgeting, are described. The characteristics of each of the controllable components are discussed, as well as the three risk dimensions for each component. In later chapters we explain how to build up budget costs for each component and how to control those components through effective use of budgeting.

BUDGETING THE DP DEPARTMENT VERSUS BUDGETING DP EXPENDITURES

The traditional approach used by DP management is to budget for the data processing department. However, this is becoming an increasingly smaller part of the organization's data processing expenditures. Many companies now state that the DP department budget is less than one-half of the organization's expenditures on data processing. Many experts have projected that by 1990 the data processing department may account for only 10 percent of the total data processing expenditures for the organization.

There is a need to address data processing expenditures at the corporate level. The principles described in this book will work equally effectively for budgeting the data processing department or budgeting data processing expenditures.

It is recommended that data processing management develop budgets for both the department and the corporation. Although data processing management may not have control over the funds allocated to other departments, the data processing manager should have influence over the use of data processing dollars throughout the organization.

The corporate comptroller cannot exercise direct control over the expenditures of departments other than his own, but he can influence the size and usage of dollars. The comptroller is responsible for safeguarding the assets of the organization. The data processing manager is responsible for data processing resources and expenditures, and is also responsible for managing and running the data processing department. These dual responsibilities require dual budgeting.

The preparation of the departmental budget will be simpler than the organizational budget. Developing an organizational data processing budget will require close cooperation with the comptroller. Special accounts will need to be set up for use by all departments for identifying data processing expenditures in the budget. For example, a common account should be established for the acquisition of personal computers.

This dual responsibility merely demonstrates the importance of the budget as a managerial control tool. Data processing management will not be able to control data processing within the organization without using the budget as a control tool. Aggressive data processing managers should begin immediately to initiate corporate-wide budgeting for data processing.

ALLOCATION OF DP FUNDS

There are many rules of thumb on what percentage of an organization's income/revenue should be expended on data processing. A 1983 DPMA survey showed that the average DP budget equaled $2\frac{1}{2}$ percent of the organization's revenue, but the range varies between 1 and 8 percent of revenue. In most organizations, the data processing budget is large, by senior management standards. As stated previously, data processing, because of its size and complexity, should be considered as a business within a business.

The use of data processing resources will vary from organization to organization, depending on the mission of the data processing department and the ways in which the function utilizes technology. There is no one right way to spend those funds, but it is always helpful to look at how the average data processing department uses its resources. However, when analyzing averages, one must always keep in mind that it is possible to drown in a stream whose average depth is six inches.

The average DP function can be constructed by extrapolating from numerous survey results published in a variety of data processing periodicals. The typical DP budget allocation is illustrated in Figure 3.1. This shows that salaries, including all benefits, are the major component of the DP budget, approximately 45 percent. Hardware is the next largest component, approximately 30 percent. Communication costs and the cost of purchasing, renting, and maintaining software from outside vendors are 10 percent each. The facilities in which the data processing department resides, together with the cost of utilities, accounts for approximately 3 percent. The remaining 2 percent is used for outside services, including training, consultants, and publications of all types.

The problem with allocations presented in this manner is that they do not represent controllable activities. Salaries could be controlled by head count, but that does not really address the mission of the data processing department. We need to control salaries by controlling such things as technical support services, systems maintenance, systems development, administrative support, and so on. Similarly, hardware is not a single thing but, rather, it is disk space, terminals, off-line printers, decollators, and so on. It is much better to control hardware based on projected usage, location of facilities, and so on, than to control it by the total dollar amount. The types and variety of hardware that can be acquired for X dollars is almost infinite.

We need to break these budget allocation categories into controllable components. After budgeting at the controllable component level, it is easy to consolidate

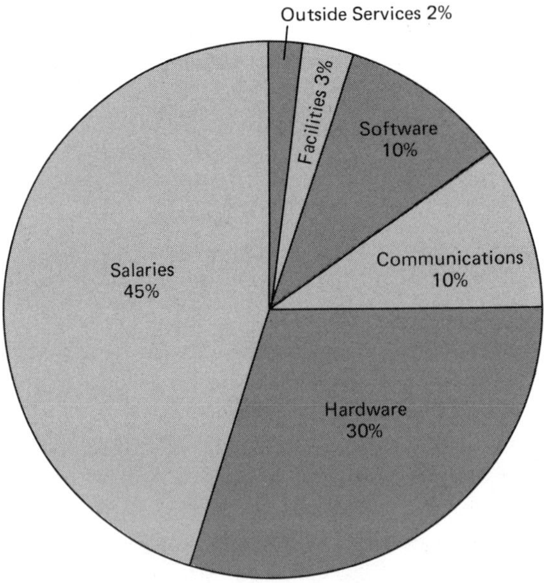

Figure 3.1 DP budget allocations.

and produce the type of breakdown shown in Figure 3.1. Frequently, such a breakdown is required by the organization for budgetary purposes. However, data processing managers must carefully differentiate between using the budget as a control tool and using it for justifying resources.

Budgetary Principle

If the data processing manager is going to use the budget as a tool for control, the budget must be developed to show the budget for those activities the manager wants to control.

CONTROLLABLE DP COMPONENTS

The literal definition of a controllable data processing component is "an activity that data processing management wants to control." There is normally a close parallel between organizational structure and controllable components. In this book we will define the *controllable component* as a major category of control, and an *activity* as the lowest controllable item. For example, systems development is a controllable component, whereas a specific project that is being developed will be considered a controllable activity.

In this section we identify and explain the controllable components. Sixteen components will be identified; however, some organizations may wish to enhance or combine these components because of their special mission or the way in which they are organized. The sixteen components recommended should suffice for most organizations.

The activities within each component (described in a later chapter) are needed to build up the cost for the component. Again, in our systems development component example, we would need to know all the developmental activities in order to calculate a total system development budget. This approach permits data processing management to control system development as a component, and then to control the individual activities within that component through the use of budgetary information. It is important for the data processing manager to keep in mind the difference between the internal DP use of the budget and the use of the budget in the organization.

The suggested sixteen controllable components, together with an overview of the characteristics of those components, are listed in Table 3.1. A more detailed description of the budgeting peculiarities of each of the controllable components follows.

DP Management and Administration Component

DP management and administration are those management activities not directly chargeable to users of data processing services. In accounting terms, these costs are referred to as *overhead*. This means that the activities are of equal benefit to all activities covered by the managers and administrators. The overhead concept states that it is fair to distribute those costs equitably among all activities rather than attempt to distribute them on a variable factor related to work. For example, overhead charges could be distributed as a percentage of resources consumed by users of the data processing facilities.

TABLE 3.1 CHARACTERISTICS OF CONTROLLABLE COMPONENTS

Controllable component	Component budgeting characteristics
1. DP management and administration	Department-wide component
2. Facilities	Department-wide component Cost related to service demand
3. Systems support	Department-wide component Cost related to service demand Easy to modify cost
4. New systems development	High technology User driven Difficult to estimate accurately Schedule dependent Limited by availability of staff
5. Systems maintenance	High technology User driven Difficult to justify Difficult to estimate accurately Schedule dependent Limited by availability of staff
6. Computer operations	Outside vendor involved High technology User driven Department-wide component Cost related to service demand Schedule dependent
7. Hardware	Outside vendor involved High technology User driven Department-wide component Cost related to service demand
8. Purchased/rented software	Outside vendor involved High technology Difficult to estimate accurately (installation cost)
9. Technical support	High technology Difficult to justify Department-wide component Limited by availability of staff
10. Quality assurance	Difficult to justify Department-wide component Limited by availability of staff

TABLE 3.1 *(Cont.)*

Controllable component	Component budgeting characteristics
11. Communications	Outside vendor involved High technology Cost related to service demand
12. Data base administration	High technology User driven Limited by availability of staff
13. Word processing/office system/ microcomputers	Outside vendor involved High technology User driven Cost related to service demand
14. Information center	High technology User driven Difficult to justify Cost related to service demand Easy to modify cost Limited by availability of staff
15. Security	High technology Difficult to justify Department-wide component
16. Outside services	Outside vendor involved Difficult to justify Cost related to service demand Easy to modify cost

For ease of illustration, let us assume that 80 percent of the DP resources is directly chargeable to users and that 20 percent represents overhead charges. This means that 20 percent of the costs must be allocated according to how the 80 percent of the resources were consumed. Since it is a 80:20 ratio, the 20 percent translates to 25 percent of the 80 percent charged to users. If the direct charges to a user were $10,000, a 25 percent overhead allocation would be added to that, making the total charge $12,500.

The mathematics above illustrate some of the mechanics of a charge-out system (the process is explained in a later chapter). For the purpose of understanding controllable components, it is unimportant how those charges are allocated. The management and administrative costs can be controlled as a component, and then through accounting procedures allocated to produce a distribution of data processing charges, if required.

It is good practice to keep management and administrative costs as low as possible. Experience has shown that organizations run better with small management staffs. The current emphasis in industry is to reduce middle management and put more responsibility on the lower-level employees.

The cost associated with management and administration is a continuous cost. It is comprised primarily of the cost of people whose salaries are fixed and continue from month to month.

Facilities Component

The organization normally provides the facilities for the data processing department. These include office space, computer room, furniture and fixtures, utilities, and other support services, such as plant protection. These other costs are normally accumulated as organizational overhead and then distributed to the various functions within the organization according to either the size of their budget or the amount of space or people involved in the function.

The costs associated with the facilities will vary depending on the mission of data processing. As the size of the function expands, so will the facilities costs. The data processing function may also have to provide facilities for users and for vendor and service personnel resident or using the data processing facilities.

Systems Support Component

Systems support is a component comprising the activities needed to support primarily the system development and maintenance activities. The major components of systems support are planning, the standards program, training, change management, and project scheduling. In some organizations, these are under a single manager, whereas in other organizations the support functions are split among several organizational areas.

The support activities are frequently considered part of departmental overhead. Activities such as standards and training apply equally to all functions within the department. The amount of support services provided will depend on the demand for those services by management and the application projects.

The systems support component contains many controllable costs. For example, outside training is a controllable cost, which is estimated in many data processing departments to consume 1 percent of the total resources. It is easy for the data processing manager to eliminate outside training if it becomes necessary to reduce costs. On the other hand, training is a means used to improve productivity, so although funds can be saved from the training budget, they may be expended several times over in increased costs to perform work because the staff lacks adequate skills.

New Systems Development Component

Systems development is the component responsible for the creation of new application systems. This may be accomplished through in-house coding, use of purchased or rented vendor-produced software, or a combination thereof. The activities involve defining user needs and then satisfying those needs through a combination of manual and automated procedures.

Budgeting for systems development encompasses the estimation of effort to produce a new application system. Variables include the knowledge of technology by the DP project staff, knowledge of DP by the user, knowledge of the technology being used, time span and staffing, management support and interest, and complexity of specified requirements. The less that is known about any of these variables, the more difficult it is to develop good budgetary information.

Some of the specific budgetary challenges are the multibudget period implications of project development. Frequently, projects extend over two or more budget years. Even if the total project is well estimated, it may be difficult to determine how much of those costs will actually be spent in each budget year. For example, if a project were budgeted to start in June but could not in fact start until November, the project would not consume all the budgeted resources that year. This would make the budgetary information look inaccurate, although the total estimate for the project might be accurate within a few dollars. These time frame and risk characteristics associated with systems development impose impediments on effective systems development budgeting. One of the variables that is very difficult to control is availability of staff at the time and in the quantity and at the skill level needed.

Systems Maintenance Component

Many data processing managers report that the majority of their systems and programming effort are now expended on maintenance, as opposed to new development. As data processing organizations mature, the percentage of resources allocated to maintenance increases. There is no reason to believe that the trend toward increased maintenance cost will abate.

Organizations define systems maintenance in many ways. The narrow definition of systems maintenance restricts the function to correcting flaws and fine tuning the application. The expanded definition includes all the activities required to manage a system in an operational stage. Using the broad definition, the costs of enhancing the application to meet changing requirements would be considered maintenance.

One of the major budgetary challenges in maintenance is identifying those activities that will be performed under the maintenance category. For example, to budget properly it would be necessary to estimate the number of defects that will occur during the year requiring correction, as well as the number of minor requests to be submitted by the user. Because these are not known a year or more in advance, budgeting for maintenance is often an allocation of the resources that management will expend on maintenance, as opposed to the maintenance needs. In other words, budgeting becomes more a level of effort than an attempt to satisfy user requirements. Provided in this level-of-effort context, maintenance is difficult to justify. It is also difficult to estimate accurately when the details of what will be done are not known.

Much of maintenance, as well as systems development, is dependent on meeting scheduled installation dates. Experience has shown that the resources required to do a task vary significantly according to the time span available for installation and the size of the staff. Nine programmers all working on the same project for a one-month period can rarely do as much as one programmer working on that project for a nine-month period, although they both consume nine person-months of effort.

Computer Operations Component

Computer operations comprise the activities needed to operate application systems. Among the more common activities are data entry operations, control function over a job submission and return, computer operators, data librarians, schedulers, and off-line data preparation activities such as printing and decollating.

The types of activities will vary based on how technology is used. The more batch systems that are run, the larger the operations staff will tend to be; however, as operations become distributed into user areas the number of operators in the data processing department decreases.

The operations activities are primarily user-directed activities. The user determines the schedule when jobs need to be run or on-line resources provided. Operations serves the entire organization, but must do it according to predetermined schedules.

The budgeting difficulty for operations is in adequately anticipating future workload. Workload can occur through increased business activities, increased data processing activities, or an increased number of defects in existing or developed applications.

Hardware Component

Hardware is a major cost component; even though the cost of hardware per unit of processing has dropped dramatically, it still accounts for a significant part of the data processing budget. For a variety of reasons, most of them valid, organizations deal with only a single or very few hardware vendors. Although the advantages of common hardware are significant, its use might restrict the flexibility of the organization in selecting lower-cost hardware alternatives.

The hardware component is defined as the totality of equipment and media needed for application processing, excluding communication equipment. This includes the computer mainframe, input/output devices, terminals, off-line hardware such as key entry devices, and computer media such as tape, disk, and printed forms, excluding those special-purpose forms charged directly to application systems.

The hardware budgeting challenge is similar to that of computer operations; it is user driven because the more service demands that are placed by users, the more hardware that is needed. An extra budgeting problem can occur if the lead time to acquire needed hardware is extensive, for example, eighteen months. In these situations, if the hardware estimates are low, the organization may not be able to get the needed hardware without paying an extensive premium or searching for alternative processing methods, such as service centers, which might drive up the cost significantly.

Purchase / Rental Software Component

Vendor-supplied software is of two types. The first type is operating system software, some of which may be provided at no cost by the mainframe vendor, and other system software, such as data base management systems that need to be acquired. The second type is application systems software. Many organizations purchase all their software system from vendors. The trend for all organizations is to purchase more and develop fewer in-house applications.

The major budgetary challenge with vendor software is the installation cost. Many organizations estimate that it takes two to three times the purchase cost to install a software package. Installation costs include learning the software, changing any necessary job control, rewriting operator instructions to the installation's standards, and any modifications or customization that needs to be made to the software package.

Technical Support Component

Technical support is the effort needed to utilize system software and to interface the software to application systems. This function is comprised primarily of systems programmers. It is one of the most technical positions within the data processing department.

The efficiency of computer operations is determined by the technical support group. It is the systems software features selected and how those features are utilized that determine the computer throughput. Unfortunately, few organizations have standards by which they can measure the performance of the technical support group. Because the group is difficult to measure, it is difficult to justify in detail what the group does. In many organizations, it is a poorly controlled function.

The specific tasks performed by the technical support component include generation of the operating system, selection of systems software, writing or specifying the interface language between application systems and systems software, and designing the parameters for effective use of the hardware.

The technical support function assists all departmental activities. Therefore, in many organizations it is considered part of departmental or operations overhead. What the technical support staff can perform depends more on the skills of the individual staff members than on the total number of systems programmers. However, for budgetary purposes it is primarily a people function.

Quality Assurance Component

DP quality assurance has the responsibility for defining the quality factors and adjusting the processes that build, maintain, and operate systems to improve the quality. This is primarily a staff function. Quality assurance is not responsible for quality but, rather, is a catalytic function that encourages and measures the level of quality in a data processing department.

Quality data processing is comprised of both quality assurance and quality control. Quality control assures that the products produced (i.e., systems) meet data processing and user standards. This is a system development and maintenance component function. Quality assurance is the quality control function for quality control of projects.

The budgeting challenges of quality assurance relate to the definition and acceptance of quality. In many organizations this function is difficult to justify. For that reason its capabilities are frequently restricted by staffing provisions. One of management's challenges is how to allocate quality assurance charges in the department. Some organizations build those costs directly into the projects in which they participate, whereas other organizations charge quality assurance to overhead. The overhead charge is the more common and preferred method.

Communications Component

Communication involves the line charges and communication control equipment (e.g., modems) needed to process information over communication lines. Communication can be by owned lines, leased lines from common carriers, microwave, voice communications, and/or satellite. It is a highly specialized aspect of data processing because of the large variety of communication options.

Many data processing organizations have found that their local telephone company is inadequately staffed to provide the assistance needed for information communication. This can complicate the budgeting process because the types of equipment or pricing options may not be readily determinable. In addition, new communication options continue to be offered, as well as equipment requiring communication capabilities.

The communication costs normally depend on the amount of communication transmitted. Some dedicated lines are leased for time periods rather than by volume of communication. Other communication contracts are based on the level of service, with charges increasing as the volume of messages increases. Therefore, the precision of the communication estimate may depend directly on the precision of the estimate of the number of messages to be transmitted during the budgetary period.

Data Base Administration Component

Data base administration is the component responsible for managing the organization's data base(s). This function normally selects the data base management system, develops the structure for the data base, instructs and works with users on how to use the data base, and has the overall responsibility for integrity of data base processing.

The use of a data base poses some unique budgetary considerations. When dedicated files are used the file structure is under the control of the project, and costs associated with that file are charged directly to the project. In data base technology, the structure is not under the control of the project. However, use of the data base is charged to the projects participating. The dilemma appears when the structure is extremely inefficient for a specific user. If the data base administrator has done his or her job properly, the data base structure has been optimized for the organization but not necessarily for each user of the organization. Some users are going to be penalized by that structure. The budgeting challenge is how to compensate users who are charged an exorbitant amount for a service that would have been much cheaper in a non-data-base technology so that other users can reap the benefits of the data base structure.

The larger the data base staff, the more service they can provide to the users. However, because these people are frequently considered to be overhead, management attempts to keep the data base staff low to a minimum. This trade-off may result in additional work being shifted from the data base function to the projects.

Word Processing / Office System / Microcomputers Component

The office systems responsibilities may be located in the data processing function. Frequently, the systems knowledge of the DP staff leads to the function getting the office systems responsibilities. In other organizations, only the office systems used by data processing personnel are within the jurisdiction of the DP department.

Office systems combine several of the larger components for centralized systems into the office systems area. For example, the group designing office systems usually selects hardware, sets up operations, acquires software, provides technical support, and may help to design and maintain systems.

The growth of data processing outside the data processing department will be one of the major challenges of the 1980s and 1990s. Word processing equipment, office systems equipment, and microcomputers are growing in capabilities. Word processing equipment is adding data processing capabilities; data processing equipment is adding word processing capabilities. Typewriters are adding disk drives with storage capabilities in the million-byte range, and with removable diskettes capabilities are almost unlimited.

Microcomputers may be the fastest-growing segment of the data processing field. Larger corporations are purchasing them by the thousands. However, the microcomputer of today is of the power and size of the mainframe computer only a decade ago. These small computers have significant processing capabilities. However, as stated several times previously, what is not budgeted will not be controlled. Without quick and effective steps to control the funding for microcomputers, the ability to control this rapidly growing part of data processing may be lost.

In some respects, the area encompasses all the budgetary challenges of the majority of the components in the data processing department. It is a microcosm of the larger environment. It is subject to the same fluctuations in estimating and precision as occur in the bigger systems.

Information Center Component

The information center is a concept by which data processing resources are used to help non-data-processing personnel use automated systems. In these instances, the user departments acquire their own computer facilities, such as personal computers, and receive assistance from data processing professionals in the use of that equipment.

Some information centers are established informally, others are formal. However, all are subject to requests by both users and management. Users want assistance in selecting, developing, and operating their equipment, as well as help in solving problems. A dilemma occurs when a user operating the semiproduction system on the user's equipment terminates or leaves and no one left is qualified to maintain or operate those systems. Management immediately calls on data processing for help.

The budgeting dilemma is how to allocate resources to this new component. It is a user-driven component, usually limited by availability of staff. It is also a function that is easy to modify; however, the cost of the information center may vary depending on management-imposed demand. It is not uncommon to have to commit extra resources to the information center to help a user get out of a serious data processing problem.

A concept closely related to the information center is the development center. Whereas the information center is an outward function assisting non-data-processing personnel in the performance of data processing tasks, the development center is an inward-looking resource used to help data processing professionals accomplish data processing tasks. Organizations that have development centers should consider them to be a controllable component and budget them separately.

Security

Security is the component charged with protecting the assets and information of the organization. Security is both physical and logical. Physical security involves primarily manual and mechanical functions designed to protect the facility, such as guards or the use of locks to enter the computer operations area. Logical security measures are those included within software systems, such as security software (e.g., IBM's RACF).

The budgeting challenge faced by data processing is the justification of the use of resources for security purposes. Management interest in computer security varies depending on recent escapades by hackers or defrauders. The greater the publicity of security violations, the easier it is to justify security budgets. However, even when funds are allocated it is difficult to substantiate that they are being used effectively.

Outside Services Component

Outside services represent assistance provided by other organizations for a fee. Among the types of services that might be contracted for are contract programmers, consultants, training courses, publications, and travel and other expenses associated with those services.

Many of these services are difficult to justify on a return-on-investment calculation. Therefore, they are an area that can easily be adjusted because the DP function rarely depends on those services for day-to-day operation of the function. Outside services tend to be increased during good economic times and decreased during poor economic times.

THE THREE DIMENSIONS OF BUDGETING

Budgets appear to be one-dimensional. This means that the budgetary estimates are for doing work for a calendar-year period. Effective budgeting considers the three dimensions of resources, risk, and time frame. Much of the problem with budgeting in data processing is that it is concentrated on the resources aspect of the budget, with little or no effort directed toward the risk and time frame.

The *resource* dimension deals with the people, equipment, facilities, and supplies estimated to be needed to accomplish a budgetary objective. The *time frame* relates to the period in which those resources will be needed. The *risk* states the probability of the estimate and/or the time frame being correct. The totality of the three will help produce better budgetary estimates.

We will examine these dimensions individually and then relate them to the sixteen controllable components. The three dimensions are illustrated in Figure 3.2 and discussed below.

Resource Dimension

The resources within the data processing department are relatively finite in nature. They include:

- Salaries
- Facility
- Hardware (including maintenance)

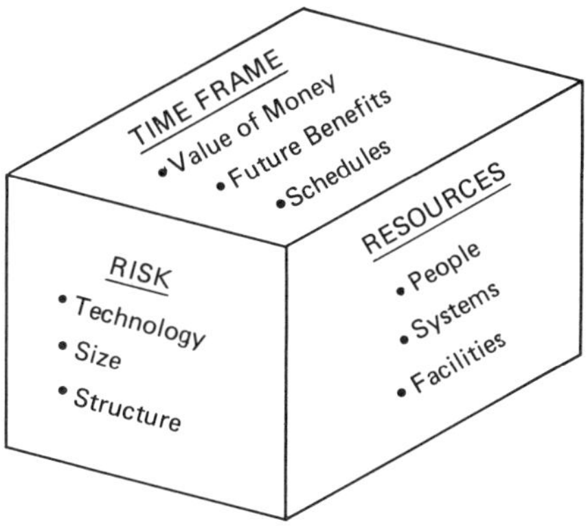

Figure 3.2 Three dimensions of budgeting.

- Purchased software (including maintenance)
- Organization overhead allocation
- Outside contracts/services
- Supplies
- Travel and entertainment

Many of these costs are reflected in costs associated with the controllable components. For example, a system development project may use hardware capacity, computer operators, outside services, and supplies. Budgetary decisions need to be made as to how those costs will be accumulated. This suggests that there can be more than one level of control over any single cost.

Let's look from two perspectives at how a single cost can be controlled by data processing management. We stated that computer hardware is a controllable component. Management should manage and control costs associated with the acquisition and operation of computer hardware. This is one level of control. That hardware can be used for systems development. The amount of hardware capacity used should be included within the systems development estimate. This provides a second level of control. One is control over acquisition and operation; the other is control over usage. Both are important.

The mechanics of excluding duplicate costs was solved years ago by accountants. The method they use is called *consolidation*. During consolidation, the charges between units of the same organization are eliminated. However, it is important that these charges appear in both controllable components so that they can be controlled by the appropriate level of management.

Budgetary Principle

It is a good budgeting practice to include costs in all activities related to a resource, even if it results in duplicate recordings. These duplications can be eliminated when budget line items are consolidated.

Time Frame Dimension

Time is important because time is money. Money has a value that must be considered in the cost/benefit analysis of computer systems. A dollar spent today may require a $2 return to break even within a couple of years. This concept is called the *present value of money*.

The present value of money is a relatively easy concept to understand. It has an important implication in data processing because DP spends dollars today to get benefits tomorrow. The concept states that tomorrow's dollars are not equal to today's in the cost/benefit calculation.

Let us assume that money is worth 10 percent interest per year. This means that $1 a year from now is only worth $0.90 today. One dollar of benefits received two years from now is worth only $0.81 today, and so on. The further in the future benefits are received, the less value they have when return on investment is being calculated. Therefore, the time when money is spent and the time when benefits are received are important budgetary considerations because they affect the return on investment from data processing projects.

The time dimension is also important because many data processing projects are multiyear projects. It would make little sense to approve funds to develop a system this year which requires two years to develop without allocating additional funds next year. This means that in DP budgeting the approval of funds in the current year may imply approval for funds in the following year. It is important that the budget make these commitments clear.

We can categorize the time frame considerations into the following four areas:

1. *Fixed continuous cost:* This type of allocation of funds is an even expenditure of funds month after month.
2. *Point in time:* This allocation of funds is directed toward using funds at a specific time. For example, we could predetermine the point at which funds would be expended to send someone to a conference.
3. *Current cost, future benefits:* This allocation of funds requires investment today to reap benefits later.
4. *Multiyear commitment:* Funds approved in this year's budget carry with them an implicit agreement that additional funds needed to complete the project will be made available in future years.

Risk Dimension

All data processing activities are not equal. Some are much less likely than others to succeed. The determination of the probability of success involves the risk dimension of budgeting.

Let's look at a few of the criteria that can cause an estimate to be incorrect:

- The technology is unknown.
- The project personnel are unskilled.
- The system is extremely complex.

The probability of success of any data processing activity is related partially to the risk inherent in completing that activity. The greater the risk, the less the probability that the project will be completed on time and within budget. For example, if a project involved the mastery of new technology, the probability of completing the project in the same time frame as could be done with current technology is low. Therefore, the estimate would need to be increased by some measure of the degree of risk inherent in performing the activity.

There are three characteristics of data processing risk:

1. *Technological risk:* This is the risk associated with new and unproven technology. The more the organization knows about the technology, the lower the risk; the less they know about the technology, the higher the risk.
2. *Size risk:* Generally, the larger the project, the greater the risk, and the smaller the project, the less the risk. For example, when more people are assigned to a project, there is a greater opportunity for miscommunication; and as components within a computer system grow in size, the difficulty of building and testing them increases geometrically.
3. *Structural risk:* As the complexity of the structure increases, so does the risk; and as the structure simplifies, the risk decreases. For example, a project involving multiple departments and several segments within data processing, such as data base and data communication, has a complex structure and thus a high risk. On the other hand, a system with a single user using simple logic has a high probability of success.

Each budgetary activity should be assessed on the degree of risk inherent within the activity. The risk needs to be viewed from two management perspectives. The first is a budgetary perspective involving whether or not sufficient resources have been allocated based on the risk. The second perspective is whether there are sufficient staff members with adequate skills to undertake a project given the degree of risk.

This concept of matching the skills of the staff with the risk of the project is called the *balanced risk portfolio concept.* It is designed to attempt to match skills with risk. High-risk projects get the more skilled personnel. If adequately skilled personnel are not available to work on a project, data processing management should seriously consider delaying the project until the appropriately skilled staff is available, contracting the project to an outside organization, or significantly increasing the budget to compensate for the inadequacy of the staff assigned to the project.

THE RISK DIMENSIONS OF THE CONTROLLABLE BUDGET COMPONENTS

Each budget component needs to be assessed from a risk perspective. In understanding the budgetary components we need to evaluate the magnitude of risk associated with that component so that we can adjust estimates accordingly. High-risk controllable budgetary components should be adjusted to reflect the risk. Budgetary components associated with low risk may need to be adjusted downward because the degree of risk may not warrant the budgetary expenditure.

Management should insist that adequate time be devoted to develop an adequate budget. This means that each component must be constructed from the bottom up, taking into account the degree of risk associated with that component. This chapter, in which the budgetary components and the dimension of risk are introduced, is designed to alert those responsible for the budgetary process to the components and risk dimensions to be considered during the process.

The risk dimensions for each of the sixteen controllable components are described in Table 3.2. This table is designed to help people who are preparing budgets to take into account the degree of risk in the budgeted activity within their area of responsibility. The three risk dimensions have been described previously, and are summarized in this table. If clarification of the figure is needed, the reader should review the specific risk dimension in question to obtain a further explanation of the specific risk dimension criteria.

TABLE 3.2 DIMENSIONS OF COMPONENTS

Controllable Components	Risk dimension		
	Resources	Time frame	Risk
1. DP management and administration	Salaries Facility Outside contracts/services Supplies Travel and entertainment	Fixed continuous costs	Size
2. Facilities	Facility Organization overhead allocation	Fixed continuous costs	Size Structure
3. Systems support	Salaries Facility Software Outside contracts/services Supplies Travel and entertainment	Fixed continuous costs Current cost—future benefits	Size
4. New systems development	Salaries Facility Hardware Software Outside contracts/services Supplies Travel and entertainment	Current cost—future benefits Multiyear commitment	Technology Size Structure

(continued)

TABLE 3.2 *(Cont.)*

Controllable Components	Risk dimension		
	Resources	Time frame	Risk
5. Systems maintenance	Salaries Facility Hardware Software Outside contracts/services Supplies Travel and entertainment	Fixed continuous costs Current cost—future benefits Point in time	Technology Size Structure
6. Computer operations	Salaries Facility Supplies Travel and entertainment	Fixed continuous costs	Technology Size
7. Hardware	Software Outside contracts/services Supplies	Fixed continuous costs Point in time Multiyear commitment	Technology Size
8. Purchased/rented software	Software Outside contracts/services Supplies	Fixed continuous costs Current cost—future benefits Point in time Multiyear commitment	Technology Size Structure
9. Technical support	Salaries Facility Hardware Software Outside contracts/services Supplies Travel and entertainment	Fixed continuous costs	Technology Size
10. Quality assurance	Salaries Facility Hardware Software Outside contracts/services	Current cost—future benefits	Size

TABLE 3.2 *(Cont.)*

Controllable Components	Risk dimension		
	Resources	Time frame	Risk
	Supplies Travel and entertainment		
11. Communication	Salaries Facility Hardware Software Outside contracts/ services Supplies Travel and entertainment	Fixed continuous costs	Technology Size Structure
12. Data base administration	Salaries Facility Hardware Software Outside contracts/ services Supplies Travel and entertainment	Fixed continuous costs	Technology Size Structure
13. Word processing/office system/microcomputer	Salaries Facility Hardware Software Outside contracts/ services Supplies Travel and entertainment	Fixed continuous costs Current cost—future benefits Point in time Multiyear commitment	Technology Size Structure
14. Information center	Salaries Facility Hardware Software Outside contracts/ services Supplies Travel and entertainment	Fixed continuous costs Current cost—future benefits	Size Structure
15. Security	Salaries Facility	Fixed continuous costs	Technology Size

(continued)

TABLE 3.2 *(Cont.)*

Controllable Components	Risk dimension		
	Resources	Time frame	Risk
15. Security *(cont.)*	Hardware Software Outside contracts/ services Supplies Travel and entertainment		Structure
16. Outside services	Supplies Travel and entertainment	Current cost— future benefits Point in time	Size

PREPARING FOR THE BUDGET PROCESS

Data processing's management assessment of the importance of the budget process will be reflected in the amount of time allocated for the process by the data processing staff. Generally, the more time that is allocated, the more effective is the budgetary process. If the preparation of the budget is shortchanged, the precision of the estimates may not be accurate enough to satisfy the desires of senior management.

In preparing for the budget, the person responsible should take into account the following three criteria:

1. *The budgeting instructions:* The comptroller of the organization normally issues instructions on budget preparation. These instructions should be studied and evaluated so that the data processing department can submit budgets that are consistent with the desires of senior management, as expressed through the organization's comptroller.
2. *Preparation of budgets at the controllable component level:* Data processing management must recognize that the budget is a valuable tool for managing the data processing department. However, there may be inconsistencies between the classification of budgetary data wanted by the organization and the classification of budgetary data needed to manage the data processing department. The preparation of a budget that cross-references the two classification needs is not a difficult task. The data processing department should collect budgetary data according to the classification of value to them. These can then be resequenced and summarized in a classification needed for the organization's budget. As the funds are allocated, data processing management can reclassify backward into those components which data processing management should control.

3. *Adjustment of budgetary items according to the risk inherent in those items:* All data processing activities are not equal; some include significantly more risk than do others. In the preparation of the budget, the degree of risk must be identified and the budgetary amount adjusted accordingly. High-risk activities should be adjusted upward to reflect the resources needed to compensate for that risk. Low-risk activities may be able to be adjusted downward because the challenge of satisfying those needs will be less.

Budgetary Principle

In budget preparation, you get what you pay for. Devoting sufficient time to constructing a budget that reflects data processing needs and risks normally returns dividends in the form of increased management confidence in data processing's ability to manage the function.

RELATING BUDGETING TO THE DP MISSION

The primary objective of the data processing function is to accomplish its mission. The mission is normally expressed in the form of an annual plan. The budget must be structured so that it is supportive of the plan and the data processing mission.

This chapter has presented a method for budgeting at the level where data processing management wants to exercise control. It is difficult to control the "people" in the data processing department, but they can be controlled once they are assigned to projects and given work. Therefore, budgeting is most effective when it is oriented toward components and activities that management wants to control.

In this chapter we have presented budgeting as a multidimensional process. This is important in both developing a budget and managing the data processing function. For example, if risk is not understood, management may fail to devote the appropriate time and effort to high-risk activities. Through the recognition of risk in budgeting, managers can direct their attention to the activities requiring management involvement.

The principles introduced in this chapter are explained in later chapters. For example, a detailed process for identifying the level of risk is described in Chapter 9. However, like the development of systems, until the intent and requirements of the system are known, the details make little sense. We will see in later chapters how the dimensions and components of data processing budgets facilitate the preparation of an effective and high-precision budget, and aid in using budgeting as a managerial tool.

4
Budgeting as a Management Tool

Budgeting is a multipurpose tool that can be used by managers to control activities reporting to them. The traditional concept of budgeting is that of cost control. However, this is only one of many uses that management can make of budgeting as a tool in fulfilling managerial responsibilities.

The use of budgeting is a two-edged sword. What you budget is what you control. Thus ineffective budgeting may result in controlling the wrong variable. This, in turn, can reduce the quality of work and the productivity of the worker. For example, if the budget process estimates and records the cost of program compilations, programmers may do more extensive manual work at a much higher cost than would occur by using the computer as a debugging tool. This would occur because the budgetary cost control identifies computer compilation cost to management, who in turn may try to control those costs.

The objective of this chapter is to define the many uses of budgeting as a tool to aid management. Seven uses of budgeting are presented and these uses related to each phase in the system development life cycle. The discussion emphasizes the need to select the appropriate budgetary line items (i.e., accounts) and suggests some new items to include in budgeting to assist in improving DP quality and productivity.

BUDGETING INFORMATION SYSTEMS VERSUS BUDGETING THE DP FUNCTION

The money expended by an organization on information processing may far exceed the budget expended on the centralized data processing function. In the past it has been possible to estimate the cost of electronic data processing in organizations by examining the data processing department budget. As stated earlier, the average data processing budget is $2\frac{1}{2}$ percent of the organization's sales. On the other hand, corporations such as IBM indicate that they expend 8 percent of their revenue on information processing costs.

It is reasonable to assume that an organization may spend between two and eight times as much on information processing as it does on the centralized data processing function. In many organizations, these costs are not consolidated and thus are not known. Another example of "what you cannot measure—you cannot control."

Let's look at examples of costs expended on information systems but not included in the centralized data processing budget:

- Personal computers in user areas
- Software/supplies acquired by users for personal computers
- Purchasing function time devoted to acquisition of computer hardware/software/services
- User training and information systems
- Data preparation/data usage in user areas
- Senior management planning committees/effort
- Non-DP effort expended to correct and remedy central computer system defects
- User effort expended to develop and modify requirements/changes
- User personnel devoted to information systems activities

The Two Information System Budgets

Information processing needs to be controlled at both the corporate and function levels. During the next few years there will be a significant shift in information system processing responsibilities. Users will take over more of the day-to-day processing and handling special requests, while the centralized data processing function will devote more effort to building corporate data bases and networks.

Information processing holds the key to productivity for many corporations. Those organizations that use information effectively will be much more competitive than those that do not. The effective use of information requires planning and management control. Budgeting is an integral part of that managerial control process. There are three general approaches that can be used to budget information systems from a corporate level.

1. *Consolidation of a revised chart of accounts:* The chart of accounts identifies the "buckets" in which cost figures will be estimated and accumulated. The current chart of accounts in many organizations does not address information system costs appropriately. A recent magazine article identified fifty ways to hide the cost of microcomputers. These practices are counterproductive to effective managerial budget controls. Under this approach, the corporate chart

of accounts as well as the uses of information system processing dollars must be studied. The chart of accounts must be standardized and implemented throughout the organization. Once done, the accounts can be accumulated to show the corporate dollars budgeted and expended on information processing.

2. *Appointment of a data administrator:* Data administrator is the common title for the position of the person responsible for information in an organization. The data administrator has the same responsibility over information as the treasurer and comptroller have over cash resources. An integral part of this position would be to collect and control information system costs. This function is sometimes headed by a person titled chief information officer.
3. *Expanded data processing function role:* The data processing department can be assigned responsibility to budget and accumulate information system costs. Although this would not have the same formality and precision as the first approach, it would provide realistic estimates and control over information processing expenditures. Normally under this approach, the data processing department works with all the users to accumulate and account for information system expenditures.

The most effective and most relevant approach would be the first. However, this requires restructuring the chart of accounts and data collection methods. Some organizations may prefer to have the expanded data processing approach precede selection between the other two approaches.

Budgetary Principle

Effective management control cannot occur when only half of the costs are accumulated and analyzed. Effective budgetary controls require the collection of all the costs.

METHODS FOR USING THE BUDGET AS A MANAGERIAL TOOL

Let's eavesdrop for a moment on a typical managerial conversation regarding the budget. Will Workman has just completed a major data processing project involving 187 consecutive days of work. Prior to the project, Will had been active in a data processing users group, and asks his boss to let him attend the next meeting. Will's boss whips out the latest budgetary printout and states in a very chagrined manner: "I'm sorry, Will, but there is no money in the budget for that trip." Both Will and his boss accept the fact that Will could go to the users group meeting if only there was money in the budget—but there is not.

Management has used the budget process in one of its most effective and widely accepted manners. This is to control costs by capping the amount of funds that can be expended for a specific purpose. However, this is only one of seven methods employed by management in using the budget to fulfill management responsibilities.

The seven methods for using the budget as a managerial tool are illustrated in Figure 4.1 and described below.

Using the Budget as a Tool to Control Economy of Operations

Management is responsible for the use of corporate assets. For corporations covered under the Securities and Exchange Commission Act of 1934, management is both civilly and criminally liable for the improper use of corporate assets. The Foreign Corrupt Practices Act of 1977, which applies to companies covered under the Securities and Exchange Act of 1934, makes senior management liable for a large civil fine as well as a criminal sentence of up to five years if corporate resources are not subject to adequate internal accounting control.

Prior to the passage of the Foreign Corrupt Practices Act of 1977, many people believed that budgetary approval was management's approval to spend. This is not true. Amounts included in a budget are considered general authorization, not specific authorization to expend funds.

Management must ensure that subordinates understand the difference between general authorization to expend funds and specific authorization. The budget is a tool that can be used for both purposes. By definition, the budget is general authorization to expend funds, and through control over each expenditure, specific authorization is given and controlled by management.

There are two ways in which a budget can be used to control economy:

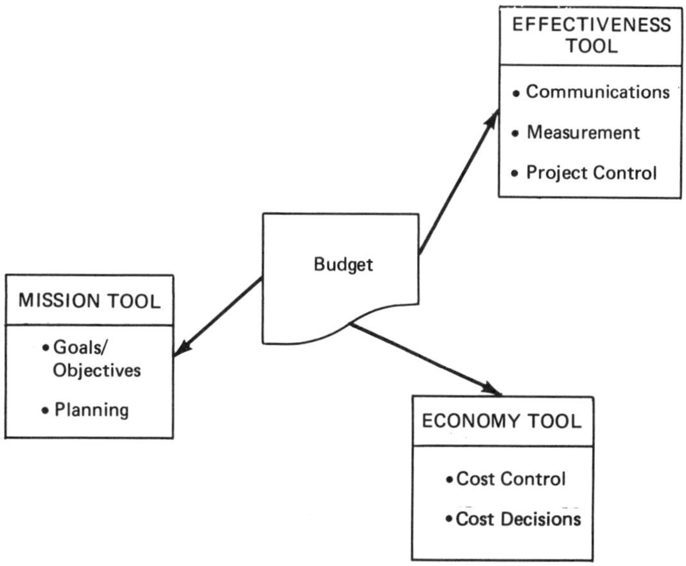

Figure 4.1 Budget as a managerial tool.

1. *Cost control:* This is the traditional form of the budget as a management tool. Management can control costs through the budgetary process, over which management has approval. By approving, reducing, eliminating, or increasing budgetary amounts, management can exercise control over the amount of funds a subordinate can expend. In addition, through budgetary reviews and adjustments throughout the year, management can keep exercising that control. For example, if sales lag expectations, management can exercise cost controls through budgetary cost constraints. For example, managers may ask subordinates to reduce their budgets by 5 percent.
2. *Cost decisions:* The budget can be used as a tool in decision making by management in any of the following three ways:
   a. *Approve or disapprove:* Knowing the cost to do a particular project or task, management can make a decision as to whether or not the task is worth the proposed expenditure of funds.
   b. *Consideration among alternatives:* Having budgetary cost information, management can decide which of several alternatives is most desirable. This does not necessarily mean the least-cost alternative but, rather, the one which, based on its merits coupled with budgetary information, appears best to meet the organization's needs.
   c. *Organization-wide comparisons.* Through the examination of budgets from multiple areas, management can make corporate decisions regarding the expenditure of funds and projects to undertake. For example, management may have to decide between a major expansion of computer activities or adding a new sales office.

Using the Budget as a Tool to Control the DP Mission

The missions of organizations change from industry to industry, but data processing is a service function that is needed to support the primary missions of an organization. The more effectively data processing fulfills its mission, the easier it becomes for the organization to meet its mission objectives.

The data processing budget is a tool that can be used by management to assist in accomplishing the information system mission of the organization. Most management information system (MIS) groups have a general mission statement and then specific mission objectives outlined in plans and budgets. It is in ensuring that these plans are accomplished that the budget can be used as a management tool.

There are two methods by which the budget can be used to assist in the accomplishment of the data processing mission.

1. *Meeting goals/objectives:* Goals and objectives of an organization are usually expressed in terms of (a) the task to be accomplished, (b) the schedule by which those tasks should be completed, and (c) the amount of funds to be expended on those tasks. By monitoring actual expenditures versus budgeted expenditures,

management can project the probability of tasks being completed on schedule and within budget. Significant budgetary overruns or underruns are indicative of project problems. Although the budget itself cannot solve the problems, it is a managerial tool for use in monitoring the accomplishment of work.

2. *Planning:* Budgeting and planning are closely related functions. In some organizations, the two functions are performed simultaneously; in others, planning precedes the budgeting process. Regardless of the sequence in which they are performed, planning is not really completed until budgeting is completed. Plans without cost estimates have not matured to the point where management can make logical business decisions regarding whether or not to adopt and implement the plans.

Using the Budget as a Tool to Manage Effectiveness of Work

Work effectiveness is one of the cornerstones of productivity. Work performed poorly is both inefficient from the perspective of the appropriate utilization of resources, and ineffective in meeting the desired objectives. Inefficient and ineffective work practices normally reduce productivity and have a negative effect on employee morale.

Management uses industrial engineers, auditors, consultants, and their own judgment to identify ineffective work practices. One of the tools that may be underutilized in evaluating work effectiveness is the budget. Inherent within the budgeting process is adequate information to evaluate and improve work effectiveness.

There are three methods by which the budget can be used to improve the effectiveness of work:

1. *Improved communication:* Accounting is the science used by management to evaluate performance. Accounting is more than numbers, it is a language for communicating quantitative information about unlike areas that can be compared and analyzed. Accounting reduces performance to numbers. These numbers can then be used as a basis of communication between two people who may not be thoroughly familiar with the other's technical expertise or managerial needs.
2. *Measurement:* The budget can be used as a tool for the mathematical measurement of performance, productivity, and work effectiveness. The budget permits performance to be converted into numbers. These numbers can then be compared to similar numbers in other areas: comparing actual to budgetary expenditures, analyzing the trend of expenditures over a period of time, and comparing expenditures against a norm. For example, there are books out that allow management to identify the approximate travel, meals, and lodging costs from city to city.

3. *Project control:* The budget can be used to control project performance. For example, in the early days of data processing, project personnel were provided with a budget to complete an entire project. Many organizations now budget only from checkpoint to checkpoint. Through this budgetary allocation of funds, management reserves the right to evaluate and approve budgetary expenditures based on project performance. Using this and similar techniques, management remains in control of highly technical projects through the effective use of budgeting.

MANAGERIAL PROCEDURES USED TO ACCOMPLISH MANAGERIAL OBJECTIVES

The use of the budget as a managerial tool is determined by management policy. A formal or informal budget policy is needed to define management's intent to use budgeting as a tool in fulfilling its responsibilities. The policy should identify which of the seven potential uses of budgeting will be used by management. The policy is needed so that appropriate procedures can be put into place to accomplish management's budgeting intent.

The procedures that can be used to ensure that the policies are implemented effectively are listed in Table 4.1 and described below by area of managerial budget control.

TABLE 4.1 HOW BUDGETING IS USED TO MANAGE

Means of managing through budgeting	Managerial procedures affected
Goals/objectives	MBO Scheduling
Planning	Projections/estimates ROI/CFRR Value of money Cost of alternatives
Communications	Financial focus Charge-out
Measurement	Actual versus budget Variance Comparisons Trends
Project control	Milestones Staffing/scheduling/cost relationships
Cost control	Establish limits Revisions Approvals
Cost decisions	Make/buy Purchase/lease Go/no go

Goals/Objectives

The procedures for this area are:

1. *Management by objectives (MBO):* This procedure establishes the objectives that management desires to be accomplished and then focuses managerial attention on the accomplishment of those objectives. This requires that budgeting be tied to objectives.
2. *Scheduling:* This process identifies specific dates for the establishment of projects and goals. Money is tied to this schedule. Scheduling can also allocate money by accounting period, such as month, quarter, or annual periods.

Planning

The budgeting procedures used as a managerial tool for planning include:

1. *Projections/estimates:* Current decisions are more effective when they can be based on potential future action. The more effectively the future can be projected, the better the management decisions that can be made. Budgetary information provides both a historical base for projecting future costs and revenue, as well as providing estimates of future costs and revenue based on management plans.
2. *Return on investment (ROI)/cash flow rate of return (CFRR):* Estimates and projections provide information which needs to be interpreted for decision purposes. Return on investment and cash flow rate of return are two similar methods for estimating an internal percent of profit that might be generated from projects. These methods are similar to the calculation of net profit, except that they frequently extend over several years and thus must take into account the present value of money.
3. *Value of money:* Money can be invested in the bank or other relatively safe investments and earn interest without any business risk. Therefore, a dollar spent today to earn money a year from now, as is common in many data processing projects, must earn more than a dollar to break even. The accounting term *future dollars* must be discounted back to present dollars in order to be comparable to current costs. This discounting, referred to as the present value of money, deals with what dollars expended and made in the future are worth in today's dollars.
4. *Cost of alternatives:* The decision-making process is one of evaluating various alternatives to accomplish the same task. For example, one might want to consider whether it is cheaper to build an application in-house, contract it to a software house, or acquire commercially available packages. An important piece of information in that process is the cost of the various alternatives. These costs can be acquired from the budgetary process.

Communications

The budgeting procedures that management uses to improve the quality of information available in making business decisions include:

1. *Financial focus:* There are many attributes for each business decision. Although these attributes need study and consideration, they normally vary from project to project. One common attribute is money, which can be provided through the budgetary process. The use of money focuses attention on a factor that is comparable from project to project. Note that because of the financial focus of accounting, some organizations split planning from budgeting to avoid that focus. On the other hand, rarely are projects approved until the appropriate focus on finances is discussed and agreed upon.
2. *Charge-out:* Many organizations attempting to promote data processing provide information system services through corporate overhead. Under this concept, the services are free (to users) and their use encouraged. Because of the "free" connotation of services of this type, many organizations switch to a charge-out method. Under this method, the costs of providing information services are charged back to users through internal corporate accounting. The objective of charge-out is to make users responsible for the resources they consume. Thus the charge-out becomes a means of communicating to users the cost of the services they are consuming.

Budgetary Measurement

The procedures used by management to measure performance and effectiveness of individuals and projects include the following:

1. *Actual versus budget:* The performance of projects can be measured by the ability of people to keep costs and revenue at levels predetermined by a budget. Actual costs versus budgeted costs can be measured at individual line items or by total projects. For example, a project may budget for people, machine time, supplies, and so on, which could be individually measured, or the project could be measured on the totality of actual cost versus budgeted costs.
2. *Variance:* Variance is a measure from what is versus what should be. Budgeting variances can be in terms of dollar variance or percent variance. Some organizations provide tolerances of budgetary performance. For example, actual cost within plus or minus 5 percent of budgeted amounts may be considered acceptable. Variances in those cases are cost or revenue which have exceeded the acceptable tolerances (high or low).
3. *Comparisons:* A powerful measurement tool is to compare two similar items. For example, if two projects are of approximately equal size and complexity, the budget estimates and/or actual cost between the two projects can be com-

pared. In other instances, budget items can be normalized for the purpose of comparison. For example, if one project is twice as complex as another, that complexity would have to be taken into account and the figures put into comparable terms (i.e., normalized) before being compared.

4. *Trend analysis:* Trend analysis shows a comparison of a single item at various times. The objective of trend analysis is to determine whether costs/revenues are increasing, staying the same, or decreasing. Trends can compare a project against a normal trend, for example, showing the trend of actual expenditures against the normal expenditure rate for a project.

Project Control

The budgetary procedures that management can use to aid in the control of projects include the following:

1. *Milestones:* Budgeted amounts can be tied to specific data processing checkpoints. If management budgets only from checkpoint to checkpoint, it can control the project status through required control points to evaluate the current status and reevaluate the project deliverables. Using this process, additional funds are allocated only when management is satisfied that the project is on target and the need for the results remains.
2. *Staffing/scheduling cost relationships:* There is a close relationship between the amount of staff required to perform a project or completed task and the schedule allocated for that task. For example, twelve people working one month will not accomplish the same amount of work as one person working twelve months, even though the same amount of labor has been utilized. The Rayleigh curve is a mathematical method that can be used for determining the optimum staffing ratio. Thus, through budgeting procedures management is better able to control project staffing.

Cost Control

The procedures used by management to aid in cost control include the following:

1. *Establish limits:* Budgets can provide a constraint on spending by establishing limits of spending. The limits can be exercised in any of the following three ways:
   a. *Budgetary period:* Individuals/projects can be allocated *X* dollars to perform certain tasks during the budgetary period (e.g., have $*X* for a year and use it any time in any way desired by the project).
   b. *Dollar allocation per time span:* Individuals/projects can be allocated money for predetermined time spans, such as weeks, months, quarters, and

so on (e.g., funds allocated monthly and project can exceed that amount during the month).

c. *Line-item authorizations:* Budgetary funds can be controlled through budgetary line items. For example, even though a budget contains X dollars, there can be limits on what an individual/project can spend for any one event (e.g., \$$Y$ allocated for a project but only \$$X$ of that can be spent on training).

2. *Revisions:* Budgets provide a vehicle for altering expenditures allocations and revenue projections whenever business conditions change. For example, in an economic downturn, budgeted costs can be cut quickly to reduce spending, or they can be increased to support increased revenues during growth periods. These revisions can be by a percentage or by line item.
3. *Approvals:* Budgets, by definition, provide only general authorization to spend. Individual items must still receive specific authorization. By withholding authorization at various levels, management can better control the expenditure of funds. This is particularly true for nonrepetitive costs such as travel, ordering new equipment, and so on.

Cost Decisions

The following are procedures that management can use to aid in making cost decisions.

1. *Make/buy decision:* Through the budgetary process, information can be provided to facilitate the make/buy decision. For example, estimating through budgetary procedures what it would cost to develop an application could then be compared to the purchase price of commercially available software so that a decision can be made regarding which is the most cost-effective use of funds.
2. *Purchase/lease:* The same type of analysis as that used in the make/buy decision can be used to decide whether to purchase or lease an item. For example, in deciding whether to buy hardware or lease it from the vendor or from a third-party leasor, the budgetary estimates frequently provide much of the information needed to make the decision.
3. *Go/no go decision:* Cost information can be used to determine whether to do or not do a project, as well as whether to stop or continue a project. The continual analysis of budgetary information provides management with the information needed to monitor and make decisions about projects. Later in the chapter the concept of "sunk costs" will be discussed, together with the impact of these expended costs on a decision to stop and abandon a project.

> **Budgetary Principle**
>
> The purposes for which the budget will be used should be determined prior to developing the budgetary process.

USES AND ABUSES OF BUDGETING

Science has proved that for every force there is an equal but opposite counterforce. This simple principle makes jet planes fly and motorboats move through the water. The principle also means that for every use management makes of the budgetary process, some employee will develop a counterstrategy to abuse that management principle.

Let us look at some of the simple but effective budgetary counterstrategies:

- *Double-cut theory:* A person asks for twice as much as he or she wants so that management can cut it in half and the person will still get the desired budgetary amount.
- *Man-on-the-moon theory:* President Kennedy proclaimed in the early 1960s that the United States would have a man on the moon by the end of the decade. We did. The theory proved by this feat is that with enough money anything is possible. In budgetary circles this means that anything is possible with a large enough budget, and that without it very little is possible.
- *Carrot-and-stick theory:* Under this theory, management promises budgetary rewards to subordinates who do good work. The managerial "favorites" get the largest budget, while the "out group" scrimps by on a razor-thin budget.
- *Creeping commitment theory:* Under this theory, the budgetary costs are known but never defined for management. For example, if data processing managers wanted a $100,000 increase in computer capacity, they might "creep" the large expenditure commitment through acquiring a lower-priced device which becomes valuable only when the bells and whistles are added.
- *The now you see it, now you don't theory:* This concept bypasses budgetary limit controls. For example, if management says that a supervisor can approve only up to a $100 purchase, and the supervisor wants to buy a $300 item, the cost is broken into three $100 purchases.
- *Rathole theory:* This is the sunk-cost concept, meaning that once expenditures have been made, they are forgotten. Future calculations using the rathole theory always discard past costs but include all future benefits.

Management needs to be aware of these budgetary abuses. Most are detectable. One good way to curb abuses is to explain them to subordinates and tell the subordinates not to use those theories on their manager. It does not mean that budgetary abuses will stop; it may just mean that the more common means of abuse are stopped.

BUDGETING AS A MANAGEMENT TOOL TO ACHIEVE QUALITY

There are two costs involved in the data processing function:

1. Cost of DP production
2. Cost of DP quality

The cost of production in most organizations encompasses the cost of quality. This is because the quality costs are not segregated through budgetary processes and are controlled through that process. When not controlled they are frequently unidentifiable. See Figure 4.2 for a breakdown of DP costs.

Most data processing budgets group the cost of DP production into the following four categories:

1. *Development:* the costs associated with the acquisition and development of software, as well as all costs required by the data processing function to get a new operation into production. If a software package is acquired, there are still costs involved to train and get the package operational.
2. *Maintenance:* the cost of repairing and enhancing existing software. These repairs and enhancements can be on both in-house-developed and acquired software.

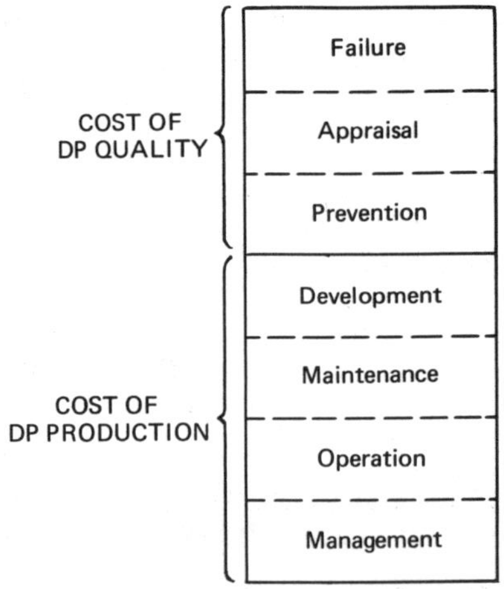

Figure 4.2 DP costs.

3. *Operation:* the costs associated with operating application software. Costs include any software needed for operations purposes, such as communication systems, library systems, data base management systems, and so on.
4. *Management:* the costs associated with housing and administering a data processing function. This includes all the costs not associated with development, maintenance, or operation. Typical costs include administration personnel, quality assurance personnel, training, standards, and general data processing management.

These budgetary costs are traditional and are discussed in depth in Part 3. The process of estimating and accumulating costs in the DP production category will be explained in a step-by-step format. A more challenging budgetary problem is the one of calculating the cost of quality.

The cost of quality is an internal budgetary measure. It measures internal performance in the same way that net profit measures external performance. The costs of quality are the costs of "not doing it right the first time."

The costs of quality are divided into the following three areas:

1. *Appraisal costs:* money spent to review completed products against requirements. Appraisal includes the cost of inspections, testing, and reviews. This money is spent after the product is built and before it is shipped to the user.
2. *Preventive costs:* money required to prevent errors and to do the job right the first time. This category includes money spent on establishing methods and procedures, training workers, and planning for quality. Prevention money is normally spent before the product is actually built.
3. *Failure costs:* all costs associated with defective products. Some failure costs involve repairing products to make them meet requirements. Other costs generated by failures, such as the cost of operating faulty products, damage incurred by using them, and the costs incurred because the product was not available. Some failure costs are experienced by the producer of the product, some by the user, and some by the user's user or customer of the organization.

Very few organizations collect these costs formally. Of the three, the prevention and appraisal costs are the best known. Failure costs are frequently known about certain unfavorable conditions, or a specific type of failure such as rerun of a computer application. Very few organizations accumulate the costs and attempt to monitor or manage them in any way. It is important to note that the three costs are interrelated. Invariably when appraisal and preventive costs go down, failure costs go up. On the other hand, money spent for appraisal and prevention normally has the positive effect of reducing failure. Organizations need to optimize the three costs to ensure that the cost of quality for their organization is minimal.

Let's look at some of the components of the three cost-of-quality categories:

Preventive cost components

- Data processing standards
- Project development methodology
- Project maintenance methodology
- Planning for the data processing function
- Training for the project team
- Training for users
- Data processing procedures
- Recommended data processing guidelines
- Configuration management

Appraisal cost components

- Error condition handling
- Unit test
- String test
- System test
- Acceptance test
- Stress testing
- Checkpoint reviews
- Inspections
- Quality assurance
- Audits

Failure cost components

- Overtime
- Maintenance repairs
- Reruns
- Project rework
- Complaints
- Lost opportunities/unrealized savings
- Incorrect decisions based on wrong information
- Noncompliance to legal regulations (with probability of fines and penalties)
- Lost assets
- Lost goodwill
- Unavailability of data processing professionals for other needed tasks
- Frustration/lack of motivation
- Employee turnover
- Excessive cost from poor design
- Excessive hardware capacity/personnel
- Cascading of errors

The collection of cost-of-quality figures involves a restructuring of the accounting system. On the other hand, until the cost-of-quality dollars are collected they cannot be controlled.

> **Budgetary Principle**
>
> The cost of DP quality in the United States is running about 50 percent of the total data processing budget. Source: *Quality Data Processing: Profit Potential for the 1980s* by Claude W. Burrill and Leon W. Ellsworth. Burrill-Ellsworth Associates Inc., Tenafly, NJ 1982.

The cost of quality is addressed in Part 3. It is an important part of the budgetary process if management is truly to control a significant data processing cost. This type of budgeting requires new data collection methods to be established which record the costs associated with preventing poor quality, appraising the quality of existing work, and recognizing the cost of failure.

> **Budgetary Principle**
>
> Until the cost of failure is known, appropriate attention is rarely directed toward reducing it.

SDLC BUDGETARY CONTROL CASE STUDY

Many managers look at budgeting as a necessary evil. It is a process imposed on them by senior management. Although many DP managers recognize the value of budgeting to senior management, they frequently do not perceive the control potential offered within the DP function by the budgetary process.

This dilemma exists because few data processing managers have been adequately trained in using budgets for managerial purposes. The following case study is designed to help explain how budgeting can be used (note that Part 3 provides the framework for using the budget to manage the DP function). The case study relates to the options available for managing an application project through budgeting.

The case study being presented is the development of an on-line inquiry system for sales personnel. The objective of the system is to provide the marketing force with computer terminals that they can carry with them to the customer's location. Using their terminals and Touch-Tone telephones, they will be provided with the capability to call the organization's computer and inquire regarding the status of inventory. If inventory is available, the sales personnel can then enter customer orders directly from the customer's place of business.

John Jones is project manager for this project. John's concern is how to ensure that the project objectives will be met within the budgetary constraints. In addition, John is looking for tools to help him manage the project more effectively.

Budgeting is a managerial tool that can be implemented into the system development process. In the case study we will look at the options available to John to control the project through budgeting. This case study is designed to illustrate the power of the budget.

The system development life cycle presented in this case study is a seven-phase life cycle. The phases are:

- *Requirements:* establishing needs
- *System design:* determining how to implement those needs on a computer
- *Programming:* the coding and testing of programs
- *Testing:* acceptance testing by users
- *Installation:* putting a fully tested system into production
- *Operations:* running the system to produce the desired results
- *Maintenance:* repairing and enhancing the application system to meet incorrectly implemented and changing user needs

Table 4.1 showed the seven means for managing through budgeting. These are the options that the manager has to control a developmental project through budgeting.

We need to look at the ways in which the system development life cycle can be controlled in each of its phases using these options as a basis for control. Knowing how budgeting can help control each life-cycle phase, John can make decisions about how to control a specific developmental project through one or more of these budgetary controls.

The system development life cycle (SDLC) phases discussed above are related to the seven means of managing through budgeting as shown in Table 4.2. This table shows which budgetary objective is applicable for the seven defined SDLC phases. For example, we see that budgeting can be used in the requirements phase in the areas of planning, establishing goals and objectives, communication, and cost decisions.

The manager of a developmental project can now begin to select which budgetary control mechanisms he wants to use to control the project. Let's examine each SDLC phase to illustrate the options available to John and the decisions he can make about using budgeting to help him fulfill his project management responsibilities.

In the requirements phase, the budgetary estimate is used in planning. The availability of funds and the potential benefits are important factors in determining when and how this system will be installed. The terminal options are evaluated by John through budgeting analyses in order to select the most cost-effective option (i.e., a cost decision). The value of having the system can be communicated by John to senior management through cost information as a basis of explaining to management the importance of installing the system. Finally, the cost information is helpful in establishing goals for usage and service to ensure that the desired benefits are received.

During the system design phase, Table 4.2 shows us four ways in which budgeting can be used. Our project manager may decide only to use budgeting for

TABLE 4.2 BUDGET AND CONTROL CONSIDERATIONS IN THE SYSTEM DEVELOPMENT LIFE CYCLE

SDLC phase	Budgeting as a managerial tool
Requirement	Planning Goals/objectives Communication Cost decisions
Systems design	Project control Measurement Cost control Cost decisions
Programming	Measurement Cost control
Testing	Cost control Cost decisions
Installation	Cost control Cost decisions
Operation	Cost control Measurement Communication
Maintenance	Goals/objectives Planning Communications Measurement Project control Cost control Cost decisions

project control purposes during design. This can be done by allocating a predetermined amount of funds for design, and then monitoring closely to ensure that the design will be accomplished within those funding limits.

Programming, testing, installation, and operation are costly phases for installing the on-line inquiry system. The manager used budgetary controls to ensure the profitability and proper design of the project. However, once the design was agreed upon, John decided to use budgeting only to control costs during these four phases. This was accomplished by allocating funds for each phase, and then receiving reports regarding whether or not the phase was implemented within those budgetary amounts.

Maintenance is a phase that was of concern to our project manager. John felt that much of the maintenance might not be needed, and thus decided to use budgeting for cost decision purposes. John decided that even though there was a maintenance budgetary amount, each change would have to be cost-justified (for use in making a cost decision).

In this case, we have seen the project manager use budgeting extensively during the requirements phase; as a tool for controlling the system design process; as a slightly different tool to control cost during the programming, testing, installation, and operation phases; and then as a cost decision tool during maintenance.

The options shown in Table 4.2 provide insight into the many ways in which budgeting can be used to control a developmental project. In our case study we saw how a hypothetical manager might select among these options as a means of implementing control over the developmental project. The means selected can vary from project to project based on the importance of that project to the organization and/or the total cost of development.

THE RESPONSIBILITY FOR USING BUDGETARY PRINCIPLES

The data processing manager is responsible for the development of budgetary procedures. Budgeting is a managerial tool; therefore, management should decide how that tool should be used. Once that decision is made, the budgetary process should be incorporated into the managerial procedures of the data processing function.

There are many options available for using budgeting, but those options should not be optional to the data processing staff. Management should select among the options and then incorporate into the data processing procedures the options selected.

Budgetary Principle

Budgeting is a project, and has requirements, design, and implementation. The project leader of the budgeting project is the DP manager.

GOOD BUDGETING DOES NOT JUST HAPPEN

In this chapter we have described the many ways in which managers can use budgeting to help fulfill their responsibilities. However, it takes work by senior data processing management to make this happen. To be effective, budgeting cannot be delegated to lower-level managers. Senior data processing managers must determine what they want controlled, and what they want budgeting used for to accomplish those controls, before the process is developed.

Much of the information presented in this and the preceding chapters is designed to help data processing management identify budgeting requirements. As with any project, the establishment of requirements is the most difficult part of the project. Once the requirements have been established, the implementation of those requirements can be controlled and managed.

The remainder of the book deals with managing, installing, and using a budgetary process to accomplish the stated budget requirements. Note that the data processing requirements must be consistent with the organization's budgetary requirements. However, the data processing requirements, although consistent with the corporate requirements, must be customized to the uniqueness of data processing and the specific control requirements of data processing management.

5
Managing the Budget Process

The concept of managing the budget process requires differentiation between the budget and the budgetary process. The budget is the physical document that contains the monetary accounts and amounts. The budgetary process is the methodology by which that budgetary product is developed. Managers manage the process and then use the product (i.e., the budget) as a tool for managing.

In this chapter we explain the principles of managing the budgetary process. The actual process itself is explained in Part 3. Senior DP management should concentrate on ensuring that "what" they desire is accomplished through the budgetary process. If the "what" is fully defined, the DP staff and accountants can decide "how" the budget is to be prepared. The process that ensures that budgeting works is a managerial quality control function which should be embedded within the budgetary process.

Thus we are able to differentiate the "what" management from the "how to" management. The "what" oriented management deals with the process, while the "how to" aspect deals with the budget product. Differentiating the two helps improve the quality and effectiveness of budgeting.

DEFINING MANAGEMENT'S BUDGETARY RESPONSIBILITIES

The four major responsibilities of management are planning, organizing, directing, and controlling. Budgeting is a tool that facilitates the fulfillment of those four responsibilities. Budgeting aids planning, supports organizations with funding, through the allocation of funds assists in directing operations, and can be used for control.

The fulfillment of management's responsibilities can be expressed from a budgetary perspective into the following three areas (see Figure 5.1).

1. *Setting budgetary objectives:* Budgeting, while used by most organizations, is not a mandatory accounting standard. Budgeting is a tool used by managers to assist in fulfilling their responsibilities. Therefore, if management selects budgeting as a tool, the objectives of using that tool should be clearly stated. Budgeting is a costly process to establish, conduct, and administer. Before the funds are allocated, managers need to assure themselves that there will be an appropriate return on investment.
2. *Developing a budgetary process:* Consistency and quality occur only when there is a process. Unless people are given a process to perform a task, management cannot rely on that task being performed the same way or with the same level of quality. The process should be designed to support the creativity and planning aspects of budgeting, while simplifying the mechanics of the budgeting process.
3. *Managing the budget process:* Management cannot rely on the budgeting objectives to be met, or the process to work correctly. Management of the budget process is necessary to ensure the probability of success. Managing the budget process includes (a) ensuring that users of the budgetary process are adequately trained, (b) measuring the performance of the process to ensure that it works, and (c) evaluating the results of the budgetary process to determine that it meets the objectives of the process.

In any organization, the budgetary responsibilities are divided between senior management and departmental management. Senior managers establish the policies, procedures, and framework for budgeting. Departmental managers must customize and implement that process within their department.

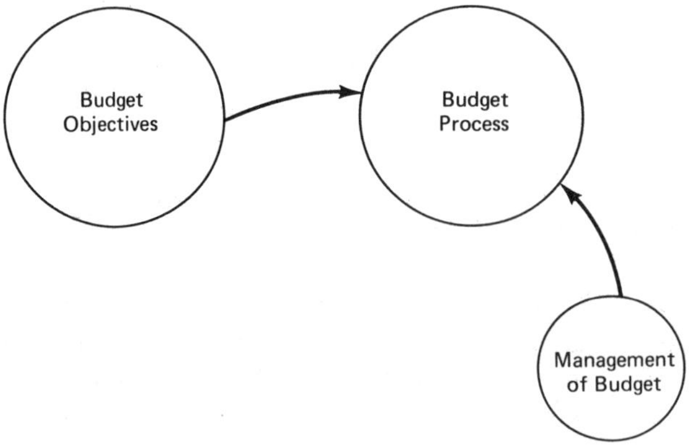

Figure 5.1 Managing the budget process.

In the data processing department, this customization must take into account the unique characteristics of the MIS function, which include:

- Long-range duration of projects
- High maintenance costs
- Reliance on technology
- Rapid changes in technology
- Interaction with all areas of the organization
- Lack of experience in implementing many MIS projects with the associated unpredictability of estimates

Budgetary Principle

Good budgets do not just happen—good management makes good budgets happen.

THE EIGHT KEYS TO SUCCESSFUL MANAGEMENT OF THE BUDGETARY PROCESS

In almost any aspect of life, there are certain keys to success. For example, being a good communicator is one of the keys to success in the marketing function. Also, there are methods and tasks which are necessary to perform tasks. Again, in marketing the types of tasks that need to be accomplished are advertising, product packaging, and distribution. However, without the "communication key" someone in marketing may have difficulty selling products even though the other elements of marketing are in place. The eight keys to managing the budgetary process successfully are listed in Figure 5.2 and described individually below.

- *Key 1: Set measurable budgetary objectives.* Unmeasurable objectives are more difficult to implement than measurable objectives. The more specific the objectives, the easier it is to determine when an objective has been achieved. For unmeasurable objectives it may be necessary to have a judge (e.g., an organization auditor) make an assessment as to whether or not an unmeasurable objective has been accomplished.
- *Key 2: Establish a formal process to accomplish the measurable objectives.* The objective of a budgetary process is to assist in the accomplishment of budgetary objectives. In Part 3 we describe a formal budgetary process.
- *Key 3: Involve budgetary users in the development of the process.* People are more willing to utilize a process which they help to develop. Industrial psychologists call this the "ownership" principle, meaning that people should own those processes in which they participate. Obviously, in the budgetary

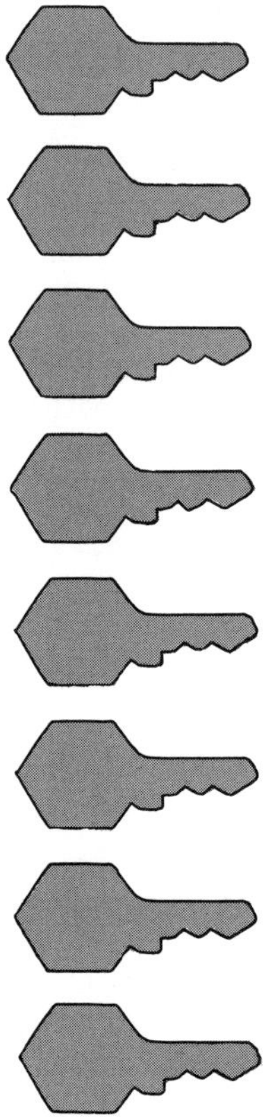

1. Set measurable budgetary objectives.
2. Establish a formal process to accomplish those objectives.
3. Involve budgetary users in the development of the process.
4. Automate the process.
5. Teach people how to use the process.
6. Subject the process to quality control.
7. Measure to determine if budgetary objectives have been met.
8. Modify the process when the measurement indicates the objectives are not being met.

Figure 5.2 Eight keys to managing the budget process.

process data processing personnel can participate in the customization of that process only for their department. However, this is normally sufficient to invoke the ownership principle, which in turn encourages active participation in the process.

- *Key 4: Automate the process.* Processes that are automated provide a higher level of quality than that of processes performed manually. Automation not only encourages consistency through systems design requirements, but also provides the opportunity to prompt and lead users in the use of the process. Many reliability problems are caused by improper use of the budgetary process.
- *Key 5: Teach people how to use the process.* Instruction is one of the keys to high-quality budgeting. If people do not understand the process, they have great difficulty in using the process correctly. Much of the budgetary process involves analysis and estimation, which is a teachable skill. Educated users of any system perform the process much better than do users with minimal knowledge in how to use the process.

- *Key 6: Subject the process to quality control.* Quality control provides the necessary review and evaluation tools to ensure that the process is performed correctly. This challenging and evaluative process is designed to produce defect-free budgets. Included with the materials on each step of the budgetary process are the quality control tools needed to verify the correct functioning of that process step.
- *Key 7: Measure to determine if budgetary objectives have been met.* The first key to managing the budgetary process was to set measurable objectives. This key utilizes those measurable characteristics to determine whether or not the objectives have been met. Measurable objectives are valuable only when the process is measured.
- *Key 8: Modify the process when the measurement indicates the objectives are not being met.* Good budgeting is as much attributable to the process as are the people that use that process. Good people and a poor process may not be able to produce a good budget. If the process is causing poor budgeting, the process should be modified as soon as the measures indicate that the budgetary objectives are not being met. To know that change is needed and not to make it is unpardonable.

Management should keep these keys in mind as they move through the remainder of the book. The combination of a good budgetary process, properly managed, will provide the data processing function with a very effective managerial control tool.

THE BUDGETARY CYCLE

Budgeting is a process. The process goes through a predetermined cycle, just as development of a system goes through a predetermined cycle. The phases within the budgetary cycle are common and predictable.

The budgetary cycle is illustrated in Figure 5.3. This cycle concept means that budgeting is an ongoing, never-ending project. Although the phases within the cycle are distinct, they are interrelated and continuous.

The budgetary cycle begins with budget requirements. The requirements come from the planning process, coupled with ongoing requirements. The requirements are normally expressed in terms of tasks to accomplish, resources to pay for, or items to acquire.

The requirements become the basis for the budget. The budget must be prepared to provide the cost and scheduling necessary to accomplish the budget requirements. Although much of the process is centered around preparation, one must remember that there are four phases to the budgetary cycle.

The prepared budget must be approved by management. In most budgetary ap-

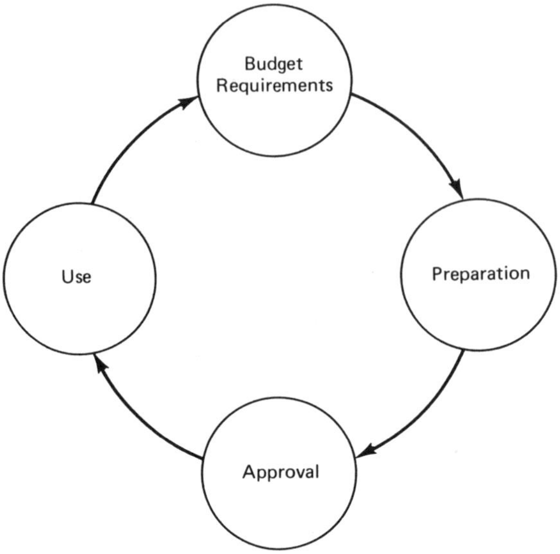

Figure 5.3 Budgetary cycle.

proval processes, there are hearings and trade-offs. A good budgetary process provides the mechanism to document budgetary requests at hearings, and to enable trade-offs to be determined quickly.

The last phase of the budgetary cycle is the use of the approved budget. This is part of the operational activities of the data processing function. Funds are utilized and budgetary status reports prepared. The use phase also includes modifications to the approved budget.

The results of budgeting are fed into the budget requirements phase. This past experience is one of the factors that determines the next budget. Thus the cycle is complete and is reborn at the same time. We look next at the factors that need to be considered in managing the budget and then discuss each of the four phases of the budgetary cycle.

QUALITY FACTORS THAT NEED TO BE MANAGED

Managers are concerned with both productivity and quality. Productivity relates to the speed at which work is performed, and the quality—the meeting of managerial intent. Experience has shown that emphasis on quality over productivity produces better budgets. The desired level of productivity can be achieved through the combination of an effective process, coupled with quality control tools.

Quality must be specified in measurable terms. This encompasses dividing quality into its component parts. Quality is achievable only when the specifics of quality are defined.

TABLE 5.1 QUALITY FACTORS TO MANAGE

Factor	Description
1. Compliance	The budget has been prepared in accordance with the policy, procedures, and standards of the organization.
2. Usable	The results of budgeting are in the proper format, sequence, and level of detail needed for ease of use.
3. Completeness	All necessary information is in the budget.
4. Reliability	The information is reproducible following the same process.
5. Validity	The information in the budget is correct.
6. Timeliness	The information is accumulated when needed.
7. Cost-effectiveness	The information is collected at a reasonable cost.
8. Maintainable	The information is in a format which is readily modifiable in the event that conditions change.
9. Realistic	The information is believable to the approving group.
10. Supportable	The supporting information for the budgetary data is readily retrievable.

The ten quality factors that require managing during the budgetary process are listed in Table 5.1 and described individually below.

- *Compliance quality factor:* Budgeting is an internal organizational procedure. It is based on organizational policy, procedures, and standards. Assuring compliance with those policies and procedures is an important aspect of ensuring a quality budget.
- *Usable quality factor:* Budgets are designed to serve managers in fulfilling their functions. If the completed budget fails to serve those purposes, it is not usable for the intended purpose. This factor also includes ease of use, which includes the sequencing of data, the level of detail, the frequency of reporting, and the amount of time taken to get a desired result.
- *Completeness quality factor:* Completeness measures the all-inclusiveness of the items included in the budget. Completeness is easy to determine during the budgetary period, more difficult to determine during budget planning and preparation. However, the failure to include items in the budget may exclude the possibility of those items being performed or acquired during the budgetary period.
- *Reliability quality factor:* Reliability is the correctness of the data included within the budget. Correctness is evaluated by the ability to reproduce the same budgetary request at different points in time and by different people. Reliability also measures the closeness of actual figures to budgeted figures.
- *Validity quality factor:* Validity relates to the state of appropriateness of the budgetary item. For example, in the budgetary abuse section the double-cut

theory was discussed. Under this theory, a person requests twice the amount needed. In that instance, the budgetary amount is not valid.

- *Timeliness quality factor:* Budgets are usually prepared in accordance with a preestablished schedule. If the needed information is not available at the appropriate checkpoint, it may not be included in the budget. Thus valid and reliable data may be omitted in lieu of rough budgetary estimates.
- *Cost-effectiveness quality factor:* The cost for preparing budgets should not exceed the benefits received from budget preparation. Note that this may be a difficult quality factor to achieve because in many organizations neither the cost nor the benefits from budgeting are formally recorded. However, this does not preclude one-time studies being undertaken to demonstrate the cost/benefit analysis of budgeting.
- *Maintainable quality factor:* Effective budgets are modified as business conditions change. This requires that the budgets be prepared and utilized in a format where the amounts are readily modifiable. At a minimum, this requires that the supporting data accompany the budget so that the details are accessible and modifiable as conditions change.
- *Realistic quality factor:* This is one of the more difficult quality factors to define and measure. On the other hand, if the budgetary amounts do not appear realistic based on the mission and task to be accomplished, those budgetary amounts may undermine the credibility of the entire budget. Realistic budgets are budgets that appear reasonable based on previous years' budgets, budgets for similar departments and functions, and are consistent with organization plans and guidelines.
- *Supportable quality factor:* Budgetary items must be supported by detail rather than by assumptions and broad estimates. This does not preclude making budgetary assumptions but, rather, that those assumptions are well documented and identified.

Each of these quality factors should be defined as part of the budgetary process. Once specified and measured, these quality factors can be managed. Budgetary processes that incorporate and manage these quality factors are more successful than those that do not.

Budgetary Principle

Quality means doing it right the first time. The quality factors define what is meant by right.

MANAGING THE BUDGETARY REQUIREMENTS PHASE

As with any other project, the requirements constitute the most important phase. If the requirements are wrong, the budget is wrong. Management should take whatever steps are necessary to verify the integrity of the requirements.

> **Budgetary Principle**
>
> The integrity of the budget can never improve after the requirements phase. The quality of budgeting can deteriorate, but it will not improve unless the budgeteers return to the requirements phase.

In this chapter we are discussing how to manage the budget process. The objective is to ensure that the process is fulfilled in accordance with the intent of data processing management. In performing this managerial role, the manager must manage from two perspectives. The first is ensuring that the work is properly planned, organized, and directed. These functions should be embedded in the budgetary process. The second perspective is quality.

The quality perspective can be managed through defining the expected budget quality. The quality factors become a basis for determining the level of quality. The quality factors must be related to budgeting criteria to be evaluated. For example, reliability is an important quality factor, but the question that needs to be determined in managing the budget process is what aspect of the process must be reliable. To do this, it is necessary to define the criteria that will be subject to the quality factors. We will do this for each of the phases of the budget process. In addition, the tools that can be used to help assess the quality of the criteria will be identified.

There are four criteria that management must consider during the budgetary requirements phase. These criteria, the tools that can be used to manage the criteria, and the quality factors for evaluating the criteria are listed in Table 5.2 and described below.

Business Plan Criterion

The business plan should be one of the basic inputs to the budgetary process. The MIS budget should be supportive of the organization's business plan. Those managing the budgetary process should ensure that the information requirements of business plans are incorporated into the budget.

The business plan is normally directed at major business objectives, such as production, marketing, and so on. The information requirements may not be stated. However, the challenge of the data processing function is to anticipate and prepare for, through budgetary procedures, the support necessary to provide the information requirements when requested.

The tools that data processing management can use in matching the business plan to data processing budget requirements are the DP mission statement, specific business objectives included in the business plan, and business systems planning. Business systems planning is a process that requires senior managers to identify and prioritize business DP projects.

The quality factors for the entire requirements phase are completeness, reliability, and validity. These are the factors by which the quality of the budgeting requirements should be evaluated. Although all the quality factors should be defined

TABLE 5.2 MANAGING THE BUDGETARY REQUIREMENTS PHASE

Budgeting criterion	Budgeting tools	Quality factors
Business plan	Mission statement Business objectives Business systems planning	Completeness Reliability Validity
DP plan	Configuration management Critical success factors Charter	
User needs	System requests Change requests User plans Trend analysis	
Quality	Quality factors definition Compliance Usable Completeness Reliability Validity Timeliness Cost-effectiveness Maintainable Realistic Supportable	

as budgetary requirements, the requirements themselves should be measured against the completeness, reliability, and validity quality factors.

DP Plan Criterion

The DP plan should be a subset, and supportive of, the organization's business plan. The DP plan is the proposed implementation of the business plan for the information requirements of the organization. In effect, the DP plan tells how the business plan will be implemented within the data processing function.

The DP plan normally takes into consideration both short- and long-range business plans. Providing the necessary capacity requires an understanding of the long-range plan. In addition, the design and acquisition cycles may encompass several years.

The tools that management can use to ensure that the DP plan is properly incorporated within the budget are configuration management, critical success factors, and the DP department charter. The charter establishes the information system responsibilities of the DP department. For example, it will indicate whether or not the DP department is responsible for personal computers in user areas. Critical success factors are a means of measuring the criteria by which the success of the DP department will be judged. Management should ensure that the budget provides a means of satisfying these critical success factors. Configuration management is a formal process of ensuring that appropriate resources are available to meet information processing requirements. This tool enables management to develop the budgetary requirements to meet the information processing needs incorporated in both the DP plan and the business plan.

User Needs Criterion

Data processing has organization-wide information system processing. The processing needs of users must be incorporated into the DP budget. In many instances, this will require the DP function to establish a process for gathering and describing user information processing needs.

In many instances, the users will either not know, or fail to describe adequately, their information processing needs. For example, many users cannot realistically anticipate the amount of software maintenance required during the year. In addition, business requirements change, and as they change they place new information processing requirements on the automated application. Data processing departments must develop mechanisms to collect and/or anticipate these types of requirements.

The tools that management has to ensure that user needs are appropriately budgeted include system requests, change requests, user plans, and trend analysis. System requests and change requests are normally methods provided users to notify the data processing function of future work. Some of these processes will be continuous, and others will be evoked especially for the budgetary process.

Data processing functions may wish to anticipate user requirements through examining user plans and trend analysis. User plans are those plans developed by individual departments to support the organization's business plans. Trend analysis is one of several statistical methods that can be used to plot changes in workload. These projected changes can then be compared against user-requested work and any significant differences investigated.

Quality Criterion

The quality of the budget should be defined as a requirement. These are the quality factors listed in Table 5.1. During the requirements process, data processing management should indicate the relative importance of these factors and the method of accomplishing them. Note that in many instances there are trade-offs between quality factors. For example, the more emphasis the department wants to place on the reliability quality factor, the less cost-effective the budgetary process may be, with a potential negative effect on the cost-effectiveness quality factor.

Ensuring the Quality of the Requirements Phase

The requirements phase should be evaluated on its completeness, reliability, and validity. A quality control checklist for these three quality factors is provided as Table 5.3. At the end of the budgetary requirements phase, this quality control

TABLE 5.3 BUDGETARY REQUIREMENTS PHASE QUALITY CONTROL CHECKLIST

Item	Response			
	Yes	No	N/A[a]	Comments
1. Has the organization's mission statement been considered when preparing the budget?				
2. Do the preparers of the budget have access to the organization's business plan?				
3. Is business systems planning used to identify and prioritize information system projects?				
4. Is the budget cross-referenced to the department's mission and organization's business plan?				
5. Is the data processing plan consistent with the organization's business plan?				
6. Has the data processing plan been prioritized?				
7. Are the resources requested consistent with the organization's configuration management plan?				
8. Have critical success factors been identified for each budgetary item?				
9. Are there adequate budgetary resources to accomplish the critical success factors?				
10. Are the budgetary items consistent with the MIS department charter?				
11. Is there a process available for users to propose systems and changes to systems?				
12. Have user requests been cross-referenced to the budgetary requirements?				
13. Are user plans reviewed to identify potential information system needs that have been omitted?				
14. Has the size of the budget been compared to processing trends and variances investigated?				
15. Is quality of budgeting a budgetary requirement?				
16. Have the ten budgeting quality factors been specified in the budget?				
17. Has the data processing management prioritized the quality factors and provided that prioritization as guidance in developing the budget?				

[a]N/A, not applicable.

checklist should be used as a means of controlling the quality of the requirements phase.

The quality control checklist is designed so that "yes" responses are indicative of good quality; "no" responses should be investigated. If the item is not applicable, the N/A (not applicable) column should be checked. All "no" responses should be explained in the comments column of the checklist.

MANAGING THE BUDGETARY PREPARATION PROCESS

The preparation of the budget uses the budgetary requirements as the base. Note that many people may be involved in the preparation of the budget. In fact, the requirements and much of the preparation may be done almost simultaneously by the same person. This information can then be forwarded to a central DP budget group for consolidation.

The criteria that management need to consider in managing the preparation of the budget are listed in Table 5.4 and described below.

Methodology Criterion

The methodology represents the procedures provided budget preparers to use in preparing the budget. The methodology provided for budgeting is normally one of identifying and recording budgetary data. Methodology is stated to begin in the preparation phase because it is in that phase that the formal budgeting begins. Most of the requirements come out of planning and thus are separated from the main budgetary methodology. However, one must recognize that the planning methodology which produces the budget requirements is also a methodology. The process described in Part 3 includes the budgetary part of the planning methodology.

The tools incorporated in budgeting methodology include forms, procedures, software, and word processing. The more traditional tools are forms and procedures. Budgeting traditionally has been a form-driven process. The procedures were aimed more at completing the forms than the budgetary thought processes.

The newer budgeting method tools are designed to automate the process. These

TABLE 5.4 MANAGING THE BUDGETARY PREPARATION PROCESS

Budgeting criterion	Budgeting tools	Quality factors

Methodology	Forms
	Procedures
	Software
	  Scheduling
	  Estimating
	  Electronic spreadsheets
	Word processing
		Compliance
		Cost-effectiveness
		Timeliness
		Maintainable

Internal management approval	Reviews Sign-off	Usable Completeness Timeliness Maintainable
Quality control	Checklists Peer reviews	Compliance Usable Timeliness Cost-effectiveness Maintainable

tools encompass both computer software and word processing. The types of software being used for budgeting include scheduling software, estimating software, and electronic spreadsheets. Word processing is used for the actual recording and maintaining of budgetary information.

Some businesses are beginning to use microcomputers for budgeting purposes. The electronic spreadsheets on microcomputers are particularly useful for this purpose. In a few organizations, the budgetary information is downloaded from corporate to the department, analyzed, developed, or modified, and then uploaded from the department microcomputer to the corporate-level mainframe computer.

Internal Management Approval Criterion

Budgets are normally prepared by individuals, projects, or areas within the data processing function. These budgets must then be reviewed by first-level supervision, and then consolidated and reviewed by departmental management.

The approval process within the data processing function is designed for several purposes. The two main purposes are to ensure the reasonableness of the budget based on managerial experience and judgment, and to eliminate redundancy between various units within the data processing function.

The two tools used by data processing management are reviews and sign-offs. Reviews are a challenging of the budget by management. Reviews can be conducted by individuals or groups of managers. The more formal the review process, the more effective they tend to be. The sign-off is a formal process of concurrence by managers. Depending on the budget item, there may be several levels of sign-off. For example, first-level supervision may have to sign off, and in larger departments there may be middle managers and top-level managers who must sign off before the budget is approved.

Quality Control Criterion

Quality control responsibility should reside with the individual or project performing the budgetary task. For example, if an application project prepares a budget for developing or maintaining that project, the project itself should be responsible for the quality of the project budget.

The two most common tools for quality control of the preparation process are checklists and peer reviews. Peer reviews use one peer to verify the quality of the work done by another peer. Note that peer reviews can be individuals or groups of peers. The objective of peer reviews is to gain the synergistic effect of multiple people working on the same budget.

Checklists provide an excellent tool for evaluating the quality of the preparation of the budget. The checklists can both ensure that all the process has been performed, and challenge the thought processes that went into completing the preparation of the budget. A checklist for quality control of the budgetary preparation process is provided as Table 5.5. This, like other quality control checklists in this

TABLE 5.5 BUDGETARY PREPARATION PROCESS QUALITY CONTROL CHECKLIST

Item	Response			
	Yes	No	N/A[a]	Comments
1. Does a formal budget preparation methodology exist?				
2. Do the budget preparers comply with that methodology?				
3. Does the methodology use formal budget requirements developed in the planning process?				
4. Does the budgeting methodology have predetermined data to be developed?				
5. Do procedures exist explaining how to comply with the budget preparation methodology?				
6. Is word processing used to record the budgetary information so that it can be easily modified and updated?				
7. Is software used to assist in the preparation of the budget?				
8. Have personal computers been considered as a tool for budgetary preparation?				
9. Are the details developed in creating the budget documented and retained with the budgetary information?				
10. Are the people who prepare budgetary items held accountable for that budgetary item?				
11. Are budgetary items cross-referenced in the documentation to the person who prepared that item?				
12. Has a formal internal data processing approval process been established?				
13. Is the formal approval process documented?				
14. Must the approving individual sign the document to indicate it has been approved?				
15. If there are defects within the prepared budget, are they noted and documented?				
16. Are the defects used to improve the budgetary process?				
17. Is the budget subject to a quality control process?				
18. Are peer reviews used to verify the integrity of the budgetary amounts?				

[a]N/A, not applicable.

book, is established so that "yes" responses are indicative of good quality, and "no" responses should be investigated for the potential impact on quality.

MANAGING THE BUDGETARY APPROVAL PROCESS

The budgetary approval process is a process external to the data processing function. At a minimum, the approval is by the person to whom the data processing manager reports. In most organizations, it may require several levels of management and a budgetary committee.

The successful DP department orchestrates this phase of the budgetary process. Good budgets may not get approved without the appropriate marketing by data processing management.

Marketing the data processing budget should be a continuous effort. It should not start when the budget is submitted and stop when the budget is approved. The data processing manager should use every opportunity throughout the year to promote the work of the data processing department, and relate that to budgetary funding.

The criteria that data processing management should use in managing the approval process are listed in Table 5.6 and described in the following subsections.

Marketing Criterion

Marketing the budget is the process of building the case for approval of the budget. The acceptance of a budget will be based partly on the credibility of data processing management and their past performance. However, the following concepts have proved helpful in marketing the data processing budget:

1. Formal sessions to present the case for the data processing budget
2. Extensive supporting detail
3. Relating the budget to the business needs of the organization

The tools that are helpful in marketing the budget include a return on investment calculation and charge-out procedures. Return on investment shows the benefits associated with the data processing budget. Although it may not be necessary to quantify the return on investment, the benefits derived from accepting the budget should be stated. Thus management knows that if they reduce or eliminate budgetary items that they also eliminate certain information processing benefits. Another effective tool is to use charge-out. This transfers the responsibility for items to users. Thus management must consider user requirements and needs when they delete data processing items. (Note that Chapter 11 is devoted to marketing the budget.)

TABLE 5.6 MANAGING THE BUDGETARY APPROVAL PROCESS

Budgeting criterion	Budgeting tools	Quality factors
Marketing	Return on investment Charge-out	Timeliness Realistic
Competition	Cross-reference to company plans	Validity Realistic
Support	Worksheets Cross-reference to DP plans	Compliance Supportable

Competition Criterion

Most organizations only have limited numbers of funds. If they give money to the DP department, they may not be able to hire additional marketing people, build a new distribution center, and so on. Thus part of the budgeting process is trade-offs among various business objectives.

Data processing management must recognize these trade-offs and be prepared to address them. Because data processing is frequently viewed as a cost center, it is not viewed as a function that generates revenue for the organization. The more closely management can relate information services to revenue generation, the better opportunity they have to be competitive with other users of organization resources.

The primary tool for addressing competition is to cross-reference DP proposals to company plans. Thus the business plans of the organization become tied to the data processing budget. In that context a cut in the data processing budget will be related to how the cut directly affects the desired business plans of the organization.

Support Criterion

In the approval process, data processing management must be able to support individual line items. If they are challenged, good support encourages approval. When support is general and vague, senior management is more likely to delete an item from the data processing budget.

The tools that help support budget items are worksheets and cross-references to DP plans. The support provided by worksheets is only as good as the information on that worksheet. Cross-referencing budgetary items to DP plans relates money to specific information system objectives. Thus, if budgetary items are cut, so are data processing plans and objectives.

MANAGING THE USE OF THE BUDGET

The budget is developed to be used. Deficiencies in the preparation must be identified and corrected during usage. The use of the budget throughout the year must be managed in the same manner that an application is managed in the production status. Senior managers and the comptroller have the responsibility to manage the budget from a corporate perspective. The data processing manager and his or her assistants should manage the budget within the data processing function.

Managing the use of the budget commences when the budget is approved at the corporate level and continues until all expenditures have been closed out for the budgetary year. The process of managing the use of the budget is one that is focused at checkpoints. In many organizations these are monthly. It is at this point that revenues/expenditures are collected and data analyzed so that the appropriate information is available to make any needed adjustments.

The criteria that data processing management should use in controlling the budget during the budgetary period are listed in Table 5.7 and described in the following subsections.

DP Management Criterion

Using the budget as a tool for managing the data processing function is a management responsibility. The methods described previously for using the budget as a managerial control tool (see Table 5.7 for a list of these methods) are the methods that data processing management should be employing on a regular basis.

There is generally a high correlation between the effectiveness of a data processing function and the reliance by DP management on budgeting as a control tool. The more effectively management uses budgeting, the more effectively and economically the data processing activities are performed. One could almost, within a few moments, get a measure of the effectiveness of the data processing function in an

TABLE 5.7 MANAGING THE USE OF THE BUDGET

Budgeting criterion	Budgeting tools	Quality factors
DP management	Management methods Goals/objectives Planning Communications Measurement Project control Cost control Cost decisions	Usable Completeness Reliability Validity
Modification	Budget defects Change requests New requirements Deleted requirements	Compliance Usable Timeliness Maintainable Supportable
Status	Written reports Screens Graphics Analysis Comparison Trends	Usable Completeness Reliability Validity Timeliness
Quality control	Audits Reviews Sampling Measurement	Compliance Usable Completeness Reliability Validity Timeliness Cost-effectiveness Maintainable Supportable

organization by asking a few key questions about how budgeting is used by that management.

Modification Criterion

An out-of-date budget is as valuable as out-of-date system documentation. Once the integrity of the budget is permitted to deteriorate, its usefulness evaporates. As much effort will be required to keep the budgetary data current as was expended on developing the budget.

The maintenance of a budget involves the same processes as are used to maintain an application system. Even the categories of maintenance are similar between the two activities. The types of maintenance that will be needed to maintain the currentness of a budget include:

1. *Budget defects:* Errors in arithmetic, recording, consolidation, and so on, must be corrected when they are detected.
2. *Change requests:* When the budgeted items no longer fairly represent the activities being budgeted, the person responsible for that information should request changes. In some organizations, these changes will have to be approved; in other instances as long as they are within accepted tolerances, changes can be made. In addition, within the data processing function, if these changes are within the stated budgetary limits and within corporate budgeted line items, they can be made at the discretion of the data processing function.
3. *New requirements:* New projects, tasks, acquisitions, or other activities undertaken by the data processing function which were not included within the original budget need to be added. Normally, these require user and/or senior management approval.
4. *Deleted requirements:* If it is decided not to implement projects included within the budget, they should be deleted from the budget as soon as that management decision is made.

Status Criterion

The effectiveness of the budget as a control tool will be dependent on two items: the quality of the prepared budget and the quality of the status reporting against that budget. If the persons reporting status "play games," the value of the budget as a managerial control tool will be diminished.

The reporting of status also involves two items: the quality of status information and the method by which that information is reported to management. Both of these items must be present for status reports to be valuable.

The budgetary status is normally reported on hard-copy reports. The information is collected in the data processing department and forwarded to a corporate budgetary system, which consolidates, analyzes, prints out, and returns that information to data processing management for analysis.

The factual information on the report normally shows budgeted and actual expenditures to date. Most budget items show the current month and year to date. In addition, the reports may show variance, trends, and year-to-year comparisons, and highlight line items of concern.

The trend is to prepare the budgetary status information on electronic media. As such, it can be called up by a terminal when needed, or downloaded to the appropriate departments on diskette for departmental analysis. Budgetary analysis through microcomputer spreadsheet packages provides the opportunity for departmental managers to play "what if" analysis and make adjustments accordingly.

Quality Control Criterion

Quality control is a tool that can be used by management to evaluate the quality of the budget. This preassumes that quality was defined in measurable terms during the establishment of budgetary requirements. If so, the quality control tools can be put into place to measure and determine whether or not the desired level of quality in budgeting was achieved.

The actual quality control measures will be related to the quality factors established during requirements. Just as the factors will be customized for each organization, so will the specific quality control measures. For example, an organization may set a goal that the budgeted estimates are reliable within plus or minus 5 percent of actual expenditures. This quality factor can then be measured and reported on throughout the budgetary cycle.

To assist in this process, a quality control checklist (Table 5.8) is provided. This checklist identifies the items that should be addressed by the budget quality control program. The checklist is designed for use by data processing management. "Yes" responses are indicative of good budget quality control practices, and "no" responses require investigation to determine whether the quality control practices should be adjusted.

WHAT IS THE PROCESS THAT SHOULD BE MANAGED?

In this chapter we have described how to manage the budget process, without explaining precisely what the budget process is. The management process has been aimed at ensuring the quality of budgeting. In this and previous chapters we have emphasized that the quality of the budget will depend heavily on the budgetary process itself. Therefore, it can be assumed that management's ability to manage will also be dependent on the goodness of the implemented budget process.

The managerial strategies, quality control mechanisms, and attitudes all help structure the content of the budget process. If managers are not fully committed to budgeting as the "key" managerial control tool, the process will become a second-class citizen. On the other hand, if managers are fully committed to budgeting, they

TABLE 5.8 EVALUATING THE BUDGET QUALITY CONTROL PROGRAM

Item	Response			
	Yes	No	N/A[a]	Comments
1. Have the budgetary quality factors been identified?				
2. Have the quality factors been defined in measurable terms?				
3. Have mechanisms been established to collect information about the quality factors?				
4. Is the collected information reported and analyzed by data processing management?				
5. Do the organization's auditors (internal and/or external) regularly review the budget process?				
6. Do the organization's auditors regularly review compliance to the budgetary process?				
7. Do the organization's auditors investigate significant budget variances?				
8. Is the quality of budgeting improving from year to year, and if not, is management satisfied with the level of quality?				
9. Is the quality of the budget made everybody's responsibility?				
10. Are defects in the budget corrected as soon as they occur?				
11. Does the budget process introduce changes, new and deleted requirements, at the point where they occur?				

[a]N/A, not applicable.

will want the best possible budget process, just as they want the best possible system development process.

In Parts 1 and 2 of this book we have dwelt on the managerial strategies and budgeting approaches. This was done to establish the need and requirements for an effective budget process. In Part 3 we explain the steps in the budget process and how to perform those steps. However, an understanding of the need, and the quality built into the process, have been the topics of the book to this point.

Part 3 The DP Budget Process

6
Building a Budget

Budgeting will be presented as a data processing project. It has the same characteristics and control needs as any other project within the data processing function. The budget cycle described in Chapter 5 will be used to identify the phases of the budget project.

There are two items to consider in building a budget: the process or methods by which the budget is prepared and the budget as a product. Both need to be addressed and controlled separately. The quality of the actual budget document issued will be determined by both the effectiveness of the budgetary process and the control exercised over the development of the budget product.

In this chapter we explain how to build a budget. The emphasis is on the process to use in developing the budget. The budget process described in this chapter is a five-step process. How to perform each of the five steps is described in subsequent chapters.

THE BUDGETARY PROCESS VERSUS THE BUDGET PRODUCT

In the early days of data processing, application systems were built using any method desired by the project leader. The project leader had discretion over how an application system would be built. Most used a lot of creativity but minimal methodology. The results were often disastrous in terms of meeting schedules, budgets, and satisfying users.

It became obvious that there must be a better way to build computer systems. When this philosophy was accepted, system development methodologies were created. These methodologies became the standardized process by which application systems were built. Through improved and more effective methodologies, the quality and acceptance of application systems improved. Data processing's ability to predict estimates and schedules also improved significantly.

The same concepts are applicable to the data processing budgeting responsibilities. The more flexibility data processing management gives its staff in budget preparation, the higher the probability that the budget estimates will not be representative of actual costs.

A good process does not guarantee a good budget. However, flaws in the annual budget can normally be traced back to problems in the budgetary process. Therefore, by continually improving the budgetary process to eliminate budgeting defects, the probability of an effective budget increases significantly.

Management is responsible for developing and implementing a budgetary process. Management has the added responsibility of establishing controls that ensure the quality of the budget itself. The establishment of a well-developed and standardized budgetary process, coupled with effective quality control procedures, provides management with the highest probability of successful budgeting.

WHY BUDGETARY PROCESSES FAIL

Budgeting is frequently looked at as a guessing game with management. It is a basis for justifying funds, but when those funds have been justified many believe that the purpose of the budget has been fulfilled.

In many organizations, expenditures are juggled to fit budgetary buckets. If a project leader manages two or more budgets, funds are diverted to budgetary categories that have not been exhausted. Frequently, there is little relationship between work performed and budgetary accounts charged.

A recent article heralded "fifty ways to hide the cost of a microcomputer." Although the words did not say it, the article implied that if one understands the budgetary process, one can acquire a microcomputer and never have it recorded as a microcomputer acquisition.

The bottom line of these budgetary attitudes is that the budgetary process is not worth much. Most believe that it is better to budget than not to budget, but they seriously question the value returned for the time expended. This incrimination of the budgetary process is frequently well founded because the same time and attention expended to develop other processes is not devoted to creating an effective budgeting process.

There are two general categories of problems with budgeting (see Figure 6.1). Using terminology borrowed from the testing profession, we can categorize these problems as white-box and black-box problems. The connotation of white and black is that white-box problems are visible through investigation, whereas black-box problems are difficult to see. For example, an error in budgetary addition would be a

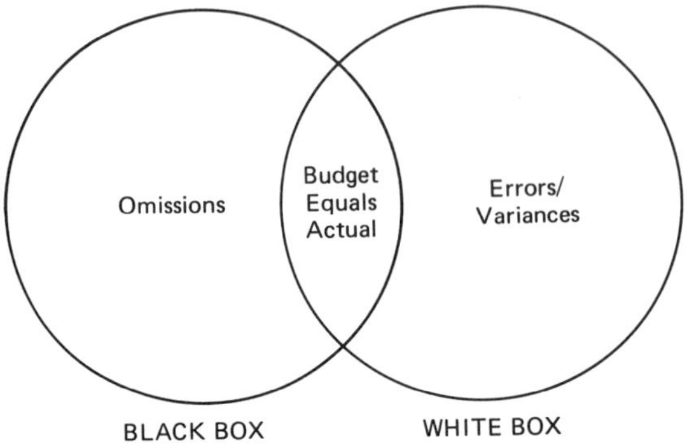

Figure 6.1 Budgeting problems.

white-box problem; failure to budget adequately for needed maintenance would be a black-box problem.

Most budgetary processes address the white-box problems; few are designed to catch errors of budgetary omission. People worry more about black-box budgetary problems than the process does. The process proposed in this book addresses both white-box and black-box budgetary problems.

White-box problems can be divided into two general categories. These are errors and estimating variances. The example of an error in addition described previously is a white-box error problem; an incorrect estimate to develop a computer application is a white-box estimating variance problem.

Much of the budgeting problem is directly attributable to the lack of managerial support for budgeting. If the managers who look at budgeting as a game fail to use it as a management tool throughout the year, or turn their back on budgetary abuses, the budget will not be implemented in a positive manner. Without strong management support, budgeting will not work.

Budgetary Principle

If there is a data processing budgeting problem, there is a data processing management problem. Budgeting without management support does not work.

INTEGRATING DP BUDGETS INTO CORPORATE BUDGETS

Data processing management operates using two budgetary processes: the corporate budgeting process and the data processing budget process. Obviously, the corporate budget process takes precedence over the data processing budget process. However, both need to be integrated to be effective.

The corporate budgeting process should explain what is needed, while the data processing budgetary process provides how to do it. The corporate requirements normally indicate:

- Forms to complete
- Accounts to use
- Calendar schedules for completion
- Budgetary constraints
- Approval processes

The data processing budget process defines how those budgetary requirements are accomplished. This customizes the corporate processes to provide:

- Assignment of responsibilities
- Third-party contacts (e.g., users, vendors)
- Estimating processes
- Quality control procedures
- Guidelines on cost/benefit components

Data processing management has the responsibility for the development of the local budgetary process, and the integration of that with the corporate budgetary processes. In smaller organizations this will be performed by the data processing manager; in larger organizations the responsibility may be assigned to an assistant manager or administrative manager. There are four tasks that are needed to integrate corporate and data processing budgetary processes. They are described in the following four subsections.

Identify Corporate Budgetary Requirements and Precision

The integration process commences with a definition of corporate budgetary requirements and desired budgetary precision. The end product of the data processing budgetary process will be input to the corporate process. Failure to meet corporate requirements negates the work performed within the data processing department.

Most organizations have budgetary procedures and forms. These are normally written by accountants for accountants. Data processing professionals may have the same problem understanding and using budgetary forms as DP users have understanding and using system development methodology processes and forms.

Data processing professionals should approach corporate budgetary requirements in the same manner they approach requirements for any other project. The better defined those requirements, the better they will be understood by the users and the easier it becomes to accomplish those requirements successfully. This may require some redefinition into terms more readily understandable and useful by data processing personnel.

Budgetary Principle

Corporate budgetary requirements are designed to collect specific pieces of information. Although it is important to gather that information, it is not important to gather it in the format proposed by corporate procedures if another process is more effective.

The corporate budgetary requirements should be obtained and each data item to be collected challenged by the following questions:

1. Do I understand the meaning and intent for collecting this piece of information?
2. Do I understand the precision required when collecting this piece of information?
3. Is this piece of information applicable to the data processing function?
4. Can this piece of information be collected within the time span required?
5. Will help be required from users in collecting this piece of information?
6. Can I relate this information to a business objective?

The answers to these questions will identify the outputs required from the data processing budgetary process.

Identify Data Processing Requirements and Precision

The data processing department will need to collect the information required by the corporate budgetary processes, but in addition information may be needed for its own internal usage. In some instances, the information needed to manage the data processing function may be in conflict with corporate budgetary requirements. For example, corporate may want information on an annual basis, while data processing needs it on a project basis, regardless of budgetary years.

In defining the data processing budgetary requirements and precision, data processing managers must define their managerial control needs. For example, if data processing management must bid against outside software houses or projects, the precision of the estimates must be high to remain competitive. On the other hand, in organizations that do not charge out their services, data processing may want to budget project by project, even though that information is not necessary for corporate records of any type.

The data processing budgetary requirements should be established by data processing management. In Part 2 we have provided information for use in developing a departmental budgetary strategy. It is generally better to collect too little information than too much. The budgetary process can be extended and modified over a period of years to enhance and refine information collected. If too much information is collected, the valuable time of the staff can be wasted, which is not recoverable in later years.

Budgetary Principle

It is better to collect too little information than too much. After all, data can be added, but work performed cannot be recouped.

Develop Cross-reference Matrix

The corporate and data processing budgetary requirements should be cross-referenced. This can be accomplished by developing a simple cross-reference matrix. An example of a cross-reference matrix is illustrated in Figure 6.2.

The cross-reference matrix shows the corporate budgetary requirements on the horizontal axis of the matrix. In general, there will be one item on the cross-reference matrix for each piece of information required by the corporate budgetary procedures. In Figure 6.2, data processing staff salaries are listed as typical of corporate budgetary requirements.

Corporate Budgetary Requirements / DP Function Budgetary Requirements	DP Staff Salaries			
Application projects	C: Average annual dollars DP: Hourly billing rate			
Software maintenance	C: Average annual dollars DP: Hourly billing rate			

Figure 6.2 Corporate to DP function budgetary cross-reference matrix.

The data processing budgetary requirements are shown on the vertical axis. In Figure 6.2, the requirements are listed which are application projects, and software maintenance projects are listed. There are requirements that require people and thus relate to salary. Note that more items would comprise data processing staff salaries than the two items listed. These are given just for purposes of illustration.

Within the matrix is shown the desired level of precision. In Figure 6.2, for example, the corporate position (designated by the letter C) indicates that salary should be provided in terms of average annual dollars per staff member. On the other hand, the data processing precision (indicated by the letters DP) is provided in hourly billing rates. Since this is the meaningful collection number from data processing staff, a recalculation will need to be made from the information collected within the data processing department prior to providing that information to the corporate budgetary process. It is frequently advantageous to collect information in one format and reprocess it to another format rather than trying to reeducate the data processing staff in corporate budgetary concepts.

Budgetary Principle

The data processing staff should be trained in only one budgetary process. If inconsistencies occur between corporate and data processing budgetary processes, they should be handled by the data processing budgetary process.

Resolve Cross-reference Differences

Differences in the budgetary process, such as that illustrated in Figure 6.2, need resolution. There are three possible resolutions. First, corporate budgetary processes can be changed. This is quite unlikely. Second, data processing function budgetary processes can be changed to bring them in compliance with corporate budgetary processes. This is very possible but violates our budgetary principle of providing data processing management with the information they need to manage. The third means for resolving the difference is to build into the data processing budget process the resolution mechanism. In Figure 6.2, this may mean converting hours charged to projects, together with other uses of DP staff, into annual salary dollars for corporate budgetary purposes. Normally, this third method of resolution is the least time consuming and complex of the three methods.

INTERRELATIONSHIP BETWEEN BUDGETING AND PLANNING

Planning and budgeting are two closely interrelated business functions. In most organizations, planning precedes budgeting, but the two are closely related. Planning is determining what should be done, and budgeting the process of allocating funding to do what is needed.

The type of budgeting required normally coincides with the type of planning required. For example, if the organization requires one-year and five-year plans, the organization normally requires one-year and five-year budgets.

The precision expected of plans and budgets are normally related to the planning and budgetary period. For example, five-year budgets would not be expected to be nearly as precise as one-year budgets. On the other hand, the same basic methods for both planning and budgeting are utilized regardless of the time span covered by the process.

Although budgeting and planning are two separate functions and processes, they should be interrelated. This is true at both the data processing function and corporate levels. Data processing plans should be interrelated to corporate plans, and data processing budgets should be interrelated to corporate budgets. For example, data processing should not be budgeting or anticipating projects which are not included in user plans and budgets. Although this principle is easy to state, it is frequently difficult to practice.

If the two processes are not firmly integrated, the three tasks described below should be undertaken to ensure integration between the planning and budgeting processes.

Identify Corporate Groups Responsible for Planning and Budgeting

The data processing department should determine who in the corporation has overall responsibility for planning, and who has overall responsibility for budgeting. At the corporate level, these processes should be integrated. The purpose of identifying these key people is to obtain access to corporate short- and long-range plans and budgets.

Acquire Corporate Short- and Long-range Plans and Budgets

The DP function must support the entire organization in information processing. That support cannot be provided unless (1) the people involved notify data processing of the needed support, or (2) data processing identifies the type of needed support through investigation. Obtaining the organization's short- and long-range plans and budgets fulfills the alternative method of identifying information requirements. Note that these requirements may not be spelled out as information processing requirements but, rather, identified as business plans as expressed in planning and budgetary documents.

Cross-reference Data Processing Budgets to Organizational Plans and Budgets

Unless there is a formal integration between planning and budgeting, it needs to be done in the data processing budgetary process. Although ideally it would be done in planning, and then have budgeting support planning, there may be inadequate time to go through these steps. Since the budget is the general authorization from management to expend funds, the integration *must* be assured at the completion of the budgetary process. Normally, this extra time expended through investigation and cross-reference is paid back with more realistic budgets.

SPECIAL BUDGETARY CONSIDERATIONS

In developing a budgetary process, management must consider and make decisions in the following three areas:

1. Management's budgeting policy
2. Expected quality of budgeting
3. Budgetary tools and practices

Prior to developing, or redesigning, a budgetary process, management should address these three areas. Management's intent in each of the three areas provides the needed direction in building an effective budgetary process. Each of these areas is discussed individually below.

Management's Budgetary Policy

The word "policy" is used to define management's budgetary intent. It is not necessary, although perhaps advisable, to develop a formal budgetary policy. However, without management's intent clearly known, budgeting may be viewed more as a game than as an important function on which people's performances will be evaluated.

The budgetary policy, like any other policy, describes in straightforward terms what management expects from budgeting. It is surprising how many people involved in budgeting have no idea of how the process is used, or management's expectations from the process. Frequently, a few simple statements from management can turn around a process which has been ineffective into one that is effective.

If a formal budgetary policy is developed, it should be comprised of three parts. Part 1 should be a general statement of the objective of budgeting. Part 2 should be the specific objectives or management intent regarding budgeting. Part 3 should explain how the implementation of the policy will be measured. All three parts are necessary for an effective policy.

A sample budget policy is illustrated in Figure 6.3. This illustration could be used as a model budget policy for most data processing functions. If adopted, it should be distributed to those responsible for budgeting at the time the budget is being prepared. It is also advisable for management to explain the policy in a staff meeting. This explanation serves two purposes: it clarifies and explains what the

> Budgeting is a tool used by management to request funding for data processing projects and to provide management with a tool to control data processing activities. It is the intent of management that:
>
> 1. Budgeting is a cornerstone of data processing management control.
> 2. Budgeting is a managerial responsibility.
> 3. There is a formal process for developing a budget.
> 4. The budget is reproducible by following the process.
> 5. The budget is reliable.
>
> The success of the budget will be determined by two factors: First, the variance between actual and budgeted amounts should not exceed plus or minus 10 percent; and second, the budgetary information must provide management with an effective tool to use for controlling data processing activities.

Figure 6.3 Sample budget policy.

policy is, and it provides management with an opportunity to explain the importance of the policy to them.

Quality of the Data Processing Budget

"Quality" literally means compliance with standards. If any product meets the standards prescribed for that product, it is considered a quality product. If a product varies beyond accepted tolerances, it is not considered a quality product. Thus quality is a predefined state rather than an expectation. Also, quality does not mean costliness but, rather, meeting prescribed objectives.

Management must define the quality standards for the budget. One of the reasons that a budget policy is important is because standards should be based on policy. Standards are the measure by which the implementation of the policy should be determined. For example, if a product were to be packaged by the pound, a sixteen-ounce standard weight would be the measure by which the packaging policy would be evaluated. If the packages weighed one pound, or within an acceptable tolerance of one pound, the standard would have been met and thus the policy achieved.

The sample budget policy illustrated in Figure 6.3 gave one specific and one general standard. The specific standard was that the actual expenditures should be within plus or minus 10 percent of the budgeted expenditures. The general standard was that the budget was an effective managerial tool. One standard is easy to interpret, the second requires judgment to determine whether it has been achieved.

Another way of describing a budgetary standard is as a success factor. The success of implementing the budget policy can be measured by factors which if achieved will make budgeting successful in the eyes of management. For managers unaccustomed to working with specific standards, the success factors may be a more realistic approach to budgeting quality.

Figure 6.4 provides a form for documenting the budgeting success factors. This

If the following factors are met, budgeting will be considered successful:

1.

2.

3.

4.

5.

6.

7.

8.

9.

10.

Signed: ______________________________ __________
Data Processing Manager Date

Figure 6.4 Budgeting success factors.

should be completed, signed, and dated by the data processing manager. The types of success factors that should be considered are those that:

1. Compare actual expenditures to budgeted expenditures.
2. Compare requested funds versus allocated funds.
3. Evaluate budgeting as a managerial tool.
4. Permit the data processing plans to be implemented.
5. Assist in educating managers and staff in the importance of budgeting and accounting.
6. Aid acceptance of the process by the data processing staff.

Budgetary Practices and Tools

Wherever possible, the budgetary process should be automated. This includes automating the collection of budgetary data, the consolidation of budgetary data, the reproduction of budgetary reports, and the reporting of status information against the budgeted amounts.

The decision to automate the budgetary process is a management decision. Which tools are selected and how they are implemented need not be decided by management. Management determines what is needed, not how it is accomplished. However, the direction to automate is both a management decision and an implementation decision.

This book assumes a management decision to automate the budget process. Therefore, in the remainder of this part of the book we discuss the tools that should be considered in automating the budgetary process. Where appropriate, multiple tools will be discussed to assist in selecting the most effective tool, one that can be implemented into existing processes.

THE STEPS IN BUILDING A BUDGET

A five-step process is recommended for building a budget. The objective of the process is to build a budgetary product. As such, it can be viewed from the same perspective by which one views a development process to build a data processing product (i.e., an application system). The four phases of the budgeting cycle (see Figure 5.3) can be considered the phases of the budget development process.

The developmental phases, and the specific steps recommended to build a budget, are illustrated in Table 6.1. This shows the four phases of the budgeting cycle plus the five budgetary development steps proposed in this book. Note that there is no development step for the use phase because at that point the budget has been developed. In Part 2 we have addressed using the budget as a management tool.

A brief synopsis of each of the phases and developmental steps follows. Although the phases are provided only for background purposes and will not be discussed in later chapters, one chapter will be devoted to each of the five budget development steps.

Requirements Phase of the Budgetary Cycle

The requirements phase in a development project defines user needs. In a budgetary process, the requirements phase identifies the needs of both the organization and the data processing department from budgeting.

The first step of the budgetary process is planning. Because budgeting is a repetitive process, as opposed to the uniqueness of a DP developmental project, the general needs have been determined. What is required is to modify and plan how to satisfy those needs during the current budgeting cycle. Thus, while this step defines requirements, it defines them within the constraints of a repetitive secular process.

The objectives of the budget planning step are as follows:

1. *Assign responsibilities:* Identify the people who will be involved in the budgetary process.

TABLE 6.1 BUDGET CYCLE AND STEPS

Budget cycle	Budget step	Objectives of step
Requirements	1. Budget planning	Assign responsibilities Train Initiate process Schedule and staff Reliability/validity
Preparation	2. Data gathering	Identify participants Distribute requirements Collect data Quality control
Preparation	3. Estimating costs and benefits	Estimate costs Estimate benefits Estimate risks Quality control
Preparation	4. Classification, consolidation, and preparation of a budget	Approve/analyze Classify Consolidate Organize Quality control
Approval	5. Marketing the budget	Package Present Negotiate
Use	Using the budget as a managerial tool	Maintain Use as a management control tool

2. *Train:* Ensure that those involved in the budgetary process are adequately skilled in that process.
3. *Initiate process:* Begin the process of preparing the budget.
4. *Schedule and staff:* Identify those people who will be involved in the process and then prepare a schedule for the tasks needed to be performed.
5. *Reliability/validity:* Ensure that the budget process produces a budget which is both valid and can be relied upon.

Implementation Phase of the Budgetary Cycle

During design and programming in the developmental process, the requirements are converted into specifications that will be executable on the computer. Before coding begins, clear design specifications are needed to solve the user need.

The early part of the implementation phase produces all the information needed to prepare the budget. Any information gathered during this phase must be classified, consolidated, and put into the budget document. At the end of these tasks, the most challenging aspect of the budgetary process has been completed.

The three steps in the implementation phase are the data-gathering step, the estimating costs and benefits step, and the classification, consolidation, and preparation of a budget step. These three steps are closely related. Although they are separate functions, they are closely interrelated and frequently are performed concurrently.

The objectives of the data-gathering step are as follows:

1. *Identify participants:* While the planning step identified the people responsible for budgeting, this step identifies the people who will receive the budgetary funds, and thus the ones responsible for defining and justifying projects and tasks budgeted.
2. *Distribute requirements:* The instructions and forms to be completed by the participants need to be distributed.
3. *Collect data:* The information needed from the participants must be collected in accordance with the budget schedule.
4. *Quality control:* The measures and techniques needed to ensure the quality of budgetary information must be put into place and exercised.

The objectives of the estimating costs and benefits step are as follows:

1. *Estimate costs:* Determine the cost for each budgetary task.
2. *Estimate benefits:* Determine the benefits associated with projects included in the budget.
3. *Estimate risk:* Determine the level of risk in accomplishing the budgeted tasks.
4. *Quality control:* Ensure the quality of the estimated costs and benefits included within the budget.

The objectives of the classification, consolidation, and preparation of the budget step are as follows:

1. *Approve/analyze:* Ensure that the budgetary items are in accordance with the intent of data processing management.
2. *Classify:* Place into the proper budgetary accounts.
3. *Consolidate:* Accumulate similar information in the same account.
4. *Organize:* Structure information in accordance with the organizational requirements.
5. *Quality control:* Ensure the integrity of the information included within the budget.

Approval Phase of the Budgetary Cycle

Testing of an approval by the user of the developed system has two primary objectives in the developmental process: to identify defects and to predict the probability of success of the product being tested.

Approving the budget has two similar objectives. The first is to determine the acceptability of the budget items with management. Although this does not remove defects in the same context as testing removes defects from an application system, it does remove unacceptable items from the budget. Note that much of this should be done prior to the final budgetary presentation. The second objective deals with the probability of success, but from the perspective of making the budget successful.

These objectives can be described as follows:

1. *Package:* Prepare a budget in a manner that increases the probability of success.
2. *Present:* Include with the budget sufficient documentation and aids to make the budget attractive to management.
3. *Negotiate:* Stay with the budget through the approval process, again to ensure the highest probability of success for the budget.

Use Phase of the Budgetary Cycle

The uses of the budget have been described earlier. It is in the use of the budget, as with the use of an application system, that the value of the budget becomes apparent. As with many aspects of business, the quality of the product will determine its usefulness. Budgets that are highly reliable are highly useful. Budgets that contain the needed information will be used. It is through an effective budgetary process that a useful document is developed.

Budgetary Principle

The key to successful budgeting is to create information that people need to perform their jobs effectively.

AREN'T ACCOUNTANTS SUPPOSED TO BUILD THE BUDGETARY PROCESS?

In this chapter we have attempted to show the relationship between the development of an application system and the development of a budget. We showed the steps and tasks that need to be performed in each phase of the budgetary cycle. We also suggested that data processing management determine the factors that would make budgeting successful in the data processing department.

Budgeting as imposed on the data processing department by senior management is normally a product of the accountants. The information, forms, and directions provided are for completing the needs of accountants and senior management. They are not designed to take into account the uniqueness or special managerial needs of the data processing function.

The budget process is too important to leave to the accountants. As shown in Part 2, the accountants have not provided the appropriate "buckets" in the budgetary process to deal with the cost of quality. The accountants have not addressed the multiyear aspects of development; the accountants have not addressed DP from a corporate perspective, versus DP from a DP department perspective. Accountants have not installed the appropriate mechanisms to control the personal computer.

Budgeting as we know it today is a product of a society oriented toward producing physical products. Many organizations are moving rapidly from a manufacturing orientation to an information orientation. The existing budgetary processes do not deal with these new requirements. The question of who should make these revolutionary budgetary changes can perhaps be best expressed through the following budgetary principle:

Budgetary Principle

If it is going to be, it is up to me!

7
Step 1: Budget Planning

Budgeting begins with planning. The planning step is limited by the constraints of the budgetary process and the budgeting objectives. Within these constraints, planning must define the responsibilities and tasks needed to build a realistic and valid budget for the forthcoming year.

The quality of the final budget will rarely exceed the thoroughness incorporated into the plan. Poor plans produce poor budgets, and good plans normally produce good budgets. As with many projects, extra time expended in planning normally has a multifold payback during the implementation of that plan. This is particularly true in DP budgeting because most of the participants lack budgetary skills.

In this chapter the five planning tasks are described: assigning responsibilities, training the budget participants, initiating the budget process, scheduling and staffing the budget process, and defining the reliability and validity of budgeting. These tasks will be related to the budgetable components described earlier in the book (see Table 3.1) and the risk dimensions associated with those components (see Table 3.2 for risk dimensions).

BUDGET PLANNING—THE MOST IMPORTANT STEP

Budgeting is a diversion from the normal activities of the data processing function. Although the concept of a budget is familiar to most professionals, the budgeting concepts and procedures are not. There is a significant variance between what a person does for one's own personal budget versus a budget prepared within a business organization.

The planning function needs to address what information is needed and how that needed information will be collected. The general guidelines for budgeting are established before annual budget planning commences. However, conditions change, the makeup and skill level of the staff change, organizational requirements change—all of these necessitating a further customization of the data processing budget process each year.

Budgeting is a widespread activity within the data processing function. It involves a large number of participants in a variety of functions. Without appropriate planning, all the pieces will not come together with the right precision and reliability at the right time.

Generally, the quality of the budget will never exceed the quality of the planning step. If this step is shortcut, the end budget will reflect that shortcoming. For example, if the question of validity is not addressed at the planning stage, the people preparing budgetary items will do it in accordance with their own definition of budget validity.

Planning encompasses all the activities that occur prior to the actual development of budgetary information. The process should involve the most senior members of the data processing department. Planning is truly a management function. Budget planning acts as a control; during the budget cycle, therefore, strong management involvement is needed during planning.

There is one concept that has been detrimental to many data processing projects: "WISCN," an acronym that stands for "Why isn't Sammy coding now?" When projects spend a large time planning, many managers push to get Sammy coding. Unfortunately, without appropriate planning, much of Sammy's coding is wasted and needs to be rewritten. The same concept applied to budgeting is "WISBN," or "Why isn't Sammy budgeting now?" Just as coding too early produces worthless code, undertaking the preparation of budgeting data too early can produce worthless budgets.

The entire budgeting process is subject to two major constraints: the budgetary process and budgeting objectives (see Figure 7.1). The steps that are followed in budgeting must stay within these constraints.

The budgetary process constraint restricts budget participants to predetermined rules. The rules state how the budget is to be prepared and the participants are expected to follow those rules. Although there should be room for creativity in budgeting, it must be done within the constraints of the process rules.

The budgeting objective constraints require that budgeting meet management's control needs. Failure to develop budgets that meet these control needs undermines the purpose of budgeting. Again, there is leeway within the budgeting process, but the objective constraints must be kept in mind.

The planning step must take into account these two constraints. Not only is planning (i.e., Step 1) subject to these two constraints, but the plan developed for the remaining budgetary steps must also abide by those constraints.

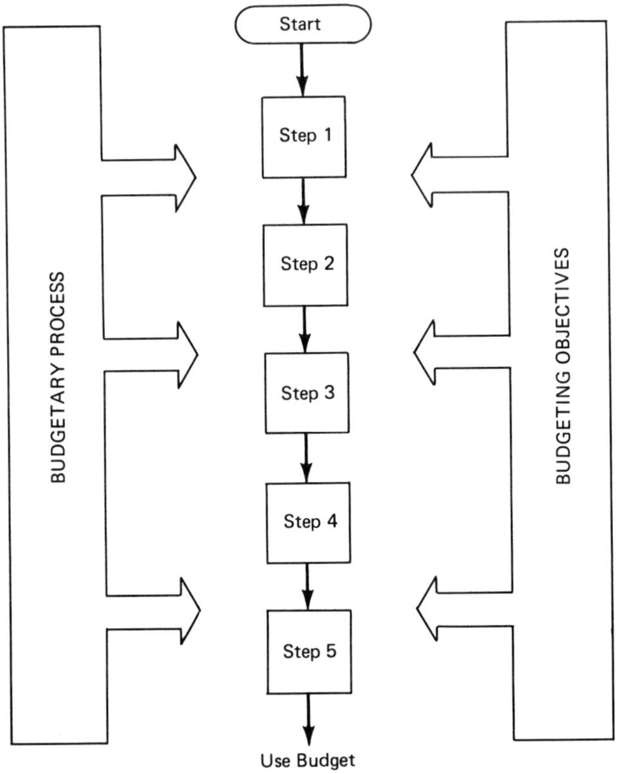

Figure 7.1 Budget planning constraints.

THE BUDGET PLANNING STEP

The budget planning step should be performed by senior management in the data processing function. In very large organizations it may be delegated to the manager of administration and/or planning. Some data processing functions have a data processing comptroller who can oversee this process. However, in the large majority of data processing departments the responsibility for budget planning should reside directly with the data processing manager.

The planning process should begin prior to the initiation of the annual organizational budgetary program. It is normally too late to begin DP budget planning once the corporate requests for budgetary information have been disseminated to the individual departments. As a general rule of thumb, budgetary planning should begin halfway through the organization's business year. For example, if the business year ends December 31, budgetary planning should begin July 1.

The budgetary planning uses the following as the basis for planning:

- Data processing budget policy or equivalent
- Organizational budgeting procedures

- Data processing management budgeting objectives
- Budget resource and time constraints

Budget planning involves the following five tasks:

- *Task 1:* Assign budget responsibilities.
- *Task 2:* Train budget participants.
- *Task 3:* Determine reliability/validity of budget.
- *Task 4:* Schedule and staff the budgetary process.
- *Task 5:* Customize budgetary process.

BUDGETABLE COMPONENTS PLANNING CONSIDERATIONS

To be workable, the budget process must divide budgeting into its component parts. The objective of introducing controllable or budgetable components is to divide budgeting into its component parts. This approach was selected because it complements most organizations' budgetable line items. For example, hardware is a line item in most budgets and therefore is defined as a budgetable component.

Each budgetable component has slightly different budgeting characteristics. For example, the systems maintenance component is a difficult cost to predict specifically for repair maintenance, whereas hardware costs are relatively stable and highly predictable costs. The budgetable characteristics of each component need to be taken into consideration during the planning process.

Planning will determine the methods to be followed in gathering budgetary data. Therefore, it is important in planning to understand the budgeting characteristics of each budgetable component. These characteristics or considerations help define the type of budgeting assignments that need to be undertaken in each of the five planning tasks.

The budgeting considerations for the budgetable components can be described through the three risk dimensions (i.e., resources, time frames, and risk). These considerations will be paramount in the selection of the appropriate practice or tool used in the budgeting process. For example, application development has a multiyear time frame, requiring that information be collected about the entire time frame rather than just the current budget year.

The considerations that need to be incorporated into the budget plan for the sixteen budgetable components are listed in Table 7.1. We will see these considerations scoping the planning tasks, defining the data collection forms used in the data-gathering step, and used again in the estimating costs and benefits step as well as in the classification and consolidation step.

The considerations related to resources are:

- *Increases in staff size:* Growth in the size of the staff requires growth in associated components.

TABLE 7.1 BUDGETABLE COMPONENT PLANNING CONSIDERATIONS

		Planning considerations for:	
Budgetable component	Resources	Time frame	Risk
1. DP management and administration	Increases in staff size Increases in salaries/benefits Increases in services Corporate constraints	Growth trends Who performs a task	Growth of function Occurrence of problems Senior management demands Skills of users
2. Facilities	Increases in services Change in business conditions Change in business programs Change in DP technology Availability of needed product	Cost trends Growth trends Who performs a task	Growth of function Occurrence of problems
3. System support	Increases in staff size Increases in salaries/benefits Increases in services Change in DP technology Corporate constraints	Cost trends Growth trends Who performs a task	Occurrence of problems Senior management demands Skills of staff Newness of technology Complexity of system
4. New systems design	Increases in salaries/benefits Change in business conditions Change in business programs Change in DP technology Availability of needed product	When time spent Priorities of work	Growth of function Occurrence of problems Senior management demands Skills of staff Newness of technology Complexity of system Completeness of design Completeness of documentation Skills of users

5. Systems maintenance	Increases in salaries/benefits Increases in services Change in business conditions Change in business programs Availability of needed product	When time spent Priorities of work	Growth of function Occurrence of problems Senior management demands Skills of staff Newness of technology Complexity of system Completeness of design Completeness of documentation Skills of users
6. Computer operations	Increases in staff size Increases in salaries/benefits Increases in services Change in DP technology Availability of needed product	Cost trends Priorities of work Growth trends Performance trends	Growth of function Occurrence of problems Newness of technology Complexity of system Skills of users
7. Hardware	Increases in services Change in DP technology Availability of needed product	Cost trends Speed of vendor response Growth trends	Occurrence of problems Skills of staff Newness of technology
8. Purchased/rented software	Change in business conditions Change in business programs Change in DP technology Availability of needed product	Cost trends Speed of vendor response Growth trends Who performs a task	Occurrence of problems Skills of staff Complexity of system Completeness of documentation Skills of users
9. Technical support	Increases in staff size Increases in salaries/benefits Increases in services Change in DP technology Availability of needed product	Cost trends Priorities of work Growth trends Performance trends	Skills of staff Newness of technology Complexity of system
10. Quality assurance	Increases in staff size Increases in salaries/benefits Increases in services	Growth trends Who performs a task Performance trends	Occurrence of problems Senior management demands Skills of staff Newness of technology Complexity of system Completeness of design Completeness of documentation Skills of users

(continued)

TABLE 7.1 *(Cont.)*

Budgetable component	Resources	Planning considerations for: Time frame	Risk
11. Communication	Change in DP technology Availability of needed product	Cost trends Speed of vendor response Growth trends	Occurrence of problems Skills of staff Newness of technology
12. Data base administration	Increases in staff size Increases in salaries/benefits Increases in services Change in DP technology Availability of needed product	Growth trends Who performs a task Performance trends	Growth of function Occurrence of problems Skills of staff Newness of technology Complexity of system
13. Word processing/office system/microcomputer	Increases in services Change in DP technology Availability of needed product	Cost trends Speed of vendor response Growth trends	Occurrence of problems Skills of staff Newness of technology
14. Information center	Increases in staff size Increases in salaries/benefits Increases in services Change in DP technology Availability of needed product	Priorities of work Growth trends Who performs a task Performance trends	Occurrence of problems Senior management demands Newness of technology Skills of users
15. Security	Increases in staff size Increases in salaries/benefits Increases in services Change in business conditions Change in business programs Change in DP technology	Priorities of work Performance trends	Occurrence of problems Senior management demands Newness of technology Complexity of system Skills of users
16. Outside services	Change in business programs Change in DP technology Corporate constraints	When time spent Speed of vendor response Priorities of work Who performs a task Performance trends	Growth of function Skills of staff Newness of technology

- *Increases in salary/benefits:* As salaries and benefits for employees increase, so do the costs of data processing services.
- *Increases in services:* If a component offers more services, for example, an information center agrees to assist users in debugging programs, the cost of those components will increase accordingly.
- *Changes in business conditions:* If the business environment changes, for example, the economy significantly improves or worsens, that normally has an effect on organizations tied to that business indicator.
- *Changes in business programs:* As a business adds additional programs, product lines, and so on, the support required increases.
- *Changes in DP technology:* Each technological advance has associated with it a learning curve. The costs associated with that learning curve are translatable into additional component costs.
- *Corporate constraints:* The data processing function may be constrained in hiring or spending money: for example, a travel ban by the corporation, which will be immediately translatable into changes in expenditures.
- *Availability of needed product:* If a needed product or service is not available, costs will not be expended until that product becomes available.

The time considerations associated with the budgetable components are as follows:

- *Cost trends:* The relationship of cost per unit of work over a period of time constitutes a cost trend.
- *Allocation of time spent:* Constraints within a function may determine when a specific task can be accomplished. Thus, work may be spread out or bunched depending on availability of time.
- *Speed of vendor response:* Costs may accelerate or decrease depending on how quickly a vendor can respond to a given situation.
- *Priorities of work:* A determination as to which project goes first can affect cost.
- *Growth trends:* The projection as to whether work is increasing or decreasing indicates the growth trend.
- *Who performs a task:* Costs can be shifted between components by shifting responsibility.
- *Performance trends:* These are trends relating to the productivity of performing a unit of work.

The risk associated with a DP task affects the cost of doing the task. Performing a high-risk task is generally more difficult than the effort needed to perform an equivalent task for a project with a low-risk rating. For example, coding a well-defined program (low risk) can be done more quickly than coding a poorly defined program of equivalent size (high risk). The risk considerations for the budgetable components are as follows:

- *Growth of function:* As functions and tasks get bigger, the risk increases.
- *Occurrence of problems:* The type and frequency of problems/defects that occur.
- *Senior management demands:* Requests made of the data processing function by senior management, for example, responding to specific problems.
- *Skills of staff:* The skill level of individual staff members, with the implication that highly skilled staff can do jobs quicker.
- *Newness of technology:* The newer the technology, the higher the risk.
- *Complexity of systems:* The more complex a system, the higher the risk.
- *Completeness of design:* The more complete the design, the lower the risk.
- *Completeness of documentation:* The more complete the documentation, the lower the risk.
- *Skills of users:* The more highly skilled the users in data processing technology, the lower the risk.

PLANNING THE QUALITY OF THE BUDGET PROCESS

An important aspect of budgeting is to ensure the quality of budgeting. It is easy to put in a process and hope that it works. It is more difficult, but normally much more successful, to build quality control procedures into the budgeting process.

Quality control is needed in budgeting for the following three reasons:

1. *Budget participants are untrained.* People unfamiliar with the task have great difficulty in determining whether or not they are performing that task correctly. Quality control tools provide a basis for people to evaluate the quality of their work.
2. *Ensure meeting budget goals and objectives.* The primary purpose of quality control is to ensure that the desired level of quality is met. For budgeting, these are the budgetary goals and objectives established by management. Quality control tools should help ensure that those goals and objectives are met.
3. *Identify variances from expected quality.* Quality control tools are means of measuring whether or not the predetermined quality standards are being met. If the process varies from those standards, quality control should detect that variance. Once detected, it can be addressed by management and corrected as close as possible to where the defect occurred.

Quality control concepts should be used because organizations cannot afford not to use them. The objective of quality control is not only to increase or assure quality, but also to reduce the cost by eliminating defects and/or correcting defects at the point where they are most economical to correct.

Budgets that include defects may undermine the credibility of the budget. If defects are detected before the budget is transmitted to senior management, the cost, pressure, and frustration of correcting defects can be eliminated.

As we discuss each of the five planning tasks, we will be reviewing how to ensure the quality of those tasks. It is important to note that quality control, like testing, can contain defects. Thus it is important to ensure the quality of the quality control process. This should be a specific responsibility of the DP manager.

TASK 1: ASSIGN BUDGET RESPONSIBILITIES

One of the key concepts of quality is to make people responsible and accountable for the tasks they perform. Work done by a committee or group is a group responsibility. Although groups are effective at performing certain types of tasks, budgeting is not one of them. There should be one person responsible for each aspect of the budgeting process.

The task of assigning budget responsibility is twofold. First, the budgetary process must be broken into pieces and one person held accountable for each piece. The end product of this step is a budget responsibility worksheet (see Table 7.2). This worksheet shows the various segments of the budget process and lists who is responsible.

There are six major segments to the budgeting process. One person should be held responsible for each segment. Note that in some instances the segment can be divided between two or more people, but the divided parts should be stand-alone pieces.

TABLE 7.2 BUDGETARY RESPONSIBILITIES

Budget segment	Responsible individual
Customizing the budget process	Data processing manager Any one person in the data processing department who is responsible for budgeting
Management of the budget process	Data processing manager (small data processing department) Data processing comptroller (large data processing department)
Budgetary training	Supervisors Manager of the budget process
Development of budgetary data	Line management
Quality control of the budget process	Everyone involved in the budgetary process
Responsibility for budget approval	Senior data processing manager Middle management, subject to approval of senior data processing manager

Listed below is a discussion of the six segments of budgeting, who is the most logical person for that responsibility, and a brief description of the responsibility:

1. *Customizing the budget process:* Each year, the budget process needs to be modified and changed. This is similar to maintenance in any other application system. The responsibility for this should be given to the person within the data processing department responsible for budgeting. In many instances, this will be the data processing manager. Note that although tasks can be delegated, responsibility cannot.
2. *Management of the budget process:* The preparation of the budget may be assigned to someone other than the person who developed the process. The manager of the budget process is the one who has responsibility for assigning the remaining responsibilities, ensuring that they are done properly, that schedules are met, and that the final product is a high-quality product. In a smaller data processing department, this would be done by the data processing manager; in a larger department it may be assigned to an assistant manager (e.g., data processing comptroller).
3. *Budgetary training:* The individual participants in the budget process must be trained in that process. Training can be instructions included with the budgetary information, formal training, or a combination of the two. In some organizations, training may be the responsibility of supervisors. Because of the uniqueness of budgeting, training normally becomes the responsibility of the manager of the budget process. Because training is so important in getting good budgetary data, the quality of training is normally directly translatable into the quality of the budget.
4. *Development of budgetary data:* The requests for funding as expressed through the budgetary process is a responsibility of line management. However, each line manager should know precisely what budgetary items he or she is responsible for. Note that the use of the budgetary components should be helpful in assigning specific responsibilities.
5. *Quality control of the budget process:* Quality is everybody's responsibility. Therefore, if people are assigned specific responsibilities, they should be assigned the responsibility for the quality of their work. To fulfill this responsibility, the manager of the budgetary process should provide those persons with the appropriate quality control tools. Note that throughout this part of the book the tools needed to ensure quality are provided.
6. *Responsibility for budget approval:* The most senior data processing manager should be responsible for approving the budget. This is normally a part of that person's job description. However, the data processing manager may want lower-level supervisory sign-offs before giving final departmental approval. If this is to occur, the middle managers should be assigned specific approval responsibility, subject to prerogatives retained by the data processing manager.

TASK 2: TRAIN BUDGET PARTICIPANTS

Using any process requires a knowledge of that process and an understanding of the tools and practices that need to be followed in fulfilling the process. Therefore, training the budget participants is an essential part of the success of budgeting. The participants need to acquire the skill used in budgeting. For example, the science of accounting is used in budgeting, which requires an understanding of the principles of accounting by budget participants.

It is unrealistic to expect people to follow the budget process properly or to develop valid, reliable budgets without training. It is of little value to spend large amounts of time and effort developing an effective budgetary process if the staff does not understand the process and thus cannot follow it.

The skills that are helpful in completing budgetary tasks are:

1. *Accounting/budgeting skills:* A basic understanding of the objectives of budgeting and the processes that need to be followed to develop an effective budget. Note that this book is designed to assist in teaching these skills.
2. *Expectations of management:* Each person should know what management expects of him or her in completing the budget. Management must explain to the staff how they intend to use the budget, what they expect of the people preparing the budget, and how good budgeting practices will affect performance.
3. *The budgeting process:* People need to understand all the steps within the budget process and how those steps are performed. Obviously, training should concentrate on that step or task performed by the person being trained, but an understanding of the entire process is helpful in getting quality budgetary information.
4. *Budget tools:* If tools/worksheets are available to assist in the budget preparation, the participants should be trained in how to use those tools.
5. *Quality control methods:* If people are held accountable for the quality of their work, they should be instructed in quality principles. This training should concentrate on specific quality control tools that a person can use to assess his or her quality of work.

The budgetary training program should include the following four training modules:

1. *Budgetary alert:* This session alerts participants to the forthcoming budget and reinforces the objectives of budgeting.
2. *Budget orientation:* The objective of this module is to introduce participants to the specific tasks that they will have to accomplish. The objective is to encourage the person to begin thinking and gathering preliminary information on

budgeting. Note that these first two modules may be accomplishable with a budgetary memo or a brief statement in a data processing staff meeting.

3. *Budget preparation training:* This is the most extensive of the training modules. It is during this module that the person receives specific training in how to perform the budgetary analysis and how to complete any required worksheets. This training could be given through a formal training session, video training course, or budgetary preparation workbook. It is at this time that the needed skills are taught.
4. *Evaluation/follow-up:* It is important to understand that the budget participants have mastered the skills for which they were trained. This last module is designed to assess the participants' mastery of the budgeting skills. This can be accomplished through feedback discussion, budgetary exercises, or review of initial budgetary work. Training can be considered completed only when the participants have demonstrated mastery of the skills taught.

TASK 3: DETERMINE RELIABILITY / VALIDITY OF BUDGET

Two of management's major concerns over the budgetary process are:

- Is the budget reliable?
- Is the budget valid?

Reliability of a budget relates to the consistency of the budget process. Reliability attempts to state that if the budgetary amounts were recreated, or if two people developed the budgetary amounts independently, they would arrive at approximately the same budgetary figure. For example, if a project leader was asked to estimate the cost to do project X, that estimate should be reproducible by another project leader.

If budgeting is to be a managerial tool, the budget estimates must be reliable. If the estimates are not reliable, all management can use budgeting for is to measure people's ability to budget. If budgeting is an art form, it must be performed by artists, not technicians.

Many automotive repair shops develop standardized estimating procedures. Thus, no matter who develops the estimate (i.e., budget to do a job) it will be the same estimate. As such, the estimates are reliable and can be used by managers to evaluate performance, charge customers, guarantee charges, and perform the other desirable effects of budgeting.

A major fallacy in budgeting is the unreliability of many data processing budgetary items. Therefore, in the planning process the person responsible for the process must address reliability. The process itself, the training, the analysis, and the approval must all be designed to ensure the reliability of the estimate.

The second major concern is the validity of the items within the budget. This relates to specific line items within the budget. For example, if a project is divided into tasks, such as time for design, time for tests, time for documentation, and so on, the question is whether the line items are valid for the project being proposed. The question management has is: Are these items valid for the function that is being budgeted?

The validity of budget items rarely relates to the mainline items of the function. For example, there is little question that systems maintenance and system development are valid items for a data processing function. On the other hand, other items within the budget, such as participation in professional societies or the acquisition of a library, a budget training program, or a documentation librarian might be questioned as a valid use of data processing funds.

Most of the challenges by senior management about a budget item relate to either the reliability or validity of the item. Therefore, it is essential that these issues be addressed during budget planning. If the data processing manager cannot guarantee the reliability and validity of the budget, he or she is in a very vulnerable position when presenting the budget to senior management. Highly reliable and valid budgets have a high probability of acceptance on face value.

Step 2, data gathering, addresses the validity issue. Step 3, estimating, addresses the reliability issue. However, the basis for reliability and validity should be established during planning.

Budgetary Principle

Reliable and valid budgets offer minimal vulnerabilities to the DP manager in justifying and defending his or her budget.

TASK 4: SCHEDULE AND STAFF THE BUDGETARY PROCESS

Budgeting should not be a time-consuming function. The cost of managerial control should never exceed the benefits derived from that control. The challenge is to obtain the highest reliability and validity for the lowest dollar cost. Scheduling the preparation of the budget is significantly easier than estimating the amount of staffing needed to develop the budget. It is advised to provide a well-defined schedule, but only issue guidelines on the effort to be used to develop the budget. This is because the process is new to many, and it is difficult to estimate how long it will take people to accomplish specific budget tasks.

A schedule can normally be prepared by backing off from the organization's budgetary due dates. Following are minimum guidelines for scheduling the budget process:

- Training and instruction: one week
- Data gathering: one week

- Estimating costs and benefits: one week (normally includes first-level supervisory approval)
- Classification, consolidation, and departmental approval: one week
- Approval and final preparation of the budget document: one week

Obviously, the process can be shortened if necessary. However, budgeting is usually a part-time function with most participants. Therefore, providing them sufficient time to enable the budget tasks to be interwoven with other tasks is normally the most efficient way to prepare the budget.

No one involved in the preparation of the budget should need to spend more than one day if the tasks are appropriately divided. Although this general guideline is not an absolute, it does indicate to people the approximate amount of time that managers believe budgeting warrants. If the process consumes significantly more than one day of a participant's time, the appropriate budgetary tools are probably not in place, forcing the participant to do too much investigation.

TASK 5: CUSTOMIZE THE BUDGET PROCESS

Each year the budget process needs customization. The objective of this task is to ensure that the budget process is consistent with the objectives of management. For example, if there were reliability problems the previous year, as experienced through missed budget estimates, the process should be adjusted to improve the precision of estimates.

The customization process should be performed by the person responsible for the budgetary process. The input to this customization should be:

- Actual results versus budget estimates for the previous year
- Changes to the corporate budgetary process
- Changes to data processing management budget objectives
- Availability of new practices and tools

Using this input, the process should be changed accordingly. However, note that slow changes are normally superior to dramatic changes unless the reliability and the validity of the process are undependable. The discussions in the following four chapters should prove beneficial in customizing an existing budgetary process.

Budgetary Principle

The credibility of data processing management will be based partially on the reliability and validity of the function's budgets. Planning is the function that must address these issues.

ENSURING THE QUALITY OF THE BUDGET PLANNING STEP

An effective way to review the quality of the budget planning process is to conduct a peer review. This is best accomplished when performed using a structured approach. The most common method for doing this in data processing currently is through evaluation checklists. These checklists provide the structure needed to ensure the adequacy of a peer review.

The person who reviews the budget plan should be someone other than the person responsible for preparing the plan. If the data processing manager prepares the plan, an assistant manager should be the reviewer. If an assistant manager prepares the plan, another assistant manager or the manager can be the peer reviewer.

The budget planning review checklist is a quality control tool for reviewing the quality of the plan. The checklist is designed to probe the completeness of the planning process. The checklist is designed so that "yes" responses are indicative of good planning, and "no" responses represent potential planning defects. All "no" responses should be investigated to determine whether additional planning is required before the budget process begins.

The review should occur at the conclusion of the planning process. If timing is critical, the review may need to be made before planning is complete. This is because if there are areas for investigation and change, adequate time must be left for those adjustments. A budget planning quality control checklist is provided as Figure 7.2.

BUDGET PLANNING IMPEDIMENTS AND COUNTERSTRATEGIES

Processes fail for a variety of reasons. People do not like them, they are difficult to use, and time pressures may encourage shortcuts. If these impediments are understood, appropriate counterstrategies can be developed which can increase the probability of success. In the planning step, the following impediments are most common:

1. *Lack of adequate time:* Budgeting is a task assigned in addition to all other tasks. Also, budgeting is a long-term project, whereas emergencies appear to need immediate handling. The net result is that budgeting is frequently put off and then not enough time is allocated to do the budget properly.

   Two counterstrategies can be used to help devote adequate attention to budget planning:

   a. *Senior management support:* The public statement by senior DP management to the budget planners about the importance of budgeting helps put the project into the proper priority.
   b. *Training:* If the budget planners are adequately trained in accounting, budgeting, and quality control skills, they have the needed background to address the budget planning task properly.

ITEM	RESPONSE			
	YES	NO	N/A[a]	COMMENTS
1. Is a budget plan required?				
2. Is one person accountable for developing and maintaining the data processing budget process?				
3. Is one person responsible for management of the budget procedure?				
4. Is data processing management responsible for the approval of budget items?				
5. Are individual budget participants responsible for the reliability and validity of the budgetary data?				
6. Are the budgetary participants responsible for the quality of the budget?				
7. Has data processing management stated to the staff its perception of the importance of the budget?				
8. Has data processing management stated its objectives from the budgetary process?				
9. Are all participants in the budget process trained in how to perform that process?				
10. Are all participants in the budget process alerted sufficiently ahead of the budget process so that they can do adequate planning?				
11. Is the budget plan a formal document?				
12. Does the budget plan contain responsibilities?				
13. Does the budget plan contain a schedule for completion of the budget?				
14. Is sufficient time allocated for the preparation of the budget?				
15. Are guidelines given to budget participants regarding how much time they should spend on budgeting?				
16. Has management stated the desired reliability from the budgetary figures?				
17. Has data processing management issued guidelines on the validity of budgetary items?				
18. Is the budget process reviewed annually to determine if changes are needed?				
19. If budgetary process changes are needed, are they made in sufficient time to be incorporated into the following budget cycle?				
20. Does data processing management review and approve the plan?				
21. Is the data processing plan coordinated with the corporate budget plan?				

[a]N/A, not applicable.

Figure 7.2 Budget planning review checklist.

2. *Lack of knowledge about corporate budgeting and planning procedures:* It is difficult to develop an effective data processing budgeting plan without a knowledge of the corporate budget plan and process. Also, budgeting should tie into corporate planning, which requires a knowledge of how that occurs and what the plans are. This type of background information is invaluable in developing an effective budget plan that will produce a product that is highly integrated into the organization's plan and budget.

   The counterstrategies that can be employed to overcome this impediment include:

   a. *Assignment to a corporate budget or planning committee:* The closer the data processing budget planners work with the corporate budget planners, the higher the probability that the two plans and procedures will be in harmony. If it is impractical to work on the corporate committees, interviews with those people and access to their budget products may also overcome this impediment.
   b. *Data processing budget plan review:* The plan developed by the data processing budget planners can be reviewed by the corporate planners for consistency with corporate strategies. This can be a formal review or an information discussion. The format is not as important as the fact that there is a positive step taken toward integration of the two plans.

Budgetary Principle

One of data processing management's major budget responsibilities should be to ensure that the data processing budget plan is integrated with and supportive of the corporate budget plan.

THE RESULTS OF PLANNING

The end product of the planning step is a chronological list of the tasks to be performed during budgeting and who is to perform them. The plan defines the expected quality of the budget and how it will be achieved. An integral part of this quality is the reliability and validity of each budget item.

Planning should not cease until the planners are convinced that the budget for the data processing function can be developed on time and at an acceptable level of quality. Although the planning document does not have to be a formal document, the steps must be well thought through. In the following four chapters we describe in detail what the plan must define. The net result of a well-thought-through plan will be minimal effort expended to develop the best possible budget.

8
Step 2: Data Gathering

It is easy to collect data. It is difficult to collect valid and reliable information. The concept between gathering pieces of data and gathering valuable information is the key concept of the data-gathering step.

In the development project, it is easy to gather ideas and general requirements from users. It is difficult to gather implementable and measurable requirements. Budget projects suffer from the same lack of good information as do system development projects.

The objective of this chapter is to identify the types of data that need to be collected for budgetary purposes. What is collected will be determined primarily from management's intended use of budgets. If budgeting is to be used as an effective management tool, the specific items budgeted become an extremely important part of the data-gathering step.

In this chapter the budgetable components are used as a base for gathering budget data. Data gathering is divided into the budget tasks of identifying participants, distributing budgeting requirements to participants, collecting data, and initiating the quality control function over the data-gathering process. The suggested tools, practices, and forms needed for this step are provided in this chapter.

YOU CANNOT CONTROL WHAT YOU CANNOT MEASURE

Budgeting is a control. The objective of a control is to minimize loss associated with specific risk. For example, there is a risk that application systems will not be adequately tested. Budgeting is a control that can help reduce that risk by allocating and measuring the use of test resources. However, if the budgeting process cannot measure the resources consumed by testing, management will have difficulty controlling the test activity.

Many data processing managers are starved for control information. In our previous example of testing, let's look at some of the control information that might be of interest to a manager:

- Amount of time expended on testing
- Phase of the system development life cycle in which testing is expended
- Percent of testing conducted by automatic test tools and percent performed manually
- Testing dollars as a percent of total system dollars
- Testing resources allocated in systems maintenance
- Testing dollars expended during emergency software maintenance

If data processing departments merely budget system development and software maintenance, they cannot control testing. On the other hand, if the budgetary and associated reporting processes budget and account for testing dollars, management can control the testing activities.

If managers do not know what testing costs, they do not know whether it needs improvement. If testing costs are known but cannot be related to events that cause them to vary, it is again difficult to improve testing. On the other hand, the more information acquired about testing, the easier it becomes to control and improve it.

The same analogy on testing can be applied to many other data processing activities. Examples of DP activities that evoke widely varying opinions about the benefit of the activity are standards, training, and documentation.

At this point in the budgetary process, the managerial control objectives for budgeting must be tied to specific budgetary line items. A line item is a controllable element of cost, such as testing costs in a development or maintenance project. Note that in doing this, the data processing budget will be much more detailed and descriptive than the budget needed for presentation to organization management for funding.

Budgetary Principle

The return on investment from an information system increases significantly as multiple uses are made of the same piece of information. Similarly, the value of budgeting increases when the budget serves multiple purposes.

IDENTIFYING CONTROLLABLE BUDGET LINE ITEMS

The budgeting process provides the opportunity for three levels of control. This three-level control concept is also applicable to security. For example, we can protect data at the file level, the record or segment level, or at the data element level. The lower the level of control, the more costly the control becomes, but it is also more effective.

The level of control that one desires is a trade-off between cost and the control objective. Controlling data at the element level is an extremely effective security procedure, but obviously costs significantly more than if security was exercised only at the file level. On the other hand, if control is exercised only at the file level, management will not know who is accessing what data elements and what records within the file.

Three levels of control are possible in a budgetary system:

1. *Corporate line item:* These are the budgetary accounts provided by the corporate budgetary system. These are normally at broad levels and include such items as salaries, travel, and space.
2. *Project level:* Data processing is primarily a job shop operation. It does a variety of projects or assignments throughout the year. These projects consume the resources in the corporate line item, such as salaries, but are more detailed and define how those salaries and other costs are expended.
3. *Project line items:* Within any given project there is a buildup of costs that is a further subdivision of the project level. For example, salaries can be divided into design, programming, testing, documentation, and other tasks performed during the execution of a project.

The question that the data processing manager must answer is: "What level of detail do I want in the budgetary process?" The answer to this question will be dependent on the level of control that that manager wants to exercise through the budgetary process. If the manager does not intend to control costs at the project line item level, it is not necessary to build the budget up at that level. If the manager does not want to control costs at the project level, it is not necessary to develop budgetary information at that level. However, what cannot be measured cannot be controlled. The lower the level of cost control, the greater the control the manager has over projects through use of budgeting.

Table 8.1 lists the sixteen budgetable and controllable components of data processing costs. For each component, a representative list of line items is provided. Note that the controllable components of budgeting and the line items in Table 8.1 do not address the project level of control. The identification of projects is a project management function, not a budgeting function. Budgeting should utilize the existing project definitions used in the data processing function.

DATA COLLECTION CONSIDERATIONS

There are two basic considerations that must be resolved prior to collecting data:

1. *Funded and unfunded costs:* There are two types of costs that organizations incur in performing work. These are funded costs, those for which cash will be ex-

TABLE 8.1 TYPICAL LIST OF CONTROLLABLE BUDGET COMPONENT LINE ITEMS

Controllable budget component	Line item
1. DP management and administration	Management reports
	Incident reports
	Fiscal reports
	Personnel reports
	Weekly activities reports
	Administrative procedures
	Purchase orders
	Cost analysis
	Contracting
	Contract status reports
	Quarterly resources reports
	Logistic support plan
	Payroll information
	Position description
	Adding/terminating staff
	General briefings
2. Facilities	Space
	Utilities
	Telephone
	Furniture and fixtures
	Processing relocation requests
	Services (e.g., typing)
	Copy equipment
3. Systems support	Planning
	Contractual services (e.g., consultants)
	Training
	Documentation libraries
	Supplies (e.g., coding sheets/forms)
	Travel/meals
	Clerical (e.g., typing)
4. New systems development	Work order requests
	Program change requests
	Data change requests
	System requirements
	System design
	Program design
	Coding
	Testing
	Installation
	Documentation
	User interface
	Status reports
	Training
	Travel/meals
	System reviews
	General briefing
	Internal management review
	Quality assurance review
	Project management

(continued)

TABLE 8.1 *(Cont.)*

Controllable budget component	Line item
5. System maintenance	Emergency maintenance
	Repair maintenance
	Maintenance due to changes in the operating environment (e.g., new equipment, new release of operating system)
	Program change requests
	Data change requests
	Compliance with new standards
	Management of maintenance
	Testing
	Error tracking
	Problem analysis
	Coding changes
	Changing system documentation
	Changing program documentation
	User interaction
	Quality assurance reviews
	Internal management reviews
6. Computer operation	Operations management
	Operation of applications
	Operations overhead (e.g., making backup copies of data bases, startup tasks, maintaining logs of work)
	Rerun (may be categorized by type)
	User inquiry (e.g., help desk)
	Updating software (e.g., installing a new version of an operating system)
	Installation of new equipment
	Disaster recovery planning
	Testing operating procedures (e.g., test of a disaster plan)
	Data library
	Off-site storage
	Supply management
	Chargeout administration
	Training
	Supplies
7. Hardware	Purchase of hardware
	Rental/hardware lease
	Maintenance
	Alternate power supplies
	Operating supplies (those that charge directly to users)
	Contractual services (e.g., maintenance)
	Installation

TABLE 8.1 *(Cont.)*

Controllable budget component	Line item
8. Purchased/rented software	Purchase of software
	Rental/lease of software
	Contractual services (e.g., maintenance)
	Supplies
	Installation costs
	Software selection
9. Technical support	Planning
	Configuration management
	Problem management
	Scheduling
	Technical consulting
	Preparation of job control statements
	Acquisition/design of software tools
10. Quality assurance	Error tracking
	Statistical quality control
	Evaluating processes (e.g., evaluating the effectiveness and usefulness of the system development methodology)
	Quality assurance reviews
	Quality assurance reports
	Special assignments
	Incident reports
	Management reports
	Management briefings
	Consulting/training (of others)
	Training
	Development of policies/standards/procedures
11. Communication	Communication lines
	Communication charges
	Communication interface equipment (e.g., modems)
	Switching equipment
	Procedures/standards
	Communication software
12. Data base administration	Data base administration
	Data definition
	Data dictionary
	Data base software
	Error analysis
	Data structure organization
	Consulting (with systems analysts and users)
	Management reports

(continued)

TABLE 8.1 *(Cont.)*

Controllable budget component	Line item
12. Data base administration *(cont.)*	Recovery procedures Backup of data base Training (of users) Training (for data base administration personnel) Resolving conflicts
13. Word processing/office system/ microcomputer	Word processing equipment Office equipment Equipment installation Training of users Administration of facilities
14. Information center	Downloading information Consulting on acquisition of hardware and software Selling hardware and software Assisting in writing and debugging programs Providing hardware backup to users Assisting users in problem solving Conducting training classes Conducting equipment demonstrations Maintaining a personal computer library Repairing equipment Updating software
15. Security	Security software Security guides Security surveillance equipment Physical security equipment (e.g., card locks) Violation reports Violation investigation Security training Security testing Developing security procedures
16. Outside services	Consulting Training Publications Acquiring training courses Attending training courses Participation in user groups Consultants Contractual programming Contractual systems design Service centers Time sharing

pended, and unfunded costs, those for which cash may or may not have been expended but whose value for that expenditure has not yet been received. Salary is normally a funded cost, whereas the depreciation associated with capital assets is an unfunded cost. Examples of unfunded costs include:

- Depreciation on fixed assets
- Prepaid expenses, such as supplies
- Employee benefit liabilities not funded; for example, some companies do not fully fund pension costs
- Amortization

The organization's budgetary procedures normally determine whether the budget will include both funded or unfunded costs. However, if the organization is going to charge out their services, or do competitive bidding against outside organizations, it is important to include unfunded costs if they are significant. If competitive bidding is to occur and unfunded costs are not included, the amounts being compared are not comparable.

2. *Data to be collected:* Organizations can collect two general categories of data. The data that have been discussed so far have been task- or work-oriented data. It was suggested that these data can be collected at the organizational line item level, project level, or project line-item level.

   The second category of data relates to the reliability of the information collected. In some organizations, this is called estimating factors or risk factors. The objective of this second category of data is to help develop a realistic dollar estimate for the work tasks. Although this information may need to be collected during the data-gathering phase, it will not be discussed until Chapter 9. This is the step where the estimating factors are used to develop budgetary estimates.

CONDUCTING THE DATA-GATHERING STEP

The data-gathering step can be performed individually or it can be performed in conjunction with the estimating step. The determination of whether the two will be performed together depends on:

1. *Skill of budget participants in estimating:* A decision needs to be made by management whether all participants will do estimating or whether estimating will be done centrally. In order to develop a reproducible estimate, it is recommended that estimating be done after the data-gathering step. If the appropriate data are gathered, the estimating step should not be a time-consuming or difficult step.
2. *Use of estimating tools:* Tools are now available that produce estimates for certain types of data processing work. For example, ESTIMACS is a software package that will estimate the cost of developing a new application system. It

requires that the appropriate data be gathered and then fed into the software package. As these tools become available or are developed, they will force a natural separation between the data-gathering and estimating steps.

The following four tasks need to be completed during the data-gathering step:

- *Task 1:* Identify budget participants.
- *Task 2:* Distribute budget requirements to participants.
- *Task 3:* Collect budget data.
- *Task 4:* Evaluate the quality of the collected data.

Tasks 1 and 2 are the primary responsibility of the individual responsible for the budget process. Task 3 must be performed by the budget participants. During the collection of the budgetary data, Task 4 should be performed to ensure that the quality desired is inherent in the data collected.

Budgetary Principle

The quality of budgetary data must be built into the process. Quality cannot be an after-the-fact task.

TASK 1: IDENTIFY BUDGET PARTICIPANTS

The planning step should have identified the participants in the budget process. These participants may be identified at the individual level or they may identify participants by the type of work they perform. For example, participants could be identified as Bill Smith or as a project leader. In the latter instances, all the project leaders would need to be identified during this step.

The most common participants (by category) for the budget process are:

- Department heads
- Project leaders
- Manager/chairman of the general function (e.g., security)
- Section/area supervisor (e.g., data library supervisor)
- Contracting manager
- Training manager

A list should be maintained of the participants for control purposes. A form for this purpose is illustrated as Figure 8.1. The information that should be collected about each participant is:

- Name of participant
- Title of participant

Number	Name	Title	Telephone	Area of Budget Responsibility	Budget Data	
					Sent	Rec'd
1	Bill Smith	Proj. Ldr.	8765	Payroll project	9/17	10/1

Figure 8.1 Budget participants control list.

- Telephone number of participant
- Area of budget responsibility (this should identify those parts of the budget for which this person should be preparing the data)

Room is then provided on the form to indicate when the budget instruction/information is sent to the participant (this is Task 2) and when those data are received back from the participant (this is Task 3). A line-item example is shown on Figure 8.1, which indicates the information that would be recorded about a typical budget participant.

TASK 2: DISTRIBUTE BUDGET REQUIREMENTS TO PARTICIPANTS

A budgetary packet should be prepared and distributed to all participants. In most organizations, some or all of this budget packet will be prepared by the corporate budgetary function. However, it may need to be customized because of the uniqueness of data processing or special control considerations desired by data processing management.

At a minimum, the budget packet should contain:

1. Budget areas to be developed. The specific project/task/line items that the participant is responsible to develop should be clearly stated in the budget packet. Note that in some cases these may be general, such as payroll project, operation of the data library, or provide secretarial services.
2. Copy of last year's budgeted items (should be the final budget showing actual costs year to date).
3. Schedule of items due.
4. Forms/worksheets to be completed (some of these may be electronic worksheets).
5. Instructions on how to perform budgetary analysis. This should include how to complete the forms and the precision required.
6. Who to contact for help (this normally would be the person responsible for the management of the budget process).

TASK 3: COLLECT BUDGET DATA

The data to be included in the budget are project and work oriented. The guidance that is needed in collecting data comprises the attributes of the data that need to be collected. As a general rule, it is better to collect data in work units and convert them to dollars than to ask participants to perform the translation from work units to dollars.

Work units vary based on the project/task to be accomplished. Suggested units for recording work for the more typical data processing tasks are:

- *Staff/operations/support personnel:* Hours of productive work.
- *Supervisors:* Number of supervisors or ratio of supervisors to subordinates.
- *Clerical personnel:* Number of clerical personnel or ratio of clerical personnel to staff and management.
- *Supplies:* Number of items (can be expressed in terms of boxes of paper, number of diskettes, disk packs, etc.).

- *Computer processing:* Expressed in terms of transactions processed or computer work units if a charge-out system is in use.
- *Space:* Number of square feet.
- *Hardware:* Number of units.
- *Software:* Number of systems to acquire/develop/maintain.
- *Training:* Number of training days in town and out of town.
- *Nonproductive work days:* Average number of days per category: for example, vacation, sickness, training.
- *Furniture, fixtures, office equipment:* Number of units needed or deleted.
- *Other:* Other costs should be identified as specifically as possible. For example, the other items that might be listed include security devices, contractual services, and insurance. Note that on many of the specialized items the cost of those items may be the most appropriate descriptor (e.g., a contract for software maintenance).
- *New system requirements/maintenance requests:* An alternative way to describe the costs of new system requirements and maintenance to existing software is to indicate the number of function points associated with that change. Functions are business functions satisfied through the change or new development. Function points will be described in Chapter 9 as a method for estimating costs.

Two forms are provided for collection of information. One form is for people (Figure 8.2) and the second is for hardware/software costs (Figure 8.3). These forms provide a framework for collecting budgetary information. The vertical axis of the matrix indicates the organizational line item/project/project line item data to be collected. In Figures 8.2 and 8.3, the items shown are geared more at the organizational line-item level. The horizontal axis of the matrix indicates the type of data to be collected. In the worksheet illustration, these categories are divided into funded, unfunded, and subdivisions thereof. The horizontal axis needs to be customized depending on the level of data wanted.

Within the worksheets at the matrix intersections is space for the data needed. In the illustrated worksheets, the information to be entered by the budget participant comprises the data used to calculate the indicated cost. For example, on the worksheet shown in Figure 8.2, the DP office personnel (administrative function) may be recorded as average number of employees per year who receive regular wages, and perhaps number of hours expected as overtime wages (if any).

When completed, the participants should send the worksheet back to the person responsible for managing the budget process. Prior to doing this, the person should evaluate his or her quality of work. In the translation and consolidation, the manager of the budgetary process should also evaluate the quality of the work.

Cost elements / Personnel	Total Annual Cost Estimate						Totals		
	Funded Costs					Unfunded Costs			
	Direct		Indirect						
	Regular Wages	Overtime Wages	Other Expenses (Training, Travel, Etc.)	Fringe Benefits	Miscellaneous Costs	Retirement, Etc.	Funded	Unfunded	Total
MIS Office									
Data Center Personnel									
Systems Analysis and Programming Branch									
Total									

Figure 8.2 Personnel budget data worksheet.

Cost Elements / Equipment and Software	Funded Costs				Unfunded Costs (Depreciation)	Total
	Lease	Rental	Maintenance	Total		
Equipment 1. Processors 2. Core Memory 3. I/O Multiplexor 4. Data Communications Gear 5. Disk Drives 6. Tape Drives 7. Unit Record Cont. 8. Printer 9. Card Reader/Punch 10. Terminals						
Equipment Subtotal						
Software 1. Operating System, Language Processors, Utilities, Etc. 2. Data Base Software 3. Applications Software						
Software Subtotal						
Total						

Figure 8.3 Equipment/software data worksheet.

TASK 4: EVALUATE THE QUALITY OF THE COLLECTED DATA

The data collection step is one involving analysis on the part of the participant. The participant must identify all the projects and all the elements of costs for those projects. Thus quality over data gathering is looking for:

1. Completeness of the information collected
2. Validity of the information collected
3. Reliability of the information collected

The most appropriate quality control tool to provide the participant is a quality control data-gathering checklist. Figure 8.4 is a proposed quality control checklist designed for this purpose. The checklist is designed to be used by each budget participant in evaluating the quality of his or her work. The checklist should be used at the end of the data-gathering process but before the information is collected. The checklist is designed so that "yes" responses are indicative of good-quality work, and "no" responses should be investigated. For example, if the item on the checklist requires some action to be taken which was not, the participant should investigate the impact on the data collected of not performing that item. If it would negatively impact on the completeness, validity, or reliability of the data collected, the person should perform that step before the data are collected.

ENSURING THE QUALITY OF THE BUDGET PROCESS

The person managing the budget process must evaluate the quality of that data-gathering process. A data-gathering quality checklist is provided as Figure 8.5. Like the preceding checklist, "yes" responses are indicative of good data-gathering practices, and "no" responses are indicative of potential quality problems. This checklist should be completed by the person responsible for budgeting after the data have been collected.

DATA-GATHERING IMPEDIMENTS AND COUNTERSTRATEGIES

In all budgeting steps, time constraints will be a continual impediment. The counterstrategies to scheduling constraints were discussed in Chapter 7. The impediments and counterstrategies are applicable to all steps in the budgetary process.

Two specific impediments to data gathering, with recommended counterstrategies, are incomplete data gathering and incorrect completion of data-gathering worksheets.

Incomplete Data Gathered

The data-gathering step is the key step to ensuring the validity and reliability of budgetary information. Also, if budgetary data are not collected, they will not be in-

ITEM	RESPONSE			
	YES	NO	N/A[a]	COMMENTS
1. Have all the items requested for budgeting been identified?				
2. Have all the elements of cost for each item of budget responsibility been identified?				
3. Have the attributes of the data (e.g., hours of work, function points, etc.) been identified for each element of cost?				
4. Has the source of those elements of cost been identified?				
5. Is the collection process for each element of data reproducible; in other words, would someone else have come up with the same data?				
6. Are the data collected reasonable for the project?				
7. If the project is continuous from year to year, are the data collected consistent with last year (changed for changing conditions, of course)?				
8. Are the items of cost reasonable based on the project?				
9. If it was your money, would you include all the items requested in the budget?				
10. If it was your money, would you pay as much to have the work performed?				
11. Have all parts of worksheets and forms been completed?				
12. Have the forms/worksheets been checked to determine that the numbers posted to the forms are correct and that they are in the correct columns?				
13. Has any requested addition been checked?				
14. Are all the items presented for budget purposes easily justified?				
15. Are you proud to have your name associated with the budgetary data that you are presenting?				

[a]N/A, not applicable.

Figure 8.4 Data-gathering quality control checklist.

cluded in the budget. If funds are needed for nonreported items, the funds will not be available in the forthcoming budget.

The counterstrategy that can be used to ensure the completeness of budgetary items is to *cross-refer to current costs*. The items and budgetary quantities for items collected can be cross-referenced to items included in similar projects for the current

ITEM	RESPONSE			
	YES	NO	N/A[a]	COMMENTS
1. Have all the budget participants been identified?				
2. Have the participants been recorded on a control list of participants?				
3. Has each participant's area of budget responsibility been documented?				
4. Has a budgetary packet been prepared and distributed to each participant?				
5. Does the budgetary packet indicate the areas for which the participant is responsible?				
6. Does the budgetary packet include a schedule?				
7. Does the budgetary packet include instructions on how to complete the budget data-gathering step?				
8. Does the packet include a schedule of when the work is to be completed?				
9. Is there sufficient time for the participants to do a high-quality job of data gathering?				
10. Have the appropriate forms and worksheets been included in the data-gathering packet?				
11. Are the participants provided a quality control checklist so that they can verify the quality of their own work?				
12. Do the participants complete and sign such a checklist?				
13. Is immediate follow-up made if the participants are late in returning their data?				
14. Are the data returned reviewed to determine that they are reasonable?				
15. Are the data returned reviewed to determine that they are consistent with previous years?				
16. Are the data returned reviewed to determine that they are consistent with management's budgetary direction and constraints for the budgetary year?				
17. Are any observed deficiencies returned to the participant for immediate investigation and correction if necessary?				

[a]N/A, not applicable.

Figure 8.5 Data gathering quality checklist.

year. If there are current cost categories that are not included in the budget, or the budgetary estimates vary significantly from current expenditures, those items should be questioned and returned to the participant for further investigation.

Incorrect Completion of Data-Gathering Worksheets

The improper classification of budgetary items, or the improper recording of those items, affects the quality of the budget. The counterstrategies that can be used to improve the quality of the form completion include the following:

1. *Give instructions and examples.* Clear instructions with realistic examples provide the guidelines needed by the uninitiated to work through and complete the worksheets.
2. *Use self-checking forms.* The matrix-oriented worksheets showing cross-reference between different attributes of budgetary data provide greater assurance of accuracy and completeness than do single-dimensional forms.
3. *Make use of quality control checklists.* Providing a tool, such as a quality control checklist provided earlier in this chapter, assists people in improving the quality of their own work. The more detailed the quality control checklist, the higher the probability of completeness. Organizations may wish to modify and customize the quality control checklist to meet their individual needs. Note that if problems recur from year to year, they should be addressed by one or more items in the checklist.

Budgetary Principle

The motto that should be provided budgetary participants regarding quality of budget data is: "Do it right the first time."

HOW DO I KNOW THAT THE DATA GATHERED ARE CORRECT?

The data-gathering phase is the time-consuming step of the budgetary process. It is during this step that the participants are asked to submit the items they want included in the following year's budget. It is the information gathered that will form the basis for the funding of the data processing function for the forthcoming year.

The assurance that the information collected is correct will depend on the previous budget steps and the steps that follow. This step is the doing step, but the preparation to the doing, and the challenging of the reasonableness of the doing, will really determine the quality of the data collected. A budgeting process is a series of steps, all of which must be performed. In developing an effective budgetary process, management cannot select some steps and discard others. It is an all-or-nothing process. To develop an effective data processing budget requires that all the steps be performed properly.

9

Step 3: Estimating Costs and Benefits

There are two primary objectives to estimating. One is to determine the estimated cost and/or benefit of performing a data processing task or activity. Second is to estimate the probability that the estimate is correct. Most data processing functions accomplish the first objective but neglect the second.

In this chapter we discuss the various methods that can be used for estimating costs and benefits. Determining risk is the method used to estimate the difficulty of completing a DP task. A risk model is proposed as a basis for adjusting a DP estimate to increase the probability of developing highly reliable estimates. The risk model can also be used to project the probability of accuracy of the estimates. As the level of risk gets higher, the probability of an accurate estimate gets lower.

Four tasks are identified in the estimating step. These are estimating costs, estimating benefits, estimating risk, and ensuring the quality of the estimates. The chapter concludes with a discussion of the impediments to estimating and proposes counterstrategies.

ESTIMATING—AN ART OR A SCIENCE?

As data processing professionals advance within their own organization, new responsibilities are added. One of those responsibilities is estimating the costs and benefits of forthcoming tasks. This responsibility becomes an increasingly important part of one's job as advancement continues.

Estimating is one of the few ''black arts'' remaining within the data processing profession. It is a skill that is passed from senior to subordinate in the middle of the night. This must be true, because it is a rare data processing department that trains or provides guidance for their staff in how to estimate.

When estimating is viewed as an art, one can draw two conclusions about a correct estimate. First, the person is good at the process and thus was able to determine the resources needed to complete a task. Second, one might conclude that the person was smart enough to make the resources consumed match the estimate.

Assuring that actual costs expended equal the estimate is perhaps more of a science than estimating. One can accomplish this coming in at budget in any of the following manners:

- Estimating high and then upgrading requirements to consume all the resources if need be
- Transferring costs between different project accounts regardless of where the work was performed
- Reducing the quality of work to keep within the budget constraints
- Doing extra, frequently unneeded and unwanted tasks to consume the budgeted resources

One organization guarantees that the user will never pay more than the estimated cost of a task. To ensure this guarantee, the estimators in the organization inflate the estimate and then take delight in completing most projects significantly under the estimate. Although this may have some positive "PR" value for the department, it sabotages estimating as a managerial control.

Estimating as an art does not develop reproducible estimates. When estimating is moved to a science any adequately skilled member of the staff can reproduce the estimate given the same data.

The approaches explained in this chapter are designed to move organizations toward the science of estimating. Estimating tools are being developed, and they are discussed in this chapter. However, it needs to be noted that many of these tools are not fully perfected today, but should be in the near future.

BUDGETS—SHOULD THEY INCLUDE BENEFITS?

Data processing departments are viewed by most senior management as cost centers. In other words, the data processing department does not generate revenue from the organization. This is not to say that it does not provide a contribution but, rather, that contribution cannot be measured in terms of revenue. It is a cost, and costs need to be controlled.

Senior managers approve costs only when they believe there will be a positive return on investment for those costs. For example, the commitment to an in-house data processing function is normally based on the belief by management that such a function is the most effective means of performing information processing. If management believed that it would be better to contract the work outside, funds would not be budgeted for an in-house function.

It is normally within the best interest of the data processing function to demonstrate a positive return on investment for the funds spent on data processing.

> **Budgetary Principle**
>
> It is better for the data processing function to identify the benefits from their services than to leave it to chance that the senior management will recognize those benefits.

Including benefits in the budget does not mean that the benefits will be budgetary line items. What it means is that the budgetary process be performed assuming that the data processing function is a profit center. A profit center concept means that the data processing function increases the profitability of the organization. It is not revenue in the context of sales revenue, but revenue in the context that the absence of certain services would result in lesser profits for the organization.

Estimating benefits should be performed regardless of whether those benefits are directly included in a budget document. Calculating benefits is an exercise that will enable the following question to be answered: Is this task/service/system worth doing?

It is strongly recommended that benefits be estimated during the budgetary process. In addition to answering the questions above, the calculation of benefits from budgetary expenditures serves the following purposes:

- Provides justification for any budgetary item challenged by senior management
- Assists data processing management in determining which services/tasks/systems should be performed first
- Demonstrates the value of the project to the persons performing the project
- Improves the credibility of the data processing function
- Provides a base to measure and demonstrate the success of the data processing function

Benefits can be calculated using many of the methods used to estimate cost. Benefits should be calculated to the same precision by which costs are estimated (e.g., nearest $100). However, it may prove more difficult at first to estimate benefits because much of the budgetary process is directed at cost estimates. On the other hand, experience in estimating benefits should prove beneficial throughout the year in negotiations with users over the value of specific projects.

METHODS TO ESTIMATE COSTS AND BENEFITS

Estimating is used in a wide variety of occupations. Some of the more common estimators are contractors, repair personnel, engineers, and marketing personnel. In some industries, estimating has become sophisticated. For example, many new car agencies have elaborate estimating methods for repair work. Not only is the estimating procedure standardized, but mechanics who work on the cars are held to those estimates. Their salary is tied directly to their ability to meet or beat estimates. Building contractors frequently go bankrupt if they estimate incorrectly.

There is an extensive body of knowledge about how to estimate. Unfortunately, little of this knowledge has moved into the data processing profession until recently. Today, some data processing departments have installed highly effective estimating procedures.

There are ten general methods for estimating costs and benefits. These are listed and briefly explained in Table 9.1 and described in detail below.

Method 1: Judgment

One of the more common methods of estimating costs and benefits is to let the senior personnel develop the estimate. This estimate is based on the past experiences of the estimator. Some use general guidelines, which is common in many industries. For example, builders know that to construct a building it will cost approximately \$*X* per square foot. Many data processing personnel have their "little black book" which gives them similar rules of thumb.

TABLE 9.1 METHODS FOR ESTIMATING COSTS AND BENEFITS

Estimating method	Description of method
1. Judgment	An estimate based on the experience of the estimator.
2. Component	Each attribute of the task is analyzed and estimated.
3. Breadboarding	Projects/tasks are compared to similar projects, with the estimate being the actual cost of the similar project.
4. Historical	Experience of the organization and staff in performing work is used to estimate future work.
5. Function point	The estimate is based on business functions performed by the work.
6. Standards	The time allocated for a specific task is predetermined and used as an estimate.
7. Centralized estimating	All estimates are passed through a single person/group for consistency.
8. Software	Attributes of the task are fed into a software package which produces the estimate.
9. Risk	Estimate is developed using the annual loss expectation formula.
10. Management edict	Management sets a budgetary amount or limit for work.

This method is as effective as the estimator's judgment. Some persons are very good at judgmental estimates, whereas others are not. The disadvantage of this method is that it is a difficult skill to teach. However, as long as an organization has a cadre of experienced people who are good at estimating, the method works.

Method 2: Component Estimating

This method coincides with structured methodologies. The components are usually identified through two dimensions. The first dimension is the product produced and the second dimension is the time span in which the product is produced. This process, when developed to its fullest, leads into standardized methods.

The work product dimension includes the items previously identified as project line items. In addition to these project line items, there are system deliverables, such as inputs read, files maintained, output reports produced, and so on.

The time frame dimension indicates when the specific task is performed. In a system development life cycle this would be the phases of the life cycle. For example, there are certain tasks performed in specifying a report during design, other tasks during coding, and still other tasks during testing. In a production environment, the time frame can be expressed in terms of daily work, weekly work, monthly work, and so on.

Once all the components have been identified, they are estimated. The estimates are then accumulated to develop a total budget estimate for the work. Note that this is extremely detailed and thus very time consuming. In addition, the amount of work is not directly related to the reliability of the estimate. It is very possible to do a very detailed job of estimating and still have the estimate vary significantly from the actual expenditure because of unidentified risk factors. For example, if unique technology is not addressed as a component, large amounts of resources may need to be devoted to mastering the technology, as opposed to doing the predescribed work.

Method 3: Breadboarding

Breadboarding is a widely accepted, but difficult to support, estimating procedure. It has also proved to be reasonably reliable. The major advantage of breadboarding is that it is economical to produce an estimate.

Breadboarding can be performed two ways. First, a task can be compared to another, similar task. For example, the effort to install a new data base may be compared to a previous installation experience. The amount of effort required for the previous work is then used as the estimate for the future work.

Breadboarding can also divide tasks into categories and then assign estimates for each category. For example, an organization can categorize repair maintenance into ten categories. Each category is then assigned a predetermined estimate. For example, category 1 might be changing a variable in a report or table and be assigned five hours. Category 2 may be slightly more complex and assigned ten hours. The range of breadboard estimates is usually taken from historical experience. Then when estimating a project, one need only categorize the task and the estimate is readily available.

Method 4: Historical Experience

History is a good teacher. Many of the previous methods, and many of the other methods to be described, use history in one form or another to assist in estimating.

A pure historical method is one based primarily on cost accounting. Cost accounting is a branch of accounting which uses historical information plus accounting theory to develop standard costs based on history. One widely used DP estimating factor that originated through cost accounting concepts is the DP budgeting estimate or factor which states that it takes one person-day to produce one executable program statement.

The historical method is the most believable method to people. However, because of the uniqueness of many projects and the technological risk, the historical method may not be highly reliable for DP projects. It is a very acceptable method to management and one that is supportable. It works well as long as the information on which the costs are estimated is continually updated.

The historical method includes RPQ (request for price quotation), vendor price lists, and vendor proposals. It is also reasonable to assume that future vendor prices will be similar to past (historical) vendor prices.

Method 5: Function Points

Function points relate to business functions accomplished through the use of information processing. The objective of function points is to relate information processing more directly to the business of the organization using those information processing systems. For example, function points are related to product sold, producing invoices, shipping product, and customer services performed.

The use of function points has been promoted within and by the IBM Corporation. To date, it has had only minimal acceptance as an estimating process. However, as information systems become more integrated into the business of organizations, one can expect the concept and use of function-point estimating to increase.

Function points has the major advantage that it integrates estimating costs and benefits into a single item. Completing the function point is the benefit, and the costs are the budget line items consumed to produce that item. For example, management, knowing that it costs $5.72 to process an insurance policy or $876 to produce a revised customer bank statement, closely relates information systems to business needs.

Method 6: Standardized Estimating

Quality estimating requires estimating standards. Quality is compliance with standards, and thus estimating will generally be unreliable until it can be standardized. This preassumes that the standards are realistic.

Standardized estimates can be automated. Once this level of estimating has been achieved, the budget process logically divides data gathering from estimating. Standardized estimating also has the major advantage of producing estimates that can be reconstructed.

The standards are normally developed by using one or more of the other estimating processes. In the standardized method, the budget group produces the standards using one or more of the estimating methods. For example, the standards might be developed using the historical or cost accounting method.

Method 7: Centralized Estimating

Many industries use centralized estimating as a practice. Again, the repair department at new automobile agencies uses centralized estimators. These are the people that diagnose the problems in automobiles, estimate the repair, and then assign the work. Several data processing organizations have adopted this same concept.

Centralized estimating can be used for individual projects and/or budgeting. Using this concept, the responsibility for estimating is assigned to a single person or group. The estimating group then identifies the data attributes needed to make the estimate. Thus the estimating group specifies the output from the data-gathering step.

After receiving the estimating data, the centralized group makes the estimate. Generally, it is then given back to the person who will be held accountable for implementing the project/task. If this person agrees to the estimate, it then becomes the estimate. If the person responsible for implementing the task does not agree to the estimate, it must go to arbitration. Normally, a member of senior data processing management arbitrates disputes.

Method 8: Estimating Software

Several vendors produce software that will estimate the cost of performing a task. These software estimators fall into two general categories as follows:

1. *Modeling software:* This category of software attempts to model the work to be performed. The model not only shows the feasibility of performing a task, but estimates how long it will take to perform the task. Modeling tends to be more effective in estimating operational costs than in estimating the development costs.
2. *Attribute estimating:* These software packages require a series of input attributes about the work to be performed. Some estimating packages use risk attributes, whereas other software packages identify the attributes of the work to be performed, for example, number of inputs, number of reports, and so on.

Method 9: Risk Analysis

Risk analysis is more attuned to calculating benefits than costs. It uses the annual expectation formula, which is

Frequency of occurrence × loss per occurrence = annual loss expectation

This formula deals with the expected costs or loss associated with an event. For example, in calcuating the cost of data entry, the formula can estimate that it costs $1 to key-enter a transaction, that 10,000 transactions will be entered in a year, and thus that the annual loss expectation is $10,000.

The major use for the formula is in calculating benefits. Benefits can be associated with cost reduction and/or cost avoidance. For example, if one wanted to know the benefit of key verification, one would calculate the cost of correcting key entry errors by multiplying the number of errors times the cost to correct. Let us assume without key verification there that were 500 errors and that it cost $30 to correct each error. Multiplying the two variables, we get an annual loss expectation of $15,000. If key verification will reduce the number of errors from 500 to 100, the benefit is calculated using the formula by multiplying the 400 errors reduced times $30, or a benefit of $12,000.

Method 10: Management Edict

This is the simplest estimating method of all. It can occur in one of two ways. First, management can state what they believe to be the estimate, and that becomes the estimate. Second, management can establish a limit on a task, for example, training will not exceed $10,000 this year.

If budgeting is to be a management control, a management edict method is consistent with the control aspects of budgeting.

Budgetary Principle

The methods of estimating are not mutually exclusive; they can be used in conjunction with one another in developing a single estimate, or can be used individually for different aspects of budgeting.

SELECTING AN ESTIMATING METHOD

The ten methods of estimating that have been described serve different budgetary purposes. Some of the methods, such as modeling software, are good for estimating operational costs using new technology. Other methods, such as the historical method, are very effective in providing estimating input into repetitive tasks that change very little over time.

This book has divided the data processing work tasks into sixteen budgetable components. The different components refer to different functions within the data processing department. Because the functions are different, the methods of estimating the costs and benefits associated with those functions also have differences. Thus it is appropriate to use different estimating methods for different budgetable components.

Figure 9.1 is a matrix showing which estimating method(s) is most appropriate for which budgetable component. The sixteen budgetable components are cross-referenced to the ten estimating methods. The check marks within the matrix represent the estimating method(s) most effective for those components. Note that this matrix is provided as a guideline, not as a standard. Circumstances may make it desirable to use methods other than those indicated in the matrix for estimating a specific budgetable component.

THE ESTIMATING TASKS

The performance of the estimating step will vary depending on the budgeting strategy and the estimating method. If the person gathering the data also estimates costs and benefits, the steps are performed simultaneously by the same person. On the other hand, if the functions are separated, the estimating is normally performed by the manager of the budgeting process.

Regardless of who performs the function, the following four tasks need to be performed during this step:

- *Task 1:* Estimate costs.
- *Task 2:* Estimate benefits.
- *Task 3:* Estimate risk.
- *Task 4:* Ensure the quality of the estimate.

Tasks 1 and 2 are normally performed simultaneously. The costs and benefits are then subject to adjustment based on the degree of risk in the task. The quality of the estimate is a process that continues from the beginning to the end of the step.

Task 1: Estimate Costs

Most data processing professionals are more attuned to costs than to benefits. Also, one's personal life is more closely devoted to managing costs than revenue, because most of the revenue comes from a single source.

The estimate of the costs for a single budgetary line item is a three-part process as follows:

1. *Identify estimating method.* Estimating begins with determining the method to be used for estimating. This assumes that the estimator has an option. If the

BUDGETABLE COMPONENTS / BUDGETING METHODS	Judgment	Component	Breadboarding	Historical	Function Point	Standards	Centralized Estimating	Software	Risk	Management Edict
1. DP management and administration				✓						✓
2. Facilities				✓						✓
3. Systems support	✓	✓	✓							✓
4. New systems development		✓	✓		✓	✓		✓	✓	
5. System maintenance	✓	✓			✓	✓	✓			✓
6. Computer operation				✓		✓				
7. Hardware				✓		✓				
8. Purchased/rented software	✓	✓	✓						✓	
9. Technical support	✓	✓	✓							✓
10. Quality assurance	✓								✓	✓
11. Communication				✓		✓				
12. Data base administration	✓	✓	✓							
13. Word processing/office system/microcomputer	✓	✓				✓				✓
14. Information center	✓	✓	✓							
15. Security	✓								✓	✓
16. Outside services	✓			✓						✓

Figure 9.1 Estimating method selection matrix.

organization has adopted a single method, for example, a standardized estimating system, this part of the estimating process has been predetermined.

If an option exists for selecting an estimating method, it is recommended that the method be selected as follows. First, determine what budgetable component is being estimated. Second, select from the estimating selection matrix (Table 9.1) the appropriate methods. If more than one method has been checked in the selection matrix, the final determination should be based on two criteria. The first is the estimator's personal knowledge of the estimating method. In other words, use the methods that you can do best. The second criterion is the acceptance by management of the estimating method.

2. *Apply the estimating method.* The estimate to perform the line item should be calculated using the selected estimating method. To develop an estimate, the estimator should follow the instructions for using the method. If the estimator must make decisions in using the method, the decisions should be documented so that the estimate is supportable and reproducible.
3. *Challenge the estimate.* Every estimate should be challenged by the person making the estimate. The following types of questions should be included in this challenge:
   - Did I collect the appropriate data?
   - Am I using the appropriate estimating method?
   - Did I use the estimating method correctly?
   - Is the estimate reasonable for the task being performed?
   - Is the estimate consistent with other line tasks?

Task 2: Estimate Benefits

Benefits can fall into one of the following four categories:

1. *Cost reduction:* This benefit is derived from reducing the cost to perform an activity/task or project. The benefit is the difference between the cost prior to the event and the cost after the event. For example, if an item costs $1,000 prior to performing an activity, and costs only $200 annually thereafter, the benefit would be $800.
2. *Cost avoidance:* This benefit is not directly measurable in reduced costs; rather, it is measurable because additional costs will not have to be paid. For example, if the data processing application enabled an organization to continue processing an increased volume without having to hire an extra person, the cost avoidance would be the salaries and benefits that would have been paid had that person been hired.
3. *Gained opportunity:* A benefit can be calculated from an increased business opportunity provided an organization. For example, if increased service enabled

an organization to add more customers, the opportunity to serve more customers and the profit derived therefrom is the benefit.

4. *Intangible benefits:* These benefits are the most difficult to calculate, but frequently are the most profitable. For example, improved customer goodwill is difficult to calculate, but it might be translatable into retaining customers, increased business from customers, and customers recommending new customers to the business.

Benefits are calculated in approximately the same manner as costs. However, the benefit calculation begins by determining the type of benefit (i.e., cost reduction, cost avoidance, gained opportunity, or intangible benefit), estimating what that benefit is, and then challenging the validity and reliability of the benefit calculation.

Many data processing personnel avoid benefit calculation because it is a less precise process than cost calculation. Costs are dollars expended and are easily measurable. The origin of cost, because it is dollars expended, is also easily determinable. For example, if the project uses more computer time, acquires an extra person, or reruns a job, the dollars expended can readily be determined.

The benefits are more difficult to determine because the cause of the benefits may be more subjective than the cause of the cost. For example, if one determined that a project benefit was the cost avoidance of hiring two more people, how can one be sure that those people would have ever been hired? Even though benefit calculation may be more subjective, what is not calculated can never be realistically addressed. For example, if one does not try to estimate the benefits from a task or project, it may be much more difficult to convince management to expend the funds than when the benefits are stated.

If the benefits are stated, the discussion over a project can be directed at the validity and reliability of the benefits. The benefit calculation focuses attention on a calculation rather than on the credibility of the person making it. The net result is decisions are made on a more businesslike basis.

Task 3: Estimate Risk

The risk in estimating is the probability that the estimate will be unreliable. Risk in estimating, like risk in general, cannot be eliminated. It can only be controlled.

Controlling risk begins with identifying risk and then measuring it. Once the magnitude of the risk is known, the necessary adjustments can be made. In estimating, this involves increasing or decreasing the estimate, or adding a probability of correctness to the estimate.

Studies by Warren McFarland at Harvard have shown a positive correlation between the degree of risk in an application system and the amount of resources required to complete that project successfully. Factors like user knowledge of data processing were identified as risk factors. The more the user knew about data processing, the higher the probability of success of that user's system. In areas where users knew less about data processing, systems were less successful. One method of improving success was to work closely with users, but that requires extra resources—thus a higher estimate for high-risk systems. Risk is applicable to both developmental and operational systems. Understanding risk, one can predict with reasonable assurance how many resources are needed to be successful. The same concept works equally well with operational systems.

High-risk systems tend to have more abnormal terminations and problems than do low-risk systems. Therefore, even in computer operations, the amount of resources to run high-risk systems will be more than for low-risk systems of equal volume and complexity. Thus, using risk in operation, one can predict much better the amount of resources needed for computer operations.

The risk factors are relatively constant from organization to organization. However, the importance of the risk factors varies from organization to organization, as does the weight that should be given to each risk factor. This makes it difficult to develop one universal risk formula applicable to all organizations.

The risk analysis algorithm needs to be customized for each organization. Two risk formulas are presented in this chapter: one for application systems under development, and the second for operational applications. Note that although organizations can use these risk analysis procedures as a starting point, they should be customized as the organization gains experience in using risk concepts.

Figure 9.2 is a risk algorithm for application systems under development, and Figure 9.3 is a risk algorithm for operational applications. The algorithm in Figure 9.3 can be used for both maintenance and operations.

The risk algorithms list the significant characteristics of an application system that correlates the risk. For example, the first factor in Figure 9.2 is the importance of the function as measured by the number of organizational units that rely on the application. The more that several organizations rely on important functions, which are satisfying several conflicting needs between the groups, the higher the risk. For example, if accounting relied on a system's information for accounting information that was processed in accordance with generally accepted accounting procedures, and marketing relied on the same information but wanted that information to reflect commitments, there would be a conflict between the two units for important functions. This would make it a high-risk application.

The objective of the risk formulas is to show relative risk. The objective is to identify those applications which are higher risk than average, and those which are lower risk than average. Determining whether an application is high risk, medium risk, or low risk is an important factor in determining the final budgetary estimates.

All the risk characteristics on the appropriate risk model (i.e., Figure 9.2 or 9.3) should be examined, rated according to the stated criteria, and then a score assigned to the application being developed. Three points are scored if the characteristic is rated as high risk, two if rated medium risk, and one if rated as low risk. Note that in Figures 9.2 and 9.3 the significant characteristics (i.e., risk factors) are not weighted. Organizations may wish to assign more weight to certain factors than to others. In those instances, they can change the point value for the factors that they believe correlate more positively to risk in their organization.

Application ____________________ Preparer ________ Date ________

Significant Characteristics	Indicative of High Risk (Score: 3 points)	Indicative of Medium Risk (Score: 2 points)	Indicative of Low Risk (Score: 1 point)	Characteristic Score
System scope and complexity				
(a) Organizational breadth				
(1) Important functions	Must meet important conflicting needs of several organizational units	Meets limited conflicting requirements of cooperative organizational units	No significant conflicting needs, serves primarily one organizational unit	
(2) Unrelated organizational units deeply involved	Dependent on data flowing from many organizational units not under unified direction	Dependent on data from a few organizational units with a common interest, if not unified control	Virtually all input data come from a small group of sections under unified control	
(b) Data processing breadth				
(1) Number of transaction types	Upper one-third of applications	Middle one-third of applications	Lower one-third of applications	
(2) Number of related record segments	Upper one-third of applications	Middle one-third of applications	Lower one-third of applications	
(3) Output reports	Upper one-third of applications	Middle one-third of applications	Lower one-third of applications	

(continued)

Figure 9.2 Computer applications development risk profile.

Significant Characteristics	Indicative of High Risk (Score: 3 points)	Indicative of Medium Risk (Score: 2 points)	Indicative of Low Risk (Score: 1 point)	Characteristic Score
(c) Margin of error [necessity for everything to work perfectly, for "split-second timing" for great cooperation (perhaps including external parties), etc.]	Very demanding	Realistically demanding	Comfortable margin	
Technical complexity (estimated)	*High, aggressive*	*Moderate*	*Conservative*	
(a) Number of programs, including sort/merge	Upper one-third of applications	Middle one-third of applications	Lower one-third of applications	
(b) Programming approach (number of module/functions interacting within an update/file maintenance program)	Upper one-third of applications	Middle one-third of applications	Lower one-third of applications	
(c) Size of largest program	Upper one-third of applications	Middle one-third of applications	Lower one-third of applications	
(d) Adaptability of program to change	Low, due to monolithic program design	Can surmount problems with adequate talent and effort	Relatively high; program straightforward, modular, roomy, relatively unpatched, well documented, etc.	
(e) Relationship to equipment in use	Pushes equipment capacity near limits	Within capacities	Substantial unused capacity	
(f) Reliance on on-line data-entry automatic document reading or other advanced techniques	Heavy, including direct entry of transactions and other changes into the master files	Remote-batch processing under remote operations control	None or limited to file inquiry	

Pioneering aspects (extent to which the system applies new, difficult, and unproven techniques on a broad scale or in a new situation, thus placing great demands on: The non-EDP departments; Systems and programming groups; EDP operations personnel, Customers or vendors, etc.)	*Aggressively pioneering* More than a few relatively untried equipment or system software components or system techniques or objectives, at least one of which is crucial	*Moderate* Few untried systems components and their functions are moderately important; few, if any, pioneering system objectives and techniques	*Conservative* No untried system components, no pioneering system objectives or techniques
Commitment by management	Senior management shows no interest in the project	Management receives reports and asks questions but are not heavily involved in the project	Senior management takes a personal interest in the project by attending meetings and providing direction
Skills of users and data processing personnel			
(a) User skill in DP	Minimal skills	Average skills	High skills
(b) DP project personnel skill in user functions	Minimal skills	Average skills	High skills
Total Score			

Figure 9.2 *(Cont.)*

Application ____________________

Preparer ________
Date ________

Significant Characteristics	Indicative of High Risk (Score: 3 points)	Indicative of Medium Risk (Score: 2 points)	Indicative of Low Risk (Score: 1 point)	Characteristic Score
System stability	*Unstable, much is new*	*Moderate change, most is not new*	*Stable, little is new*	
(a) Age of system (since inception or last big change)	Less than 1 year	1 to 2 years	Over 2 years	
(b) Frequency of significant change	More than 4 per year	2 to 4 per year	Less than 2 per year	
(c) Extent of total change in last year	Affecting more than 25% of programs	Affecting 10 to 25% of programs	Affecting less than 10% of programs	
(d) User approval of specifications	Cursory, essentially uninformed	Reasonably informed as to general but not detailed specifications; approval apt to be informal	Formal, written approval, based on informed judgment and written, reasonably precise specifications	
Satisfaction of user requirements	*Low satisfaction, many problems*	*Reasonable satisfaction, some problems*	*High satisfaction*	
(a) Completeness	Incomplete, significant number of items not processed in proper period	Occasional problems but normally no great difficulties	No significant data omitted or processed in wrong period	
(b) Accuracy	Considerable error problem, with items in suspense or improperly handled	Occasional problems but normally no great difficulties	Errors not numerous or of consequence	
(c) Promptness in terms of needs	Reports and documents delayed so as to be almost useless; forced to rely on informal records	Reports and documents not always available when desired; preset timetable inconvenient but tolerable	Reports and documents produced soon enough to meet operational needs	

(d) Accessibility of details (to answer inquiries, review for reasonableness, make corrections, etc.)	Great difficulty in obtaining details of transactions or balances except with much delay	Complete details available monthly; in interim, details available with some difficulty and delay	Details readily available
(e) Reference to source documents (audit trail)	Great difficulty in locating documents promptly	Audit trail excellent; some problems with filing and storage	Audit trail excellent; filing and storage good
(f) Conformity with established system specifications	Actual procedures and operations differ in important respects	Limited tests indicate that actual procedures and operations differ in only minor respects and operations produce desired results	Limited tests indicate actual procedures and operations produce desired results
Source data origin and approval	*Leaves much to be desired*	*Reasonable*	*Sound procedures, well carried out*
(a) People, procedures, knowledge, discipline, division of duties, etc., in departments that (1) Originate data (2) Approve data	Situation leaves much to be desired	Situation satisfactory but could stand some improvement	Situation satisfactory
(b) Data control procedures outside the EDP organization	None or relatively ineffective (e.g., use of noncritical fields, loose liaison with EDP department, little concern with rejected items)	Control procedures based on noncritical fields; reasonably effective liaison with EDP department	Control procedures include critical fields; good tie-in with EDP department; especially good on rejected items
(c) Error rate	Over 7% of transactions rejected after leaving source data department	4–7% of transactions rejected after leaving source data department	Less than 4% of transactions rejected after leaving source data department
(d) Error backlog	Many 30-day-old items	Mostly 10- to 15-day-old items	Items primarily less than 7 days old

(continued)

Figure 9.3 Computer applications operational risk profile.

Significant Characteristics	Indicative of High Risk (Score: 3 points)	Indicative of Medium Risk (Score: 2 points)	Indicative of Low Risk (Score: 1 point)	Characteristic Score
Input data control (within EDP department)	*Leaves much to be desired*	*Reasonable*	*Sound, well executed*	
(a) Relationship with external controls	Loose liaison with external control units; little concern with rejected items; batch totals not part of input procedures; only use controls such as item counts; no control totals of any kind	Reasonably effective liaison with external data control units; good control over new items, but less satisfactory control over rejected items; batch totals not received, but generated by computer	Good tie-in with external control units for both valid and rejected items; batch totals received as part of input process	
(b) Selection of critical control fields	Control based on noncritical fields	Control based on a mixture of critical and noncritical fields, with effective supplementary checks	Control established on critical fields	
(c) Controls over key transcription	Control based on batch totals	Control based on transmittal sheets; batch totals and key verification of critical fields not batch-controlled	Control based on transmittal sheets, batch totals maintained on data logs, key verification of fields, and written "sign-off" procedures	
Data validation (computer editing)	*Few, relatively simple tests*	*Reasonably effective tests*	*Extensive, well-designed tests*	
(a) Edit tests	Alphanumeric tests	Range and alphanumeric tests	Range, alphanumeric, and check-digit tests	
(b) Sophistication	Simple, based on edit of one field at a time	Simple editing plus some editing based on the interrelationship of two	Simple editing plus extensive edit tests based on the interrelationship of two or more fields	
(c) Application to critical data	A considerable amount of critical data is not edited	A few critical fields are edited only indirectly	Editing performed on critical fields	

(d) Error balancing, retrieval, and correction procedures	Error rejected by system and eliminated from controls; treated as new items when reintroduced	Number and value of rejected items carried in suspense account without electronically maintained details	Error carried in suspense account in total and in detail until removed by correction
Computer processing control	*Limited—excessive reliance on manual procedure*	*Reasonable*	*Comprehensive and automatic*
(a) Controls within machine room	Informal operating instructions	Written operating procedures	Operations are based on a schedule, use up-to-date instructions
(b) Manual and electronic safeguards against incorrect processing of files	Tape library controls by serial number; no programmed checks	Tape library controls by serial number; programmed checks applied to file identification	Programmed label check applied to serial number, expiration date, and file identification
(c) Recording of run-to-run debit, credit, and balance totals for both transaction processing and master file records	Run-to-run totals not used	Run-to-run totals printed and compared manually	Run-to-run totals printed and compared by program
(d) Documentation status	Poor or no standards; uneven adherence; not part of system and program development	Adequate practices not uniformly adhered to; documentation done "after the fact"	Excellent standards closely adhered to and carried out as part of system and program development
(e) System test practices	Some transaction paths not tested	Each transaction path tested individually	Each transaction path tested in combination with all other transactions
Output control	*Essentially lacking*	*Reasonable*	*Good in DP and user department*
(a) Quantitative controls (1) In DP department	Virtually nonexistent	Hard to tie back meaningfully to input controls	Tied back to input controls

(continued)

Figure 9.3 *(Cont.)*

Significant Characteristics	Indicative of High Risk (Score: 3 points)	Indicative of Medium Risk (Score: 2 points)	Indicative of Low Risk (Score: 1 point)	Characteristic Score
(2) In user department	Virtually nonexistent	Hard to tie back meaningfully to input controls	Tied back to input controls	
(b) Qualitative controls	Documents and reports accepted virtually without review	Sample documents and reports receive limited review	Documents and reports tested in detail, in addition to receiving a "commonsense" review of reasonable data limits	
(c) Distribution controls	No routine report distribution procedures	Routine procedures for distribution limited to list of users and frequency of report delivery	Written procedures requiring that control log indicate receipt by user, time of accrual, accounting for each copy, etc.	
On-line processing controls				
(a) Data transmission controls, including (1) Error detection (2) Error recovery (3) Data security	The front-end control program does not validate operator identification codes or message's sequence number and does not send acknowledgement to origin	The front-end control program checks terminal and operator identification codes and messages sequence number, sends acknowledgement to origin, and provides a transaction log	The front-end control program validates terminal/operator identification codes plus transaction authorization codes and message sequence number and count, corrects errors, sends acknowledgement to origin, and provides log of transactions plus copies of updated master file records	

(b) Data validation controls, including error detection and correction	Neither the front-end control nor the application processing program checks for authorization approval codes; no check digits are used with identification keys; there is little use of extensive data relationship tests; erroneous transactions are rejected without analysis or suspense entry	The application program checks approval codes for key transaction types only, but check digits are not used with identification keys; extensive data relationship tests are used; erroneous transactions are sent back to terminal with a note, but no suspense entry is made	The application program validates approval codes for all transactions, and check digits are used with identification keys; data relationship tests are used extensively; erroneous transactions are noted in error suspense file when sent back to terminal with note	
(c) Data processing controls, including: (1) Error detection (2) Transaction processing controls (3) Master file processing controls (4) File recovery provisions	Application program produces a total number of transactions processed; no master file processing controls; file recovery provisions limited to periodic copy of master file	Application program produces a summary record of all debit and credit transactions processed; no master file processing controls; file recovery provisions limited to transaction log and periodic copy of master file	Stored validation range values are used to validate transaction fields; application program summarizes all transactions processed by type, with credit and debit values for each terminal, and uses a master file control trailer record that is balanced by program routine; end-of-processing file recovery provisions include transaction log of active master file records	
Total Score				

Figure 9.3 *(Cont.)*

After all the factors have been evaluated on either figure, they should be accumulated to provide a total risk score. This score then needs to be interpreted to determine how to adjust the estimate developed in the previous tasks.

Adjusting the estimate for development task. Figure 9.2 has sixteen risk factors. If the high-risk characteristic is selected, 3 risk points are awarded, 2 points for an average risk, and 1 risk point for the low-risk characteristics. This means that the total score will range between 16 (lowest risk) and 48 (highest risk). The estimating procedure for an organization for systems under development should assume that all systems are of equal risk. This means that risk is ignored when the estimate is made. Estimates can be developed using any of the ten estimating methods. The completed estimate is adjusted based on the degree of risk. Table 9.2 identifies how to adjust the estimate:

TABLE 9.2 PERCENT TO ADJUST DEVELOPMENT ESTIMATES BASED ON RISK

Risk score from Figure 9.2	Factor to multiply estimate to adjust for risk
48	2.0
42	1.5
36	1.2
32	1.0
28	0.8
22	0.67
16	0.5

These multiplication factors may need to be adjusted as an organization gains experience. They are presented as a starting point based on the experiences of a limited number of organizations. With some fine tuning to the weight of each risk factor and the multiplication factors, organizations should be able to improve the budgetary estimates significantly.

Operational risk factors. Figure 9.3 lists thirty-three risk factors for operational applications. This will result in a risk score in the range of 33 (lowest risk) to 99 (highest risk). Table 9.3 indicates what factors should be used to multiply the estimate by which is based on the risk score developed for that application.

Task 4: Ensure the Quality of the Estimate

The quality of the estimate is the responsibility of the estimator. The estimator should be given a quality control tool for use in evaluating the reliability and validity of individual estimates.

TABLE 9.3 PERCENT TO ADJUST OPERATIONAL ESTIMATES BASED ON RISK

Risk score from Figure 9.3	Factor to multiply estimate to adjust for risk
99	2.0
88	1.5
77	1.2
66	1.0
55	0.8
44	0.67
33	0.5

Figure 9.4 is a quality control checklist designed for use by estimators. The estimator should be familiar with these questions prior to estimating, and then be able to answer the questions positively at the end of the estimating process. The items that receive "yes" responses are indicative of quality estimates, and "no" responses should be investigated for the potential impact on the quality of the estimate.

ITEM	RESPONSE			
	YES	NO	N/A[a]	COMMENTS
1. Did the source of estimating data come from a reliable person?				
2. Are the data used for estimating reasonable based on the task being estimated?				
3. Is the estimate produced reasonable based on the task being estimated?				
4. Is the estimate consistent with other estimates for like projects?				
5. Has the mathematical accuracy of the estimating procedures been verified?				
6. Was the appropriate estimating method used for the estimate?				
7. Was the estimating method applied correctly?				
8. Was the correctness of the estimate challenged, and was the challenge responded to satisfactorily?				
9. Has sufficient documentation been retained to support and justify the estimate?				

[a]N/A, not applicable.

Figure 9.4 Estimating quality control checklist.

ENSURING THE QUALITY OF THE ESTIMATING STEP

There are two quality concerns about estimating: one is the quality of the estimate and the other is the quality of the estimating process. In general, reliable estimates cannot be developed unless the estimating process itself is reliable. Task 4 of the estimating step was related to the quality of the estimate. This section deals with the quality of the estimating process.

Figure 9.5 is a quality control checklist for the estimating process. This is designed for use by the person responsible for the estimating process. At least once per year, the quality of the estimating process should be evaluated using this checklist. As with other checklists, this is designed so that "yes" responses are indicative of good quality practices, and "no" responses should be investigated to determine the potential impact on estimating.

ESTIMATING IMPEDIMENTS AND COUNTERSTRATEGIES

The data processing profession has a reputation of being a poor estimator. In the early days of data processing, estimates were off by factors of 3, 4, 5, or greater. While the situation has improved, many data processing functions still carry the reputation of poor estimators. Part of this is due to lack of training, but part is due to impediments for which appropriate counterstrategies can be developed.

The two major estimating impediments and suggested counterstrategies follow:

1. *Lack of data processing processes:* Estimating is effective only when it is applied to a science. If the work being estimated is not repetitive in nature, estimates are extremely difficult to develop. In other words, as long as data processing is an art it is difficult to determine how long an artist will take to do a job. On the other hand, once the methods of performing work are standardized, the estimator knows what steps and processes must be followed to make that function work. Thus the impediment of data processing being an art and difficult to estimate can be overcome by the following two counterstrategies:
   a. *Adopt data processing processes.* Much of the work performed by data processing is repetitive. These require processes for system development, maintenance, testing, computer operation, installing application systems, and so on. Once these processes have been put into place, it is much easier to estimate how long it will take to perform those tasks.
   b. *Develop standards of work.* Standards go hand in hand with processes. Once the process has determined how a task should be performed, a standard can be developed to measure the actual performance of that task. The standards then become the basis for highly reliable estimates, which can quickly lead into software estimating packages.

ITEM	RESPONSE			
	YES	NO	N/A[a]	COMMENTS
1. Have the estimators been trained in estimating?				
2. Have the estimators been provided the appropriate estimating tools (e.g., methods of estimating)?				
3. Have the estimators been instructed in how to select the appropriate estimating method for the item being estimated?				
4. Have the estimates from last year's budgetary process proved to be reliable and valid?				
5. If the response to item 4 is "no," has the cause of the problem been investigated and the process changed accordingly?				
6. Are the estimates challenged first by the person and then by an independent party?				
7. Are benefits estimated as well as costs?				
8. If the costs exceed the benefits, is the reasonableness of undertaking the item challenged?				
9. Does the estimating process provide sufficient documentation to support the estimate?				
10. Would the same estimate be developed if the process was performed individually by two people?				
11. Does the estimating process include appropriate quality control tools?				
12. Are the quality control tools used?				
13. Are the estimators provided feedback on the reliability and validity of their estimates?				

[a]N/A, not applicable.

Figure 9.5 Quality control checklist for the estimating process.

2. *Lack of estimating tools:* It is difficult to perform any job without the appropriate tools. When people are neither instructed on how to do a job, nor provided tools with which to do the job, it is not unusual for the job to be poorly performed. In many data processing areas, the people doing the estimate must make up their own process and their own tools. Since this is not their profession, many of the processes and tools are ineffective. This impediment can be overcome using the following counterstrategies:

a. *Introduce estimating tools.* Ten different estimating methods have been discussed in this chapter. From this list, tools should be selected and the people doing the estimating trained in how to use the tools.

b. *Automate the estimating process.* Reliable, reproducible estimates will occur only when they are performed by computers. This should be the goal of organizations in implementing good estimating processes.

Budgetary Principle

The ability to automate a process means that the process is understood. Whatever part of budgeting can be automated should be automated.

THE VALUE OF A GOOD ESTIMATE

Estimating serves many purposes in the data processing area. In this chapter we have discussed estimating as a budget tool. It is also a means of communicating information to users to make go/no go decisions on projects, and it can be used to measure performance of data processing personnel.

Good estimates facilitate these objectives and increase the credibility of the data processing function. Poor estimates undermine staff morale by providing unrealistic targets (either high or low), contribute to poor user decisions, and contribute to ineffective budgets.

Many business contractors who estimate jobs incorrectly go out of business. This is because they lose money on projects, or they fail to win jobs. As data processing becomes more available from sources other than the centralized data processing function, data processors may find themselves in the same position as contractors. Those functions that master the estimating art will survive, and those that do not can expect serious competition from other alternative sources of information processing.

10

Step 4: Classification, Consolidation, and Presentation of a Budget

At the conclusion of the estimation step, all the information needed for budgetary purposes has been produced. This information represents a "first cut" at the budgetary process. The proposed projects, and estimates, may exceed the capabilities of the data processing function and/or senior management budget constraints.

This step is designed to transcribe the information produced in Steps 1 through 3 into a budget that data processing management is ready to present and justify. The step involves the budgeting tasks of evaluating and modifying the budgeted projects and estimates, classifying the data into the form prescribed by the corporate budgetary systems, consolidating the data and eliminating duplication, organizing the material for presentation, and ensuring that the tasks meet quality control standards. Finally, the impediments to this presentation step and the counterstrategies that can be used to improve the acceptability of the budget are discussed.

ADDING THE FINISHING TOUCHES TO THE BUDGET

At the start of this step the information needed to prepare the budgeting has been collected. If this were a system development process, we would have completed the design phase and be ready for coding. It is not the end of the process. All the pieces must now be put together and made to work. In budgeting terms, this is the final preparation of the budget document.

This step is equivalent to trying to funnel a lot of information into a small container. Normally, there are too many requests to go in the budget; as a result some will not make it through the funnel but, rather, will fall by the wayside. Ensuring that all the essential items get included in the budget is management's responsibility.

The first three steps are performed primarily by first-line supervisors and the data processing staff. This step should be conducted by the person responsible for assembling the budgeting and by senior data processing management. Knowing what is necessary, what is acceptable to senior management, and what is accomplishable by the existing staff is an important part of senior data processing management's responsibilities.

Data processing management must develop a budget that has a high probability of success. After all, data processing personnel will be judged on what they do, not by the size or format of their budget. Much of the problem in the data processing profession has been rapid growth in staff and large budgets but without the ability to perform the budgeted work properly. This inability to produce is a predictable phenomenon and as such, appropriate counterstrategies can be developed during the budgeting process.

Budgetary Principle

It is not the magnitude of the budget that counts but, rather, the ability to perform the budgeted tasks.

PREPARING A WINNING BUDGET

A winning budget is one that can be implemented. To justify funds for projects that cannot be implemented successfully undermines the credibility of the data processing function. It is far better to have fewer funds and to implement them successfully than to do projects poorly or have to turn money back because the talent is not available to utilize the resources.

A winning budget has the following characteristics:

- Funds are related to business functions.
- Budgeted tasks are recognized as important.
- Items in the budget can be executed with existing or expected staff.
- Budget provides for risk contingencies.
- Data processing resources will enable tasks to be completed to the satisfaction of users.

Data processing managers do not submit budgets unless they believe that the success criteria listed above are present within the budget. The problem that managers face is that although they may believe it, they do not have the tool that measures the probability of success. Such a tool is called the "balanced risk portfolio."

Balanced Risk Portfolio Concept

A balanced risk portfolio is one that balances the risk of budgeted tasks against the capabilities of the data processing resources to accomplish those tasks. The concept is quite simple. It requires that the risks of budgeted items be determined. Next, it requires that the capabilities of the data processing resources be determined. The two are then balanced.

The concept states that high-risk tasks should be performed by highly skilled people. If there are more high-risk projects than there are highly skilled staff, the budgeted portfolio of work is out of balance.

A prime cause of failure of the data processing function to satisfy users and management is an unbalanced portfolio of budgeted items. It is the equivalent of mismatching two football teams. If one is significantly stronger than the other, the outcome of the game is never in doubt. The strongest team will win. If the risks of the budgeted items far exceed the skill of the resources, there should be little doubt about the outcome of work from the data processing function.

If the risk of the work significantly exceeds the resources of the data processing function, data processing management has three options:

1. *Delay projects.* It is far better to delay a project than to agree to do it and fail. Failure is measured in terms of user dissatisfaction as opposed to the fact that the basic attributes are not performed. For example, systems could be run on the computer, but always late due to problems, and thus have a very dissatisfied user.
2. *Extend the time period for performing the task.* If a task is staffed with people who are less than adequately skilled, one should not expect that task to be accomplished within the normal budgeted time or resources. If the resources allocated are extended significantly, perhaps by a factor of 3, 4, or 5, the probability of success again can be slanted in the favor of the data processing function. Note that with less than fully skilled people significantly more supervisory time will also be required.
3. *Contract the task to outside organizations.* If the data processing personnel recognize that they cannot perform a task successfully, it is better to contract it out and lose the work in-house than to attempt to do it and not succeed.

The concept of balanced risk portfolio is one that measures the skill level of tasks against the data processing resources. Let's look at some of the reasons that the data processing staff may be less than adequately skilled:

1. *Lack of experienced staff:* Possibly many of the staff members are junior members and thus lack the experience needed to overcome problems.
2. *Lack of skilled supervisors:* Supervisors perform planning functions and compensate for weaknesses within project staffs. If there are too few skilled super-

visors, it may result in the lack of consistency of purpose of the project group, and perhaps coordination problems between users and data processing staff.

3. *Unfamiliarity with technology:* If the projects require technology new to the organization, the unfamiliarity with the technology can result in excessive time expended on learning technology.
4. *Unfamiliarity with user requirements:* A lack of knowledge about the business area in which the data processing staff is involved can result in difficulty in understanding and successfully implementing user needs. Although the project team may understand the requirements, they do not have adequate background to challenge or question basic misunderstandings or improperly stated requirements.

There are several ways of rating the skill level of project personnel. In general, it makes little sense to develop a special skill level rating system when most organizations already have an individual performance appraisal system. A combination of the following four factors would seem to provide all the information needed to rate the skill of the data processing staff:

- Pay grade/position
- Years of data processing experience
- Performance appraisal ratings by supervision
- Educational/business experience

It is generally satisfactory to use a subjective judgment for individual skill levels. The foregoing four factors, coupled with the success rate of a person in prior projects, should permit people in each job classification to be rated in one of the following three categories:

- Highly skilled for position
- Average skills for position
- Low skills for position

These skill levels can then be compared against the task risk that was developed in Chapter 9. Matching highly skilled persons against high-risk projects balances the budgeted portfolio for risk. A balanced risk equals a high probability for success.

ANOTHER IMPORTANT ELEMENT OF SUCCESS—PRIORITIZATION

If the balanced risk portfolio analysis determines that the data processing function cannot perform all the items included in the budget, those with the highest priority should be selected for the budget. In addition, there might be more items than budgetary limits will permit to be accomplished. Again, budgeting needs to prioritize projects for selection purposes.

There are four basic means of selecting projects, as follows:

1. *Squeaky wheel concept:* Under this approach, the person/function that yells the loudest gets the project done. The "squeaker" can do it by lobbying the data processing manager, getting senior management to intervene, or just pressuring the data processing manager by whatever means gets the desired project approved.
2. *Big budget bucks:* Large clients as measured by the charge-out systems, "favorite sons" departments, or organizations with large budgets may have sufficient clout to get a specific item approved and budgeted. This approach favors the departments with larger budgets. When charge-out systems are used, this is one of the more common methods of determining priorities.
3. *Management edict:* This option can occur as a result of an edict by either data processing management or senior management. In organizations with strong data processing functions, the data processing manager frequently determines which projects will be implemented and which will not. This approach may cause resentment toward data processing by departments whose projects are eliminated from the budget.
4. *Formal prioritization:* The only selection method that is defensible and reproducible is one that uses a scheme for prioritizing projects. There are two types of prioritization. First is prioritization within the function, and second is prioritization within the organization. The tendency has been to move from prioritization within a department or function to organization-wide prioritization. One method of doing this is to set up a senior planning committee to make decisions on what projects are to be implemented and in what sequence.

Business System Planning Prioritization

What appears to be the best and most preferred method for prioritizing work within a data processing function is to set up a planning committee. One name for such a committee is "business systems planning" committee. The objective of this high-level management committee is to determine what data processing tasks are implemented. The committee is usually comprised of representatives from all major areas within the organization. They determine not only the priorities of business applications, but also priorities for internal data processing activities, such as installing data base technology.

The objective of a business system planning committee is to ensure that the data processing resources are allocated to the projects having the highest business priority. This concept is predicated on the fact that there are normally more projects than there are resources. One study by the IBM Corporation indicated that the average data processing function had a three-year backlog of work. Given this, it would be unfortunate if the wrong projects were picked from that backlog.

One method that is used to help business system planning groups prioritize is to

Erroneous record keeping is the recording of financial transactions contrary to established accounting policies. The errors may involve the time of recognition, value, or classification.

Unacceptable accounting is the establishment or implementation of accounting policies which are not generally accepted or are inappropriate to the circumstances. This could also lead to further exposures such as statutory sanctions.

Business interruption may include anything from a temporary suspension of operations to a permanent termination of the enterprise. At the extreme, this also affects the accounting principle regarding a "going concern."

Erroneous management decisions are objectionable in themselves but may also lead to other exposures. Such decisions may arise due to misleading information, lack of information, or errors in judgment.

Fraud and **embezzlement** may be perpetrated at different levels—*against* management or *by* management. Direct misappropriation of funds is only one ramification of fraud. Deliberately misinforming management or investors is also fraudulent, even if only to keep one's job.

Statutory sanctions refer to any of the penalties which may be brought by judicial or regulatory authorities having jurisdiction over an organization's operations.

Excessive costs include any expense of the business which could be readily avoided. A related exposure is also a loss of revenues to which the organization is fairly entitled.

Loss or **destruction of assets** refers to the unintentional loss of physical assets, monies, claims to monies, or information assets.

Competitive disadvantage relates to any inability of an organization to effectively remain abreast of the demands of the marketplace or to respond effectively to competitive challenges.

Figure 10.1 Business system exposures. (From *Computer Control and Audit,* by William C. Mair, Donald R. Wood, and Keagle W. Davis, QED Information Sciences, Wellesley, Mass., 1978, pp. 11–12.)

indicate the business objective of an application system. A methodology for categorizing business activities/events for the purpose of determining the impact of those activities/events on the organization was developed by Touche Ross & Co. This classification scheme is illustrated in Figure 10.1. For example, one of the classifications is business interruption. If data processing proposed a project to use resources on a disaster planning project, the business classification for that project would be business interruption. By using such a classification scheme, the budgeted activities can be categorized by how they affect the business organization, and as such can be more effectively prioritized by a business system planning committee.

PERFORMING THE CLASSIFICATION, CONSOLIDATION, AND PREPARATION STEP

This step converts the budgetary items and estimates into a finished product. It serves the same function in budgeting as coding does in system development. It is the step that produces the desired result.

The performance of this step is the prime responsibility of senior data processing management. Much of the actual work may be performed by the staff responsible for budget management. However, the step requires some direction and decision, which can usually be provided only by senior data processing managers.

This step includes the following five tasks:

- *Task 1:* Analyze/approve budget items.
- *Task 2:* Classify budget items.
- *Task 3:* Consolidate budget items.
- *Task 4:* Organize budget items.
- *Task 5:* Ensure the quality of the final budget document.

These generally are not time-consuming tasks. Much of the classification can be performed during the budget preparation, and the consolidation done by computer. The execution of each of the five tasks is described in the following sections.

TASK 1: ANALYZE AND APPROVE BUDGET ITEMS

The responsibility of the staff during budgeting is to identify and budget those tasks/projects which they believe are needed for information processing. The staff gathers much of their information from users and past experiences. Much of the staff will not be privy to organizational business plans or the most current management budget directives. Data processing management must evaluate budgetary items in conjunction with organizational business plans and current directives.

Data processing management also has the responsibility to supervise and protect subordinates. If budget items are unrealistic, improperly prepared, or incomplete, management analysis should uncover these defects.

The major effort in analysis and approval is to select those budgetary items that will meet management's needs and provide the data processing function the highest probability of success. This involves analyzing the totality of the proposed items from the concept of balancing the risk. The result of this analysis will be the elimination from the data processing budget of items for which there is a low probability of success. Note that this elimination may be a result of negotiation with user and/or senior management.

At this point, management should begin prioritizing projects. The prioritization can be used two ways: first, to determine the sequence in which activities/projects will be executed; and second, to determine which items will or will not be included in the budget. However, using priorities to eliminate items may not occur until the consolidation task has been performed.

TASK 2: CLASSIFY BUDGET ITEMS

A properly prepared budgetary process includes in the preparation process the classification of the item. This is normally accomplished using a chart of budgetary accounts. Organizations that have a budgetary process have a budgetary chart of accounts as part of that process. If this chart of accounts meets the needs of the data processing department, it will be used in developing the data processing budget.

If the budgetary objectives of data processing management are more extensive or different than the organization, a budgetary chart of accounts for data processing may be needed. The reconciliation between the organization's chart of accounts and the data processing chart of accounts should have been done during the planning phase (see Figure 6.2). If the budgeted items were classified by the data processing chart of accounts, they must now be reclassified in accordance with the organization's chart of accounts. The most common reclassification will be salaries. In most organizations' charts of budgetary accounts salaries are a single line item, while within the data processing function they are divided among activities and projects.

Budgetary systems that are automated can have this reclassification performed automatically. The end product of this task will be the capability to produce two budgets: one for data processing management, and one for senior management of the organization.

An important part of the classification task is to cross-reference budgetary line items to the supporting information. This will enable data processing management easily to retrieve the supporting documentation in the event that a budgetary line item is challenged or questioned by senior management. It is good practice to incorporate the supporting data into a binder or notebook, cross-referenced to the budgetary line item.

TASK 3: CONSOLIDATE BUDGET ITEMS

The consolidation step takes the individual budgetary items and accumulates them into a single budget document. This step is designed to accomplish two objectives. First, it accomplishes the mechanical and mathematical functions of accumulating data. Second, and most important, it reduces redundancies between budgetary items. For example, if computer operations included the cost of operating an application and a project area also included that cost, it should be included only once in the budget.

Redundancy can be addressed from two perspectives. First, the budget planning process should identify potential redundancies and determine who should include an item. Second, if the budget data are at a sufficiently detailed level, an analysis of line items consolidated by budgetary chart of account number can quickly identify redundancies. Thus the consolidation process should produce the following three documents:

1. Budget consolidated by data processing chart of accounts
2. Line items listed by chart of account number (done to identify potential budgeting redundancies)
3. Budget consolidated by organization's chart of accounts

After this has been accomplished, management must make decisions about the size of the budget they wish to submit. If there are budgetary guidelines and constraints, projects/activities may need to be eliminated. The elimination should be done using one of the prioritization systems described earlier in this chapter. If a business system planning approach is used, the data processing manager may need to call that group to make priority decisions.

The items included in the final consolidated budget should be the high-priority projects/activities. At this point, the budget that data processing management is willing to defend should be together in a single document. The sequencing and supporting materials may yet need to be added, but the budget as it will be presented has been developed.

TASK 4: ORGANIZE BUDGET ITEMS

The objective of this task is to rearrange budgetary information in the order in which it will be presented. For example, the consolidation may list all the individual projects. For purposes of presenting it, those data may need to be reorganized by user area, types of projects, and so on.

The major challenge of the organization task will be gathering together the data needed for the final budget presentation. The information needed will include the following:

1. Consolidated budget information (prepared in Task 3)
2. Organization budget presentation requirements (usually provided by the corporate budgetary group)
3. Project justification material (normally included in the budgetary supporting information—this was cross-referenced during the classification task)
4. Organization and data processing short- and long-range plans (needed to relate budget items to approved plans)
5. Operational facts to include in budget (items such as volume of work, both actual and projected, which will be used to support and explain the budget)
6. Data processing overviews (prepared by data processing management to support budget)

The end product of the organization phase is a rough first draft of the budget document. This rough draft should be in the format and style required by the organization. At the end of this task, all the information that will be given to senior management to support the data processing budget has been developed and is in the structure and format required for budget presentation.

TASK 5: ENSURE THE QUALITY OF THE FINAL BUDGET DOCUMENT

The quality of the classification, consolidation, and preparation of a budget step is the responsibility of data processing management. The step begins when the staff has completed the detailed budgetary work, and concludes when the information is organized into the structure needed for presentation.

ITEM	RESPONSE			
	YES	NO	N/A[a]	COMMENTS
1. Is each budgetary line item classified by both the data processing budgetary chart of accounts and the organization's chart of accounts?				
2. Has the validity of the classifications been reviewed?				
3. Has each item in the budget been approved by management?				
4. Has the risk associated with each line item been calculated?				
5. Has the skill level of each person in the data processing department been identified?				
6. Are there adequately skilled resources within, or planned, to accomplish the budgetary line items?				
7. Does the data processing department have a formal prioritization scheme for projects/activities?				
8. If yes, have all the budget line items been prioritized?				
9. If items need to be deleted from the budget, are they deleted in priority sequence?				
10. Are items that cannot be completed successfully due to inadequate skills been deleted or renegotiated with users?				
11. Has the budget been consolidated?				
12. Are line items listed so that redundant line items can be eliminated?				
13. Has the quality of the steps within this task been ensured through appropriate quality control measures?				

[a]N/A, not applicable.

Figure 10.2 Classification, consolidation, and budget preparation quality control checklist.

As with other steps, the responsible people should be given quality control tools. These tools enable people to evaluate the quality of their work. Quality control tools also improve productivity by increasing the number of productive units of work produced.

Figure 10.2 is a quality control checklist for this step. "Yes" responses to the items on the checklist are indicative of good quality work; "no" items should be investigated further. The final budget step should not be entered until the quality of this and the preceding steps has been verified.

ENSURING THE QUALITY OF THE CLASSIFICATION, CONSOLIDATION, AND BUDGET PREPARATION PROCESS

The budget preparation process needs to be quality-evaluated continually, as do the products produced by that process. Quality is a never-ending challenge of the budgetary process. The continual attention and review of the budgetary process is a major step in improving the quality of the budget product. Generally speaking, the final budget is no better than the process that produced it. The failure of the staff to follow the budget process is indicative of a poor quality process. The process is a combination of management support of the process, the process itself, the training of the people using the process in the procedures, and the review and evaluation of the performance of the task within the process.

Figure 10.3 is a quality checklist for the classification, consolidation, and budget preparation step process. As with other quality control checklists in this book, "yes" responses are indicative of good quality practices, and "no" responses are indicative of potential process problems. The "no" response items should be investigated to determine whether improvements need to be made to the process. The impact of "no" items should also be assessed on the budget product.

IMPEDIMENTS AND COUNTERSTRATEGIES TO CLASSIFYING, CONSOLIDATING, AND PREPARING A BUDGET

This step is an essential step, one normally performed under the direct control of management. Therefore, there is little difficulty in getting the step performed. The major impediment in the performance of this step is failure to develop a budget that provides the data processing function with a high probability of success during the year as projects are implemented. The solution to that impediment, as discussed in this chapter, is the balanced risk portfolio approach. This relatively simple procedure may do more for improving the credibility and success of the data processing function than any other single item. It enables data processing management through risk analysis to improve their probability of success significantly.

ITEM	RESPONSE			
	YES	NO	N/A[a]	COMMENTS
1. Does the data processing function have a process for classifying, consolidating, and preparing a budget?				
2. Does that process include a prioritization scheme?				
3. Does that process address the risks associated in performing budgeted tasks/activities?				
4. If item 3 was answered "yes," has the risk of performing each line item been determined?				
5. If item 3 was answered "yes," has the skill level of the data processing staff been determined?				
6. Does the organization have a formal prioritization scheme?				
7. Does the prioritization scheme prioritize by business priorities, as opposed to individual user priorities?				
8. Does the organization have a business systems planning committee or equivalent to set data processing priorities?				
9. Does the budgetary process require that supporting documentation be cross-referenced to budget line items?				
10. Is the data processing budgetary chart of accounts cross-referenced to the organization's budgetary chart of accounts?				
11. If two separate charts of accounts exist, are two consolidated budgets prepared, one using each of the two charts of accounts?				
12. Does the budgetary process indicate all the information that must be collected for use in preparing the final budget?				
13. Does the budgetary process include a quality control procedure for the people responsible for performing this step?				

[a]N/A, not applicable.

Figure 10.3 Classification, consolidation, and budget preparation step process quality checklist.

Budgetary Principle

Budgeting can serve the dual purposes of providing a basis for funding the data processing function *and* providing a blueprint for ensuring the success and improved credibility of the data processing function.

11
Step 5: Marketing the Budget

There is a feeling of relief when the budget document is assembled. Although the feeling may be "my work is done, now it's up to management," the budget preparation work is not done. The final measure of success of a budgetary process is an approved budget. If the approved budget does not contain the needed resources, the process should be judged less than fully satisfactory.

This step begins when all the budgetary information is prepared and concludes with senior management sign-off on the actual operating budget. The data processing budget is one of many budgets presented and reviewed by senior management. The marketing step is designed to ensure that the data processing budget receives the most favorable treatment by management and to improve the probability of the acceptance of the budget.

This step involves the tasks of packaging the budget, presenting the budget, and negotiating with management on items within the budget. These tasks should be preplanned, not spontaneous events. Management reaction should be anticipated and counterstrategies developed ahead of time on addressing management challenges. In this chapter we explain how to preplan and conduct marketing the budget.

THE KEY TO SELLING THE BUDGET

The person who first said that if you built a better mousetrap people would beat a path to your door did not understand marketing. Marketing is the science of creating a demand for a product where that demand may not have existed before. Marketing is the totality of events that causes a product to be sold.

The key to marketing is known and quite simple. The key is to find the customer's "hot button" and then direct the marketing toward that hot-button area so that the customer sells himself or herself on the product. Any good salesperson understands and exploits this marketing ploy.

Visualize for a moment a teenage customer going into an automobile agency to buy a car. The teenager is fascinated with speed, so the salesperson markets his dealership's automobile based on the power of the engine, acceleration of the car, and suspension to handle the power. Shortly afterward, an accountant enters who is concerned about the cost of operating the car. The salesperson now talks about the economy engine and miles per gallon, automotive guarantee and free service of the dealership, plus the low-maintenance track record of the automobile. After that, a family enters and the salesperson discusses the roominess of the car, the size of the trunk, and safety features designed to protect the family. At the end of the day, a music lover hears from the salesperson how great the sound system is and of all the unique sound options and speaker systems available for the automobile. What the salesperson has done is identified for each customer what each is looking for and then has slanted the sales pitch toward satisfying that unique need.

Highly skilled marketeers all appear to be low-keyed. If at the end of the sale you conclude that the salesperson was wonderful, applied no pressure, and seemed to understand you and your needs, you have been marketed. All the salesperson did was let you identify your hot button, and then the salesperson helps you let you sell yourself on the product. All the salesperson does is help lead you, drop hints, and agree with your conclusions.

Out of this marketing key, we see two basic concepts emerging:

1. Focus the justification of the budget on the needs and desires of the person approving the budget.
2. Help the person approving the budget convince himself or herself that the items in the budget are correct.

This approach requires the data processing function to identify the important issues for senior management. This is normally quite easy to do. All that is needed is to maintain records on the issues raised by senior management and then keep frequency counts on the number of times those issues come up in memos and discussions.

This counting concept was the basis for the book *Megatrends,* published in 1982. The author of that book, John Naisbitt, and his researchers counted the number of newspaper lines devoted to topics such as relocation to the Sun Belt. Since newspapers, like management, have limited opportunity to communicate, they pick the most important topics to discuss. Naisbitt was able to develop two conclusions about topics. One was that the amount of space devoted to a topic was an indication of the importance of that topic. Second, the trend in allocating newspaper space was indicative of a genuine national trend. Those topics to which significant space was allocated, and for which space was increasing, were the trends reported in the book *Megatrends*.

If the same concept is applied to senior management, data processing can determine not only the important issues to senior management, but also the trends for senior management thinking. For example, let us assume that cost cutting was an issue raised frequently in memos and discussions by senior management, and that the number of times the issue was raised has been increasing. Data processing management can then conclude that cost cutting is an important issue to senior management and could justify the use of data processing resources based on that cost-cutting theme. This might be done by emphasizing the cost-avoidance and cost-reduction benefits associated with information processing systems.

These concepts are not presented as a devious device but, rather, as a realistic approach to budgeting. Senior management is charged with establishing organizational policy and direction. If information systems can be supportive of those policies and directions, the function will be more successful in fulfilling its information processing mission.

Budgetary Principle

The budget that is acceptable to management is the budget that best satisfies the needs and objectives of senior management.

ANTICIPATING MANAGEMENT'S BUDGET CHALLENGE

One supervisor stated that he believed it was management's responsibility to reject all proposals presented to them. He felt that management suffered from "request pollution." Request pollution was described as "everybody wanting something from senior management." In response to request pollution, management rejected all proposals initially and then waited for the second and third requests of the most pressing needs. The supervisor reasoned that if a presenter was uncertain of the value of a request and it was rejected, that request would die. On the other hand, if the request was valid, the requester would present it again at the point where the pollution had subsided slightly.

Marketing experts state that the average sale is made on the third call. If a salesperson gets discouraged at one or two rejections, he or she will never make the majority of sales. The salespeople who are successful are the ones with perseverance to make the third and fourth calls. Good sales personnel also know that preparation for the sale is an essential ingredient of selling. Those salespeople who prepare and rehearse for sales are much more effective than those who just call on a potential customer and then "play it by ear."

Some years ago I headed a major research project funded by the IBM Corporation. The project was funded by an outright grant, so that IBM's involvement in the project was minimal. The involvement was one of a grantor wanting to ensure that the desired results occurred as a result of the research funded by the grant. The project lasted approximately three years. At the end of the three years, the reports were prepared, and as project manager I developed a press release that I hoped IBM would issue announcing to the data processing press the completion of the project. IBM responded favorably but stated a need to prepare for questions from the press before the press release was issued. My initial reaction was that this was unnecessary, as I had spent three years on the project and knew all the answers. IBM finally convinced me through a few embarrassing questions that I might not be as prepared as I thought I was. After a week of counseling and preparation by public relations personnel, I was truly prepared for the challenges thrust at me by the press after the notification of the project completion was released.

A good salesperson making an important call will spend time prior to the call anticipating why the customer might not buy the product. The salesperson identifies all the reasons why that person would not want to buy the product, and then develops counterarguments for those reasons. For example, if the salesperson believes that the product may not be purchased because it is too expensive, a counterstrategy may be the long life of the product because of its quality, or the ability to buy the product over time.

In marketing a budget, the data processing function must anticipate all of the reasons why management may not approve the budget as is. If a feasible counterstrategy cannot be developed, data processing management must seriously consider the merits of the proposal(s) included within the budget. Not only is this a good marketing principle, but it makes common sense to avoid embarrassment during budget hearings and presentations.

Budgetary Principle

If scientific theories can be applied to budgeting, we would say: "There needs to be an equal and opposite reaction for every budgetary challenge." The opposite force is the counterstrategy by data processing management for anticipated senior management budgetary challenges.

After the budget has been prepared (at the completion of Step 4), a list of potential senior management challenges should be identified. This identification should be a two-level identification. The first level is the general category of challenge; the second level is a specific line item within that category that might be challenged.

The general categories of management challenge are:

- *Inadequate return on investment:* The proposed project/activity either costs more than it contributes to the organization, or the contribution is inadequate or questionable enough that management proposes that the activity be deleted.
- *Inconsistent with the organization's long- and short-range plans:* Specific activities may be counter to the plans and directions established by senior management for the organization. For example, senior management may want

to decentralize functions, while data processing is proposing an increase in the centralized processing facility.

- *Unreliable cost or benefit:* Management challenges the reliability and/or validity of a proposed cost or benefit included within the budget. For example, the data processing budget might propose introducing data base technology for *X* dollars, and senior management does not believe that it can be made operational for that amount of funds.
- *Redundancy of expenditure:* The same item is requested two or more times. This may occur within the data processing budget or may be an interbudget redundancy. For example, the data processing function may budget for personal computers, and users may budget for the same facility.
- *Inadequate resources to accomplish:* The budget may appear too ambitious to senior management. It may include too many new activities that management believes cannot all be accomplished within the same budgetary period.
- *Project unnecessary:* An item included in the data processing budget may be viewed as a task or activity that senior management does not feel is worthwhile. For example, the data processing department may include funds to establish an information center but senior management does not believe the facility is necessary.
- *Funds unavailable to support new activities:* Management may not object to the item being budgeted but wants to place a cap on growth. Growth can be restricted by curtailing or eliminating any new activities or activities that require new people.
- *Inconsistent with the personal likes and desires of senior management:* Some projects are challenged just because they include an activity or concept that is counter to senior management's thinking. For example, they might object to a project because it includes a product from a vendor they do not like, replaces a product which they personally developed or supported, or is for an area or person who has fallen into disfavor.

The second level of challenge identification requires data processing management to look at each line item in the budget. For each line item, management should ask the following questions:

1. Is this project essential to the day-to-day operation of the organization?
2. Is this a project/activity that currently has strong management support?
3. Can this project/activity be justified to the point where it would be extremely difficult for management to reject the item?
4. Is this a project/activity that would be difficult to delay?

If any of these questions are answered "no" for any line item, data processing management should be alerted to a possible management challenge for that line item.

The potential challenge should first be categorized into one or more of the foregoing categories. Second, the specific challenge should be identified and a counterstrategy developed for that challenge(s). As stated previously, if strong counterstrategies cannot be developed, data processing management should reconsider the inclusion of that item in the budget.

CONDUCTING THE MARKETING-THE-BUDGET STEP

Marketing occurs before the budget is prepared, within the budget itself, between the data processing budget and other budgets in the organization, and after the budget has been presented to senior management. It is a continuous process with potentially large paybacks if done effectively.

Marketing the budget is a data processing management responsibility. The responsibility begins with the senior data processing manager and includes every member of data processing management. It is a function that should be continuous year round, and each member of management should utilize the opportunities available to market the data processing function, specifically the resource needs of that function as described in the budget.

There are three marketing tasks that need to be conducted during this step:

- *Task 1:* Package the budget.
- *Task 2:* Present the budget.
- *Task 3:* Negotiate the budget.

The importance of marketing should not be overlooked. It need not be a time-consuming function and is perhaps more of an approach and mental attitude toward budgeting. It is important for senior data processing management to keep the need for marketing data processing uppermost in the minds of other data processing managers.

TASK 1: PACKAGE THE BUDGET

The budget is a representative of data processing management. It represents them in budgetary discussions by senior management. It is important that this representative be packaged to make the best possible impression. Budgets, unlike impressions made by people, do not sell on first impression. On the other hand, the impression given by the budget package should not be discarded.

The options available in packaging the budget may be restricted by the organization's budgetary procedures. In many organizations, the forms for use in budgeting and the structure of the document are prescribed by organizational standards. However, it is unusual for some leeway in presentation not to be permitted by those standards. This does not mean that new forms should be developed but, rather, that modern packaging methods be utilized in creating the budget document.

The principles of effectively packaging a budget are:

1. *Inclusion of a management summary:* Budgets, by nature, are long and detailed documents. It is helpful to orient management with a few key points prior to analyzing and approving the budgetary detail. The management summary is an opportunity to get the analysis started on the right foot. The summary should emphasize the two or three key points that data processing management feels need to be made. If the management challenge analysis demonstrates that there will be one or two key challenges, for example, cost cutting, the management summary provides an opportunity to address that challenge head-on before management even looks at the budget.
2. *Attractive physical packaging:* The physical package itself should be made as attractive as possible. Even with prescribed budgetary forms, some creativity can be added. Among the different approaches to physical presentation are:
   a. *Varying type fonts:* Change in type fonts can make reading easier and at the same time highlight certain items. Even changes in the pitch of type, making some items physically larger than others, can help emphasize points.
   b. *Underscoring and highlighting:* To emphasize key benefits or points, certain items may be underscored or highlighted in yellow. This approach draws the reviewer's attention to those items that data processing management feels warrant management attention.
   c. *Use of graphics:* Computer plotters provide unique opportunities to present data in graphic format. The old proverb that a picture is worth 1,000 words holds true in budgeting. Bar charts, pie charts, and so on, particularly in color, are very effective ways to explain and justify budgetary items.
   d. *Use of different colored paper:* Budgetary forms can easily be reproduced on different colors of paper. This can be used to highlight data processing activities, such as presenting the development budget on blue paper, operations on brown paper, support activities on yellow paper, and so on. It can also be used to draw attention to specific activities by highlighting that activity on different-color paper.
   e. *Colored pencil notations on a typed budget:* Special notes by the data processing manager in red, green, or other colors can draw attention to specific items. Also, special notes regarding the importance of an activity, or a supporting statement by a user, may help sell a difficult-to-sell item.
   f. *Supporting testimonials/survey results:* Management often wants to know the opinion of others regarding a new service or activity before that service or activity is initiated. For example, if data processing management has proposed an information center, a series of testimonials from users or a survey mailed to users with the results included may help sell a difficult-to-sell activity.
   g. *Neatness and accuracy:* Attention to detail is always warranted. Columns that do not add correctly, misspelled words, or sloppy work plant the idea in

management's mind that if the document contains physical errors, it may also include errors of reliability and validity. Physical errors can snowball into negative attitudes and rejection of valid proposals.

The packaging ideas listed above are representative of what some data processing functions do to ensure the success of their budget. Packaging is merely one aspect of marketing a budget, but an important one. It must be remembered that the budget document frequently must defend itself without the assistance of data processing management, and the credibility of data processing is based partly on the budget presented to senior management by data processing management.

TASK 2: PRESENT THE BUDGET

There are two basic methods for presenting the budget to senior management for approval. One is to forward the budget to management for their analysis. Under this approach, data processing management believes the budget to be a stand-alone documentation and thus does not feel the need to make a formal budget presentation. The second approach is one in which data processing management uses budgeting as an opportunity to market the data processing function and to justify and support the requested resources.

A formal budget presentation is an additional opportunity to market the budget. Failing to take advantage of this opportunity is a lost opportunity for data processing management. It is quite likely that if the budget runs into difficulty (i.e., management challenges items within the budget) that management's minds may be hardened to the point where the item can no longer be marketed.

The procedures that an organization follows in developing budgets may call for, or may preclude, a formal budget presentation. If the opportunity is required, or exists, it is strongly recommended that data processing management make the most opportunity out of this presentation.

Two concepts need to be embedded into the budgetary presentation:

1. Attendees of the presentation will take away with them only two or three concepts. Therefore, it is important for data processing management to predetermine what those two or three pieces of information will be.
2. The budget document will be taken away from the presentation and used for future evaluation. Therefore, the presentation should be complementary to, not a reiteration of, the budget document.

Budgetary Principle

Budget presentations should present information in addition to the budget document. If a budget presentation was only a restatement of the budget document, it would not be necessary.

The budget preparation should be used for two purposes:

1. Highlight the three major features of the budget.
2. Provide the support needed for the manager to approve the budget and justify it to his or her superiors.

Previous discussion in this chapter identified how to select the two or three key features. However, if the budget contains a unique or important new activity, such as an information center, that should be highlighted in addition to addressing what data processing management believes will be senior management's major budgetary challenges.

The senior manager who must approve the data processing budget and then defend it to other senior managers needs the necessary support for that approval and defense. The type of support that should be given in a presentation is that which is complementary to the managerial style of that person. Let's look at the four general managerial styles to determine what information needs to be included in a budget presentation:

1. *Driver managerial style:* This person is willing to champion a cause. All that the person needs to know is why that cause/activity will be beneficial to the organization. For example, the discussion to a driver on a proposal to install an information center should highlight the advantages of that information center to the users and the organization.
2. *Consensus managerial style:* This manager does not want to pioneer new concepts. This person's managerial style is similar to that proposed by Nasser in describing his role as leader of Egypt. He stated that the role of the leader is to find out which direction the mob is going and then get in front and lead the mob. The consensus manager wants to know that everyone is in agreement about a decision before the decision is made. In presenting to a consensus manager a proposal to initiate an information center the presentation would want to emphasize all the managers in the organization who are currently behind the concept.
3. *Idealist managerial style:* This type of manager thinks in terms of big pictures and long-range solutions. The person is not as concerned with the day-to-day implementation problems as with global solutions to major problems. This type of manager does not want to know the details or impediments but, rather, wants to discuss business theory and philosophy. Details tend to bore this type of manager. When presenting a proposal to install an information center to this type of manager, the budgetary presentation should emphasize what other corporations are doing, how the concept incorporates into managerial styles, and the type of major corporate problems that can be addressed by an information center, such as raising the skill level of users in DP concepts.

4. *Analytical managerial style:* This type of manager wants to have had a complete investigation undertaken before a project is improved. The analytical manager is impressed with large volumes of detail that support proposals. For example, the estimating method of breadboarding would not be acceptable to this type of manager; the component or attribute estimating method where volumes of detail are accumulated provides the type of support this manager looks for. In presenting an information center proposal to an analytical manager, the presentation should include an identification of the users, the frequency of services that they are likely to ask for, the costs and benefits of each of those services, and so on. The more the detail, the better, for this manager.

TASK 3: NEGOTIATE THE BUDGET

Artful negotiation is an important skill for the data processing manager. Few functions within an organization get all that they want. Those that are good negotiators normally get more resources than the poor negotiators.

Negotiating is a give-and-take proposition. The objective from a budget preparer's perspective is to get more than you give. Unfortunately, senior management usually writes the negotiating rules.

In negotiating a budget, data processing management must view senior management comments as challenges as opposed to cuts. Cuts are finite, challenges are not. If all management concepts are viewed as challenges, there is the opportunity to negotiate what, if any, cuts will actually occur.

Any successful negotiator holds the following two trump cards:

1. *Additional unstated benefits/advantages:* A good negotiator *never* includes all the arguments for an activity/project in the budget or in the beginning negotiations. If a negotiator states all the advantages and benefits for doing a task, and management still objects, the proposer most likely loses. For this reason, one or more key benefits/advantages should be held back and not used until absolutely essential. In the game of negotiating, data processing management should attempt to get senior management to indicate all the reasons why an item should not be approved, and at that point play this trump card.
2. *Know your personal priorities:* Sooner or later, good negotiators are prepared to give up something. Knowing what can be safely given up, and in what sequence, is an important part of negotiating. Obviously, the negotiator does not want the other party to know what compromises will prove acceptable. In the beginning of the negotiation, arguments should indicate that nothing is expendable, and continue that argument until the point of impasse, at which the second trump card of sequence of compromise comes into play.

Some of the guidelines to follow in successful negotiations are:

- *Never address issues personally:* Negotiators should talk about budgetary items as inanimate objects. They should talk about project X, line 17, and so on. If budget negotiations turn into personality duels, it is no longer negotiations but, rather, arguments.
- *He or she who speaks first loses:* Many negotiations involve frank and direct questioning. The answer to many of these questions from senior management will determine whether or not an item will be accepted. Frequently, it is better to endure a period of silence until senior management commits itself on the direction they desire for budgeting. The experience of silence can be an invaluable negotiating tool.
- *Limit negotiating periods:* Extensive negotiating periods generally are not effective uses of time. Negotiating sessions should be limited, for example, to one hour. If items cannot be resolved satisfactorily within that time, additional negotiating sessions should be scheduled.

Many times, senior management will cease negotiations with a budgeting edict. It is generally best to accept the edict at that time. There will be later opportunities to negotiate the edict, but the point at which the edict is given is normally not that time.

The major argument in negotiation will be the benefits to be derived from information system projects. These benefits will be compared by senior management to other projects of other areas. The better prepared data processing managers are to discuss and present benefits, the more likely they are to be successful in negotiating information system projects over other projects by other areas of the organization.

MARKETING IMPEDIMENTS AND COUNTERSTRATEGIES

Marketing is as much a part of the budgeting process as is data gathering. It is of little value to build a good budget and have many of the key items turned down by senior management. Marketing is a step that increases the probability of successful budgeting.

In today's business environment, managers are looking for a win/win situation. This is a situation in which both parties to an event win. An objective of marketing should be to enable senior management to win and data processing management to win. Following the principles laid out in this chapter, the win/win situation can occur.

The two impediments to successful marketing and recommended counterstrategies to that impediment are:

1. *Marketing is viewed as an unnecessary function for a technical profession.* Many data processing professionals believe that their mission is to be of service

to users and to provide information services to their organization. Although this is true, they also have the obligation to provide direction in building and operating information systems. Marketing is a prerequisite to fulfilling this second information system objective successfully.

The counterstrategies that can be used to overcome the unwillingness to initiate a marketing campaign for a budget include:

a. *Past history of success:* If the data processing function has been less successful than they would like, the need to change tactics should become apparent. History tends to be an excellent teacher.

b. *Conferring with colleagues in other corporations:* Identify the experiences of other data processing managers in getting budgets through senior management successfully. Determine if the more successful data processing managers market their budget, and if there is a correlation between failure to market and failure to get desired projects approved.

2. *The staff lacks marketing skills.* One of the reasons people fail to perform a needed function is that they do not possess the necessary skills. It is difficult to do a task for which you have never been trained or given guidance as to how to perform. Computer science schools do not teach marketing. This may be unfortunate, because marketing is one of the skills missing from the background of many data processing professionals.

   The counterstrategies that can be employed through lack of training and skills include:

   a. *Marketing training:* The people involved can attend a conference or college course in basic marketing and/or advertising principles. This will not teach a person how to market a data processing budget, but will teach the basic concepts of marketing which the data processing professional can then apply to their budgeting challenge.

   b. *Making use of common sense:* Much of selling a product is just using everyday common sense. If people think for a moment what would appeal to them and then build a budget presentation that meets their own acceptance criteria, there is a high probability that the presentation will appeal to others.

Budgetary Principle

There is no greater finale to the budgeting process than the statement "Your budget is approved."

Part 4 Using and Evaluating the Budget

12
Living with Your Budget

The approval of the budget document by senior management can be viewed as the end or the beginning of the budgetary process. It is the end of the preparation of the budget, but it is the beginning of the use of the resources included within the budget. The budget, like an application system, is developed for use. Also like an application system, a well-developed application system (and budget) serves the user well.

In this chapter how to "live with" or use the budget effectively is explained. Discussed also are the four challenges in using a budget: allocating funds, managing with the budget, managing a changing workload, and surviving managerial budget edicts. These are continuous activities that begin when the budgetary year begins and frequently extend past the budgetary period. This is because the final expenditures and accounting may continue past the end of the budgetary year.

SO NOW YOUR BUDGET IS APPROVED!

The approval of the budget solidifies the data processing plan for the forthcoming year. This book has emphasized building a budget that offers a high probability of success. The management and use of those resources must also be geared to ensuring the success of the data processing function.

Data processing departments must literally "live" with and within the budget. The living concept implies a changing environment and adopting the budget to that changing environment. The budget is a starting point which should not be used to constrain success but, rather, to encourage and complement successful operations.

If the budget is used as a harness, it can stifle creativity and progress. This is not to state that projects and activities should not live within budgetary constraints but, rather, that the budget should be used as a tool to help encourage success. This involves integrating the budget into the day-to-day planning and implementing the mission of the data processing function.

Living with a data processing budget involves the following four tasks:

- *Task 1:* Allocating funds.
- *Task 2:* Managing with the budget.
- *Task 3:* Managing the changing workload.
- *Task 4:* Surviving managerial budget edicts.

These are four concurrent tasks. Data processing management and the people responsible for using resources must work together in this process. The effective use of budgets is a challenge to all concerned, but when performed properly, budgeting can be a tool to improve the productivity of the data processing function.

Budgetary Principle

Budgeting is one of the least recognized productivity tools. Budgeting's contribution to productivity is manyfold, including early identification of defects, ensuring the appropriate use of resources, early abortion of ineffective projects, and assuring managerial involvement in projects.

TASK 1: ALLOCATING BUDGETARY FUNDS

In accounting terms, the budget is general authorization to expend funds. This means that management of the organization has allocated funds for the use of the data processing department. However, it does not mean that the data processing department has the right to use those funds.

In the mid-1970s, several large U.S. corporations were charged with improper use of corporate funds. The U.S. government charged that those funds were used for improper purposes and that senior management of the organization should be held responsible for the use of those funds. The case centered around the fact that funds included in the budget for one purpose, frequently legal fees, were used for purposes that the U.S. government charged were improper, such as bribing officials of other governments to get a favored position in contractual negotiations. The people involved stated that the approved funds in the budget was their authorization to expend those funds for whatever purposes they deemed necessary. Senior managers reported that although they did not approve of the action taken by their subordinates, they had little opportunity in their corporate headquarters thousands of miles from an operating division to direct the specific use of funds.

In reaction to the cases prosecuted by the Securities and Exchange Commission, the Foreign Corrupt Practices Act of 1977 was passed. This Act specifies that corporations must maintain systems of internal control that provide for both general and specific authorization to expend funds and to ensure that funds are expended in accordance with the intent of management.

General authorization to expend funds is the budgetary process. Specific authorization to expend funds deals with specific use of funds, such as the purchase of software, travel funds to take a trip, and the approval of employee overtime. These and all other specific uses of funds must be individually authorized by management. Data processing management is normally delegated that responsibility, except in those instances where the funds will be used personally by themselves. In those instances, a higher level of management, either within or outside the data processing department, depending on the rank of the data processing manager, must approve a specific authorization of funds.

Budgetary Principle

The budget does not provide for the use of funds but, rather, the allocation of funds for a general purpose. The use of the budget requires the specific authorization of each expenditure by management.

Management has two primary responsibilities regarding the use of budgeted funds.

Apportionment of Budgetary Funds

Most departments/activities within an organization are provided leeway in the apportioning of budgetary funds. Note that this varies from organization to organization, and as such, data processing management should clarify their apportioning responsibility. This concept means that funds included within one budgetary account may be transferrable in part or in total to other budgetary accounts. For example, funds allocated for training may be usable to acquire publications for a library or even a personal computer for use in a data processing function.

Reapportioning budget resources among accounts may occur because:

1. Budgeted projects are canceled.
2. Unbudgeted items need to be accomplished.
3. Projects are completed using fewer resources than budgeted.
4. Projects require more resources than are budgeted to be completed.
5. Technology changes requiring new studies/investigations.
6. New technology offers new methods of accomplishing budgeted tasks, but the funds required to use that new technology will be less than or greater than the budgeted amounts.
7. The scope of projects change, requiring more or less funding.
8. The volume of transactions changes, requiring more or less budgeted resources.

9. Unique opportunities arise: for example, the opportunity to buy needed computer equipment early at significant discounts, which requires additional resources.

Data processing management has three options when resource requirements change. First, funds can be reapportioned from one budgetary account to another. This assumes that management has this authority and that it will not adversely affect other budgeted items. This reapportionment permits the data processing function to operate within its budget but to reallocate those funds as workloads and priorities change. Second, additional funds can be requested. Data processing management always have the prerogative to go to senior management and request additional funds to handle changing workloads and/or priorities. Under the first option, data processing management could make the decision, but under this option the decision on whether to act or not to act is left to senior management. Note that under this option, funds can also be returned to senior management for use in other areas of the organization, although it normally does not take senior management approval. The third option is to request senior management's approval to change priorities of work. This option is similar to option 1 except that the impact of the reapportionment is usually more significant, and thus data processing management feel that senior management should be involved in the reapportionment.

Specific Authorization to Expend Budgeted Funds

All the resources expended within the data processing area must be specifically authorized by management. As noted earlier, with the exception of personal expenditures made by the most senior data processing manager, such as his or her travel expenses, data processing management can provide the needed specific authorization.

Some of the considerations that need to be taken into account in providing specific authorization include:

1. The budgetary periods in which the funds are allocated; for example, annual funds may be allocated in monthly or quarterly allotments.
2. The amount of overage leeway permitted; for example, in some organizations management can exceed the budget by 5 percent without additional approvals.
3. The person who is given authority to provide specific authorization. This should be determined ahead of time. Each person within his or her job description should have stated the types of specific authorization to expend which they are authorized to approve.

There are two general types of specific authorization: one is for nondiscretionary expenditures, and the second is for discretionary expenditures. A *nondiscretionary expenditure* is one for which data processing managers have little choice as to the expenditure, and *discretionary expenditures* are those for which data processing managers have sole authority over the expenditure of funds.

Nondiscretionary expenditures normally receive specific authorization when the commitment for that expenditure is made and then again after it has been made. For example, the salaries and benefits associated with a data processing staff are nondiscretionary expenditures. Specific authorization is made prior to hiring a staff member, and then again to indicate that that staff member is still on the payroll by approving a weekly or monthly statement that that employee is still at work. The rental of computer hardware is the same type of nondiscretionary expenditure. It is approved prior to acquiring the hardware, and then at those points where the vendor invoices the organization for rental and/or maintenance. Note that in these types of expenditures it is not necessary to provide specific authorization before each payroll period or billing period.

Data processing management should approve each use of discretionary funding prior to the use of those funds. The following is a list of typical data processing discretionary expenditures:

- Overtime for employees
- Purchase of books/training courses
- Employee travel
- Employee overtime
- Hiring of consultants
- Acquisition of office equipment
- Reconstruction of office space

Specific authorization to act does not always need to be in writing. However, it is good practice to put specific authorization to expend in writing. Note that some organizations give verbal approval for the discretionary use of funds, and then provide their specific authorization in approving the actual invoice/expense account/expenditure.

TASK 2: MANAGING THE DP DEPARTMENT WITH A BUDGET

In earlier discussions we explained the value of a budget as a managerial control. Part of that control function has been exercised in the preparation of the budget. However, the primary control uses for a budget occur during the budgetary period. It is during this time that management will be able to exercise control over projects/people through the effective use of budgetary procedures.

The actual control will occur through specific authorization to expend, allocate, and reapportion funds. These are the end results of the managerial control process, not the control process itself. Control through budgeting means managerial involvement in the use of those resources in accomplishing the data processing mission.

In determining whether to give specific authorization, apportionment, or reapportionment of data processing budgeted resources, data processing management can use one or all of the following four control methods:

1. Budgetary status reports
2. Monitoring and modifying risk variables
3. Budgetary reviews
4. Trade-offs and priority considerations

Method 1: Budgetary Status Reports

Organizations that have budgetary systems normally also have budgetary status reports. In most organizations these occur monthly. The expenditure information and changes in budgetary allocation information are posted to the corporate accounting systems. These are closed shortly after an accounting period. At this time, status reports are prepared and disseminated to the appropriate people within the organization.

These budget status reports normally show the following four pieces of information:

1. Budgeted amount for year, year to date, and budgetary period (i.e., a monthly period)
2. Actual expenditures for year to date and budgetary period
3. Variance between budgeted allocation and actual expenditures (may be expressed as a percent, actual dollars, or both)
4. Any changes this period in budgetary allocation/reapportionment

If the data processing budget line items are different from the organization's budgeted line items, the data processing department may need dual status reports. The organization status report will be needed because senior management will evaluate the performance of data processing management partly on that report. In this context, the budget is used as a senior management control over data processing management. However, for data processing management to use it effectively over their subordinates, a more detailed budgetary breakout may be necessary.

The data processing department normally has an advantage over other departments in this detailed breakout. This is because the accounting budgetary system is normally a computerized information system. In most instances, data processing systems analysts/programmers have built the system. As such, they can normally either modify the system or capture input to the system for their function so that they can provide that detailed breakout. In addition, some data processing departments may want to use their own internal accounting systems to provide that type of information. For example, project status reporting systems and job accounting systems may contain the detailed information needed to determine the budgetary status of projects.

Some of the accounts included in the data processing budget will not be needed to monitor the tasks/activities of subordinates. For example, overhead funds, telephone, and so on, may not be needed in evaluating the status of specific projects and activities. In some instances information other than financial figures (for example, workload figures and hours) may provide better information for analyses.

Based on the budgetary status information, data processing management must continually perform analyses and make decisions. In most instances, these analyses are either an investigation of a variance, or a comparison of expenditures against project/activity status reporting, indicating the percent of work done. Based on these analyses, data processing management will make one of the following decisions:

1. Do nothing—the project/activity looks on target.
2. Become more involved in the project to avoid a potential disaster indicated by a too rapid use of resources.
3. Stop the project, or delay the project, because the use of resources does not appear to warrant a continuation of the project.
4. Change the budgetary allocation. Either allocate more or fewer funds to the project.

Method 2: Monitoring and Modifying Risk Variables

In the preparation of the budget, it was recommended that the risk variables of each activity/project be identified. The purpose of identifying these variables was to determine the probability of the project being completed within what would be normal budgetary allocations. If the variables indicated that it was a high-risk project/activity, it was suggested that the normal budget allocation be increased. On the other hand, if the variables indicated that it was a low-risk project, the normal budget estimate could be lowered.

These same risk variables can be used in monitoring and adjusting projects. Let us assume that a project that was considered normal and receives the normal budget allocation. However, after some months of activity the actual expenditures appear to be outrunning the budgeted expenditures. This is a typical management dilemma. Without risk analysis, the management options are more involvement, or changes in budgetary allocation. With risk analysis, they can focus in on a specific risk variable that may be causing the problem. There are several reasons why the use of risk variables would not produce a correct estimate, such as:

- Risk variable was incorrectly estimated; for example, the number of programs (i.e., size of systems) was misestimated.
- Errors in the risk estimating formula; for example, certain factors were not appropriately weighted.
- A risk variable of significance was excluded through omission.
- Changes to the project/activity have changed the risk variables; for example, new requirements have increased the size of the project.

In monitoring budget variances, any noted variance indicates only a variance. The cause of this variance is not obvious in a budgetary status report. Using this managerial method, the risk variables will be examined as part of the investigation. If management perceives a potential project/activity problem, they will immediately begin investigating the risk variables.

This investigation should be limited to projects that management believes are potentially in trouble. It is suggested that management recalculate the risk score using the risk analysis worksheet provided earlier in this book in Figures 9.2 (Computer Applications Development Risk Profile) and 9.3 (Computer Applications Operational Risk Profile). After the risk score has been recalculated, management will have a new score, as well as the indicated risk variables. The management analysis should be first to examine the two scores and then the individual variables that comprise those scores. If there is a significant change in the risk score and variables, the cause of the budget variance will probably have been identified.

Management can then adjust the probability of success of the project by changing the risk variables. For example, if the project is currently comprised of very large programs and that is a changed variable which adds to the risk, management can recommend those programs be divided. This reduces the amount of risk and thus increases the probability of success.

Budgetary Principle

Managers have two methods available to eliminate unfavorable budget variances: first, they can change the amount of resources; and second, they can change the risk variables of projects/activities.

Method 3: Budgetary Reviews

A budget review is a control that is most effective in a developmental activity. The objective of the budgetary review is to evaluate the use of past funds, reconsider the use of future funds, and make decisions regarding the direction and/or continuation of the project.

Budgetary reviews are practical only in developmental activities that are built using a developmental process that contains checkpoints. Each checkpoint in the developmental process must be keyed to predetermined deliverables so that project status can be measured against predetermined expectations. Although budgetary reviews could be held in a noncheckpoint process, they tend to be less effective because it is more difficult to identify the actual activity status.

The objective of a checkpoint is to have predefined managerial reviews during development. If these reviews are tied to budgetary allocations, they take on much greater significance. Many organizations only allocate project funds from checkpoint to checkpoint. This means that projects are, in effect, out of funding at the end of a checkpoint and cannot continue until they receive appropriate managerial review. Based on that review, management then allocates additional funds based on the decisions made during the review.

The steps that management would follow in a budgetary review are:

1. *Evaluate project status.* This is a comparison against expected deliverables at a specific checkpoint versus actual deliverables. Not only are the deliverables examined to determine that they are complete, but the quality of the deliverables is evaluated.
2. *Determine status of budgets.* A determination needs to be made as to whether the project has reached the checkpoint within budgetary tolerances, or whether it is over- or underfunded.
3. *Determine the probability of successful completion within budgeted resources.* Management must make an estimate based on the current and expected project condition regarding the probability of the project being completed on time, within budget, and meeting the project specifications.
4. *Make managerial budget decision.* At the checkpoint, management must decide what should be done, and then how much funding should be allocated for those tasks. Based on this, the project is either terminated or continues until the next checkpoint review, at which time these steps are repeated.

Method 4: Trade-offs and Priority Considerations

The data processing department is charged with completing a mission. The mission is usually expressed in terms of an annual plan and an annual budget. Based on changing conditions and the unpredictability of estimating, it is unusual that all the planned items will be completed within the budgeted amounts.

At each budget status reporting period, the plan and budget should be reevaluated. This reevaluation looks not only at the status of expenditures and individual variances, but it is an opportunity to reassess priorities and make project trade-offs.

This method requires the performance of the entire budgetary process on a miniature scale. Management must plan this review; gather the data regarding existing budgets, actual expenditures, and actual and projected workload changes; develop estimates for completing the projected budgetary year workload; prepare a new budget and improve it; and if changes in funding are required, marketing and presenting those changes to senior management may also be required.

Note that many organizations have formal corporate-wide budget reviews. Determining the priorities of current and projected workload, together with any desirable trade-offs, is a prerequisite to data processing management for attending those corporate budgetary reviews.

TASK 3: MANAGING THE CHANGING WORKLOAD

It is almost impossible to project eighteen months in advance the tasks that a data processing function will be performing eighteen months hence and the complexity of those tasks. Budgeting is destined to remain part science and part art. It would only be possible to develop highly predictive budgets if business conditions, workloads, and performance of staff remain constant. They do not.

If budgeting is viewed solely as a means of acquiring resources, maintaining the currentness of budgetary data will appear unimportant. Only if additional funds are needed is the importance of updating budget information recognized. If budgeting is used as a managerial control, it will be only as effective as the currentness of the budgetary data.

There are two categories of data used in budgeting: one is the estimated or budgeted resources, and the second is the actual expenditure of resources. Errors on either side (i.e., budget and actual) can lessen the effectiveness of the budget as a managerial tool.

The methods by which management can ensure the currentness, reliability, and validity of budgeted data include:

1. Require budget data to be changed when project data are changed.
2. Continual review of the budgeted data by the budget participants. When the participants recognize that the integrity of the budgeted data is lost or lessening, they should revise those budgeted amounts (note that this does not mean that the budget document itself will be changed, just that new projections will be included with the original estimate as a basis of control).
3. Changes in management plans/priorities need to be reflected immediately in actual budgeted data. For example, if there is a 5 percent across-the-board budgetary cut, that should be reflected at least in the next budget status report, and earlier if the effect of any change will be significant.
4. Reflect priority changes and managerial actions as they potentially affect the budget. Budgetary actions should also be reflected in budgetary status reports. For example, if a project is significantly over budget, but management has adjusted the risk variables and now believes that the project will be completed within budget or close to it, that action if shown in the budget would help others interpret status.

Most management action will be taken based on the variance between budgeted and actual amounts. If the actual amounts fail to reflect actual activity, inappropriate action will be taken. For example, if a project leader is playing with budgets so that the budgeted numbers work out correctly, but they do not reflect the amount of resources being expended, management will have lost the ability to control the use of expenditures. It is possible that the project that is consuming excessive resources, but whose use of resources is hidden through budgetary shenanigans, would have been canceled by managers had they known the actual cost.

The actions that management can take to improve the integrity of actual resource usage reporting include the following:

1. *Use of automatic data collection procedures:* Automation improves the integrity of data collection. The more actual data that are collected through automatic means, the higher the integrity of the data collected.
2. *Explaining the importance of accurate reporting:* Many subordinates do not understand the use of budgets or the importance of good budgetary information for management. Many come to believe that the most important thing is to complete the project within budget. Any means, such as switching funds between budgetary accounts, that accomplishes that objective may be viewed as good by subordinates.
3. *Integrity audits:* Periodic investigations by supervision over the integrity of data, such as questioning people, helps prove the reliability of reported data. It also provides another advantage. This is the value of the audit process, which is concern on the part of people that if they report incorrect data they may be identified and reprimanded accordingly.
4. *Requiring reported data to be signed and verified:* People may put incorrect data on a worksheet, but if they are required to sign that sheet attesting that the data are correct, they are less likely to report incorrect data. The integrity can be improved by also requiring a supervisor to sign verifying the correctness of the data. This "personal pressure" is another means by which management can communicate the importance of receiving correct data.

TASK 4: SURVIVING MANAGERIAL BUDGET EDICTS

Many key aspects of the budget process will be beyond the authority of the data processing manager to control. Budgeting is a process that originates in functions such as data processing and then moves upward through a budgetary review process. The data processing manager can control what goes upward but may not have much control over the edicts that come downward. Note that the marketing step was designed to increase the probability that favorable decisions would come down from senior management regarding budget resources.

During the budgetary process, and during the budget cycle, management edicts can significantly change the amount and purpose for which resources are allocated. Management edicts can include:

- Across-the-board budget changes (e.g., a 5 percent cut)
- Changes in operating plans, such as the elimination or addition of a product line
- Requirements to comply with governmental regulations (e.g., the requirements that banks withhold tax on interest paid)

These edicts can occur at any time. A drop in sales can be reflected immediately in budgetary reductions; an increase in sales may result in new projects to be completed. Data processing management must be prepared to adjust workloads to reflect these budgetary edicts.

This preparation should result in the development of three potential budgetary scenarios:

1. *Budget amount does not change but workload does.* Under this scenario, data processing keeps the same budgeted amount but will do work different from that included in the budget. The previous tasks have addressed the strategies that can be used to survive a changing workload edict. Note that this edict may occur as a result of senior management decrees, new user requests, and/or internal data processing requests.
2. *Cuts are made in budget resources.* Management may make an across-the-board budget cut or a cut in specific project areas. When this happens, data processing will need to modify workload and possibly size of staff. This scenario requires data processing management to preplan where across-the-board cuts might be made should they occur. It also requires the determination of who should be cut in the event that staff need to be reduced. A cut does not need to name specific persons but, rather, projects/activities.
3. *Budget resources are increased.* It would seem that getting more money would be a desirable event, but it may not be. Having resources does not predefine success. After the funds are received, data processing management must still develop the plans and strategies to ensure that the predescribed missions are successfully accomplished. Because it is difficult to acquire skilled, knowledgeable people on a short-term basis, the function may not be able to accomplish the required tasks. The objective of this scenario is to predetermine how the data processing function might build up their capabilities to do additional tasks on a short-term basis. For example, the scenario might include contract help or contracting work.

Scope and Extent of Budget Scenarios

Budget scenarios need not be a time-consuming activity. The objective of the scenario exercise is to be prepared for the unexpected. The scenario strategies need not be worked out in detail, but at a minimum the options should be identified. If this is done, data processing managers are prepared to answer such questions as: "Can we install the changes necessary to withhold tax on our savings interest by June 30?"

Budgetary Principle

Preparedness is a key to data processing credibility. Predeciding how data processing will react to changing budgetary conditions is an integral part of that preparedness.

13
Assessing the Effectiveness of the Budgetary Process

Processes need to be adjusted to keep in tune with changing business requirements. This is because the process itself may be faulty, which can result in incorrect budgetary estimates. Also, the process should be modified periodically to develop and utilize data processing budgets more effectively.

Identified in this chapter are four ways in which the budget process can be evaluated: to survey participants, use judgment, identify attributes, and utilize budgetary metrics. We also warn of evaluation dangers and discuss how to avoid these in assessing the adequacy of the budget process.

EVALUATE THE PROCESS, NOT THE PARTICIPANTS

Two evaluations need to be made about any event. One is the evaluation of the outcome from the event, and the other is the process by which the event was conducted. To fail to do both, or to confuse the two, negates the evaluation process.

Let's look at an evaluative example of a football game. The first evaluation is of the event. In evaluating the event, we can look at the final score to obtain a rating about the performance of the individual participants. This is obviously an important evaluation, because decisions about whether to keep players, additional player training, and positions of weakness can be identified. However, in many ways the second evaluation of the process is more important. In this, we evaluate the merits of the game plan, the adequacy of the training given the players, how well the players were prepared for the game by the coaching staff, and the ability to adjust the game plan as the game proceeds. Note that it is possible for all the players to be playing up to their individual expectations, yet lose the game.

It is generally easier to evaluate the participants than the process. If a systems analyst develops an estimate to do a project, and then fails to complete the project within that estimate, we can conclude that the systems analyst did a poor estimating job. On the other hand, it would be just as easy to conclude that the analyst had not been provided the adequate tools to develop realistic estimates.

It is the responsibility of supervision to evaluate the performance of the budgetary participants. This is an important responsibility but is not addressed in this chapter. It is excluded because the evaluation must take into account personal skills, motivation, and performance.

It is the responsibility of the data processing manager to evaluate the budgetary process. This DP manager should identify each budgetary flaw and then investigate to determine whether the flaw is associated with the process or the person. If the flaw lies with the process, a decision needs to be made regarding whether the process should be modified.

METHODS FOR EVALUATING THE BUDGETARY PROCESS

In any evaluative process, the evaluator must determine the objectives of the process. The objectives will be based partially on the formality of the process. For example, informal processes need to be evaluated on subjective criteria. Very formal processes can be evaluated on a more scientific process.

The type of evaluation will also depend on the intended use of the results. If the results will be used exclusively by the evaluator, then as long as the process is effective it need not be formal. On the other hand, if the evaluator must substantiate his or her evaluation to other parties, the process will need to be more formal and documented. Sometimes one spends more time explaining an evaluation than making it.

It is good practice for the evaluator to discuss the evaluation process with the budgetary participants. Their insight into the attributes and fairness of any evaluation process could prove extremely helpful. This insight should be obtained whether or not the participants will see or be personally assessed on an evaluation of the budget process.

When people are involved in determining the evaluation process, they are more likely to change their behavior based on the results of the evaluation. For example, if one believes that the budgetary process should be evaluated partially on its ability to produce a risk score, then if the risk score proves to be a poor predictor, the people who believe in its importance will be more inclined to work on a revised risk formula than they would if they did not believe it to be an important evaluative criterion.

The following four methods are the most common for evaluating the effectiveness of the budgetary process:

1. *Judgment:* an independent assessment by an expert regarding the effectiveness of the budgetary process
2. *Participant survey:* an attitudinal evaluation by the participant about the goodness or problems associated with the budget process
3. *Attributes method:* an identification of the attributes, such as risk analysis, that should be included within the evaluation process, and then evaluating the budget on those attributes
4. *Budgetary metrics:* a mathematical assessment of the effectiveness of the budgetary process

These four evaluation methods can be used individually or in conjunction with one another. For example, the budgetary process might first be evaluated on attributes, and then a judgment made regarding the effectiveness of the budgetary process that would use those attribute assessments as input to the judgment. Each of the methods is discussed individually.

METHOD 1: JUDGMENT

A judge is a recognized expert in a particular area or activity. The judge is engaged to evaluate the performance of others. Therefore, the judging means that an expert in the budgetary process will evaluate the effectiveness of the budgetary process.

Judging is associated more with an art form than a science. For example, an ice-skating competition requires a judge because such things as artistic impression need to be evaluated. On the other hand, it is not necessary to engage a judge to evaluate whether or not an automobile engine is performing correctly. This can be done by a machine that evaluates the functioning of the individual components.

Judgment is normally a process in which the judge compares the performance of the process being evaluated against processes the judge has experienced previously. The key to judgment is normally the totality of the experience of the judge. If the judge has never experienced a condition or attribute applicable to the existing process, there is little basis for the judge to determine the relative goodness of that process.

METHOD 2: PARTICIPANT SURVEY

The users of the budgetary process have firsthand knowledge of the usefulness and effectiveness of the process. The participants are instructed in the process, use it to create a budget, and then operate during the year using the budget in which they participated. As a result of these experiences, the participants are in a good position to evaluate the effectiveness of the budgetary process.

Surveying participants serves the following purposes:

1. Provides an evaluation based on experience in using the process
2. Identifies dissatisfaction with the process
3. Provides an opportunity to obtain recommendations on how to improve the process
4. Encourages greater participation if the recommendations and criticisms are addressed adequately by the group conducting the survey
5. Is a relatively inexpensive evaluation process

The survey should be conducted several months prior to beginning the next budgetary cycle. At this time, the frustration and effort associated with budget preparation has long passed, and the person can perform a more realistic evaluation of the process. Also, the person has had several months' experience in living with the developed budget. It also provides time to change the process prior to the next budgetary cycle.

The extent of the survey can include all budget participants or a representative sample of the participants. If the group is large, sampling is an equally effective method to get an evaluation, assuming that the sample is representative of the participant population. However, if one of the objectives is to gain the cooperation of the participants in the next budgetary cycle, all the participants should be surveyed.

The survey should not consume more than fifteen minutes of the participant's time. If it does, the response rate will normally be very low. Short surveys of an important topic tend to get good response rates. A good response rate is needed to gain the appropriate insight into budgetary effectiveness.

Generally, the questions should be in short-answer, multiple-choice, or a Likert-scale form. The Likert scale permits a person to show a range of attitudes about a question. For example, a Likert-scale question on a topic such as ease of use of the budgetary process would be as follows:

In preparing last year's budget, did you find the process:

Hard to Use					Easy to Use
1	2	3	4	5	6

The person completing the question marks the scale as to whether he or she feels that the process was easy to use or hard to use. The closer the X mark comes to Easy to Use, the higher the ease-of-use rating. Likert scales can be converted to numbers (1 through 6) so that the rating can be converted to a mathematical quantity.

Following are questions that are helpful to ask on a user survey:

1. Did the budgetary process satisfy your needs?
2. Were you given adequate training?

3. Were you provided adequate tools to develop budgetary estimates?
4. Were the developed budgetary estimates accurate? If not, explain the magnitude of inaccuracies.
5. Did you have adequate time to complete the budget?
6. What was the most difficult part of the budget process? (Normally, leave room for three items.)
7. What was the easiest part of the budget process? (Normally, leave room for three items.)
8. Does the budget help you perform your job? (This is an ideal type of question for a Likert scale.)

The surveys can be handled in one of two ways. The participants can indicate their name on the survey, and then the survey team can follow up for further explanatory material. The survey can also be returned anonymously. There are pros and cons to both approaches. The advantage most frequently cited for the anonymous survey is that it will tend to be more honest.

METHOD 3: ATTRIBUTES

An attribute is a characteristic about the budgetary process that can be used to evaluate the process. Under this method, the evaluation process is predetermined. All the attributes that will be used for evaluation are listed, and then the process is evaluated by those attributes. This is similar to the judgment method, except that the attributes are predefined and known to all involved.

The more specific the attributes, the more effective the process. For example, one of the attributes could be completeness. Completeness means that all the steps of the budgetary process were completed. If the steps can be defined in detail, judgment is not needed in evaluating completeness because of the detail of the definition.

Attribute evaluation is normally less threatening than judgment. Under judgment, a person rarely knows the exact criteria by which they will be evaluated. Under the attribute method, the criteria are known well in advance.

The attribute method of evaluation should be used if the evaluation is performed by lower-level members of management. This is because it is easier to criticize through predetermined attributes than it is to criticize through judgment. Less-experienced people are reluctant to make a negative judgment but have no problem in rating an attribute low.

The following are the most common attributes for evaluating the budgetary process:

- *Completeness:* performance of all the steps within the budgetary process
- *Portability:* effort required to transfer the budgetary process from one project/activity within the data processing function to another project or activity

- *Supportability:* amount and thoroughness of the documentation supporting the budgetary line items
- *Reliability:* extent to which a budgeted program can be expected to perform its intended function with the required precision
- *Validity:* extent to which items included within the budget are realistic based on the expected effort required to accomplish the mission
- *Usability:* effort required to learn, operate, prepare input, interpret output, and operate within the budget
- *Risk analysis:* extent to which the measurement of the risk variable is appropriate as a modifier for the budget estimate for an activity/project developed without regard to risk
- *Maintainability:* effort required to identify and change a budgetary estimate during the budgetary period
- *Reproducibility:* capability of the process to produce the same estimate by the same person at two different times, or by different people at the same time
- *Efficiency:* amount of resources required to develop and utilize the budget
- *Interoperability:* effort required to interconnect the data processing budgetary system with the organization's budgetary system

METHOD 4: BUDGETARY METRICS

A metric is a mathematical measure used to evaluate an activity or a process. Most professions and sciences create metrics to evaluate the work performed by that profession or science. It is a very precise way of evaluating effectiveness.

The accounting profession uses metrics to evaluate the performance of an organization. These metrics are called gross profit, net profit, and inventory turnover. Engineers use metrics to evaluate the correctness of their construction. These metrics are called load factors and stress. Doctors use metrics to determine the health or sickness of a patient. These metrics are called blood pressure and temperature.

A metric is a relationship between two variables. For example, in accounting the net profit metric is the relationship between the income from an organization and the amount left after all expenses are deducted from that income. Note that in this instance a metric can be both positive and negative.

The primary metric used in budgeting is the relationship between budgetary estimates and actual expenditures. The metric is called variance. Variance measures the difference between what was estimated to be expended and what was actually expended. This has proved to be a very effective evaluation of budgeting. Unfortunately, sometimes it measures the effectiveness of the person doing the budgeting, and at other times measures the effectiveness of the budgetary process.

Some of the other metrics that could be used to evaluate the budget process are:

1. *Budgeted projects versus actual projects completed:* The objective of budgeting is to provide the resources to complete projects. A better measure of the effec-

tiveness of the budget may be to measure the percent of work completed using the budgeted resources, as opposed to the amount of resources used. Obviously, both metrics provide value in assessing the adequacy of budgeting.

2. *Stratification of budget variances:* This measure provides an evaluation of the percent of budgeted line items that are within varying stratas of actual amount. For example, the metric would state that 80 percent of the projects are completed within plus or minus 5 percent of their budgeted amount. The recommended strata are:
    a. Plus or minus 5 percent
    b. Plus or minus 10 percent
    c. Plus or minus 15 percent
    d. Plus or minus 20 percent
    e. Plus or minus 25 percent
    f. More than plus or minus 25 percent.

    Note that the plus and minus variance can be combined or they can be listed separately.
3. *Budget trend variance:* This metric indicates the trend for variance, as opposed to the variance itself. For example, it might show the trend of variances over a period of two or more years. For example, if the average variance for one year was 5 percent and the average variance for the next year was $7\frac{1}{2}$ percent, this metric would indicate that the variance has increased 50 percent during the past year.
4. *Cost of budgeting as a percent of the data processing budget:* This metric indicates how many data processing resources are expended on the budget process.
5. *Cost of budgeting as a percent of data processing administrative costs:* This metric relates the amount of administrative resources expended for budgeting versus the total administrative costs. The objective of this metric is to show what percentage of data processing administration is expended for budgeting.

USE OF THE EVALUATION

The primary purpose of the evaluation is to approve the budgetary process. Rarely can organizations install an effective budgetary process the first time. The really good budgetary processes are bootstrapped and approved over a period of years. If organizations fail to update and improve the process continually, they will never produce a really effective budgetary process.

> **Budgetary principle**
>
> What cannot be done all at once can be improved over time—and at relatively low cost.

Index

Accountants, 112–113
Accounting skills, 4
Across-the-board-cut theory, 28
Administration, 39–41
Administrative costs, 9
Allocating funds, 202–205
Apportionment, 203–204
Appraisal costs, 71
Approval phase, 112
Approval process, 91–93
Approvals, 68
Assessing budget process, 213–219
Assets, unrecorded, 25, 32–33
Attributes method, 217–218
Authorization, specific, 204–205

Backlog, 181
Balance sheet, 8
Balanced risk portfolio, 52, 179–180
Benefits, estimating, 150–176
Black box, 99–100
Breadboarding, 154–155
BSP, 24
Budget abuses, 69–70
Budget actions, 17–20
Budget, building a, 98–113
Budget challenge, 191–194
Budget classification, 177–188
Budget components, 36–57
Budget consolidation, 177–188
Budget, customize, 128
Budget cuts, 212
Budget data collection, 142–145
Budget dimensions, 36–57
Budget document, 186
Budget, evaluating, 201–212
Budget fit, 29–31
Budget increases, 212
Budget, living with, 201–212
Budget management, 205–209
Budget marketing, 189–200
Budget metrics, 218–219
Budget, negotiate, 198–199
Budget packaging, 194–196
Budget participants, 140–141
Budget planning, 114–131
Budget policy, 106–107
Budget practices, 108–109
Budget preparation, 56–57
Budget, present, 196–198
Budget presentation, 20, 177–188
Budget process, 11
Budget process, assessing, 213–219
Budget process management, 77–97
Budget quality, 107–108
Budget reliability, 126–127
Budget responsibilities, 76–79, 123–124
Budget schedule, 127–128
Budget self-assessment, 12–17
Budget staff, 127–128
Budget steps, 109–112
Budget tools, 108–109
Budget, use of, 93–96
Budget, using, 201–212

Budget validity, 126–127
Budget value, 35
Budget versus actual, 128, 218–219
Budget, why fail, 99–100
Budget, winning, 178
Budgetable components, 117–122, 134–139
Budgetary alert, 125
Budgetary considerations, 106–109
Budgetary cycle, 81–82
Budgetary period, 67
Budgetary reviews, 208–209
Budgeting differences, 21–24
Budgeting strategies, 21–35
Business plan criterion, 85–86

Carrot-and-stick theory, 69
Case study, 73–76
Centralized estimating, 156
CFRR, 65
Changing workloads, 210–211
Charge-out, 66
Chart of accounts, 59
Checkpoints, 208
Committee, 131
Communications, 46
Competition criterion, 93
Completeness factor, 83
Compliance factor, 83
Component estimating, 154
Computer operations, 44
Consolidation, 4, 50
Contingencies, 7
Controllable components, 39–49
Corporate budget group, 105
Corporate requirements, 101–102
Cost avoidance, 160
Cost control, 67–68
Cost-effectiveness factor, 84
Cost estimate, 158–160
Cost of quality, 70
Cost of sales, 9
Cost reduction, 160
Cost relationships, 219
Cost trends, 121
Costs, classification, 18
Costs, estimating, 150–176
Costs, recording, 18–19
Counterattack theory, 29
Credibility, 29
Creeping commitment theory, 28, 69
Cross-reference matrix, 103–104

Data administrator, 60
Data base administration, 46–47
Data collection considerations, 134–139
Data gathering, 132–149
Defects, 95
Depreciation, 139
Discretionary expenditure, 204
Diverse function, 33
Documentation, 122
Double-cut theory, 27–28, 69
DPMA, 37
DP management, 39–41
DP management criterion, 94–95
DP plan criterion, 86–87

Economy tool, 61–62
Edicts, surviving, 211–212
Effectiveness tool, 63–64
Efficiency, 218
ESTIMACS, 139
Estimate, automation of, 176
Estimate benefits, 160–161
Estimate, quality of, 172–173
Estimate risk, 161–172
Estimate, value of, 176
Estimates, 19
Estimating, 26, 150–176
Estimating methods, 152–158
Estimating, selecting method, 157–158
Estimating tasks, 158–173
Estimating tools, 175
Evaluation, 146–149
Evaluation methods, 214–219
Expenditures, 204
Exposures, 182

Facilities, 42
Failure, 5
Failure costs, 71
FCPA, 61, 202–203
Fit, 29–31
Fixed assets, 139
Forms, 144–145
Fraud, 182
Function point estimating, 155
Funded costs, 134–139
Funds allocation, 37–39
Future dollars, 65

Games people play, 27–29
Gimme theory, 28
Golden rules, 6–8
Go/no go, 68
Growth, 122

Hardware, 44
Historical estimating, 155

IBM, 24, 48, 155, 181, 191, 192
Impediment, 3–6
Implementation phase, 110–111
Information center, 47–48
Intangible benefits, 161
Integrating budgets, 100–104
Interoperability, 218
IRS, 2, 22

Judgment method, 215
Judgment estimating, 153–154

Keys to success, 79–81

Likert scale, 216–217
Limits, 67
Line items, 133–134

Maintainability, 218
Maintainable factor, 84
Maintenance, 25, 43, 70
Make/buy, 68
Management approval criterion, 90
Management edict estimating, 157
Management tool, 59–76
Marketing budget, 189–200
Marketing concepts, 190
Marketing criterion, 92
Marketing steps, 194–199
MBO, 65
Measurement, 63, 66–67, 132
Megatrends, 190–191
Methodology criterion, 89–90
Metrics, 218–219
Microcomputer, 47
Milestones, 67
Mission, 57
Mission tool, 62–63
Modification criterion, 95
Monitoring budget, 207–208
Multidepartment projects, 23–24
Multiyear commitment, 51

Negotiate, 112
Negotiate budget, 198–199
New-ballgame theory, 29
New development, 70
New systems development, 42–43
Nondiscretionary expenditure, 204

Outside services, 48–49
Overhead, 9
Overtime, 205
Ownership, 35

Packaging, budget, 194–196
Participants survey, 215–217
Performance measurement, 30
Pioneer/pathfinder theory, 29
Plan, 13
Planning strategies, 21–35
Policy, budget, 106–107
Precision, 102
Preparation process, 89–91
Preparation steps, 182–187
Present budget, 196–198
Preventive costs, 71
Prioritization, 180–182
Priority considerations, 209
Product uniqueness, 24
Project delay, 179
Project control, 64
Projects expensed, 22–23
Purchase/lease, 68
Purchase/rental, 44–45

Quality, 70–73
Quality assurance, 45–46
Quality control criterion, 90–91, 96
Quality criterion, 87
Quality factors, 82–84

RACF, 48
Rathole theory, 28, 69
Realistic factor, 84
Redundancy of expenditure, 193
Reliability, 218
Reliability factor, 83
Replacement cost, 2
Reproducibility, 218
Requirements phase, 84–88
Resource dimension, 49–50
Review, 131
Revisions, 68
Risk, 26–27, 121
Risk analysis, 218
Risk, applying, 172
Risk characteristics, 163–172
Risk dimension, 51–56
Risk estimating, 157
Risk factor, 172–173
Risk modification, 207–208
ROI, 65
RPQ, 155

Salary, 121
Schedule extension, 179
Scheduling, 65
Security, 48
Self-checking forms, 149
Senior management, 4, 10
Size risk, 52
Software, 143
Software estimating, 156
Source statements, 2
Specific authorization, 204–205
Squeaky wheel, 181
Staff size, 117
Standardized estimating, 155–156
Standards, 174
Statement of income and expense, 8–9
Status criterion, 95–96
Status reports, 206–207
Strategy, 3
Stratification, 219
Structural risk, 52
Structure, 31

Support criterion, 93
Supportable factor, 84
Supportability, 218
Survey, 215–217
Systems support, 42

Technical support, 45
Technological risk, 52
Technology, changing, 24
Testing, 133
Tight budget, 31–32
Time frame dimension, 50–51
Timeliness factor, 84
Trade-offs, 209
Train, 110
Train participants, 125–126
Training, 129, 200
Trend analysis, 67, 219
Trial-balloon theory, 28
Turn-the-tide theory, 29

Unfunded costs, 134–139
Usability, 30–31, 218
Usable factor, 83
Use phase, 112
User management, 10
User need criterion, 87

Validity, 218
Validity factor, 83–84
Value of money, 50, 65
Variance, 66

White box, 99–100
WISCN, 115
Word processing, 47
Workload, 210–211